CASE STUDY APPLICATIONS FOR TEACHER EDUCATION

Cases of Teaching and Learning in the Content Areas

Edited by

Mary R. Sudzina

The University of Dayton

Allyn and Bacon

Boston • London • Toronto • Sydney • Tokyo • Singapore

Vice President, Editor in Chief, Education: Sean W. Wakely
Editorial Assistant: Jessica Barnard
Marketing Managers: Ellen Dolberg and Brad Parkins
Editorial Production Service: Chestnut Hill Enterprises, Inc.
Manufacturing Buyer: David Repetto
Cover Administrator: Jennifer Hart

Internet: www.abacon.com

Between the time Website information is gathered and published, some sites may have closed. Also, the transcription of URLs can result in typographical errors. The publisher would appreciate notification where these occur so that they may be corrected.

Library of Congress Cataloging-in-Publication Data

Case study applications for teacher education : cases of teaching and
    learning in the content areas / [edited by] Mary R. Sudzina.
        p.   cm.
    Includes bibliographical references and index.
    ISBN 0-205-28762-X (pb)
    1. Teachers—Training of—United States.   2. Case method.
    I. Sudzina, Mary R.
    LB1715.S796   1999
    370'.71—dc21   98–38837
                                                         CIP

Printed in the United States of America

10 9 8 7 6 5 4 3 2 1   03 02 01 00 99 98

CONTENTS

PART III *Mining the Chapters*

FOREWORD

Now that I have passed the half-century mark, I find myself thinking more about the past than I used to. Some of my behavior might be attributed to my daughters who, when I stopped to notice, turned out to be adults. And some more of my thoughts have surely been triggered by witnessing the uneven and inevitable decline of my mother. "Reflecting on the past" seems too sophisticated a phrase for rambling through my cluttered mind. But if I am not always thinking quietly, calmly, systematically about the past, I am certainly thinking about it more often—not just my own but others' histories as well.

I recall from a college history course or two that the great British historians both documented the past and shaped their readers' views of how history should influence the future. Edward Gibbon wrote of societal progress as occurring in steps or stages. In doing so he quite naturally influenced his readers to assume a similar teleological view of history, one upon which he imposed his own morality. Thomas Macauley tried to capture what he characterized as the public mind by writing of the relationship between people's thoughts and feelings and their immediate circumstances. His sense of drama helped readers imagine how the past must have played on the larger stage of world history. Thomas Carlyle singled out certain heroic figures and endowed them with messianic qualities of truth and foresight. Not surprisingly, Carlyle's form of hero worship appealed to a number of twentieth-century dictators. These historians have been celebrated and vilified for their writings—writings shaped by their own personal histories.

Modern American historians reinforce lessons taught by their predecessors and teach some new ones too. In his biography of Walter Lippman, Ronald Steel demonstrates how one life well lived and well documented can stand for the history of a nation. Beyond Harry Truman's romanticized upright nature and gritty determination to succeed at all costs, David McCullough makes us feel Truman's humanness as a team player in Tom Pendergast's Kansas City political machine. And most all of us have been touched directly or indirectly by John Hope Franklin's understanding of the slave family in America and his realization that much of what has passed for decent behavior toward African Americans has been less favorable than many care to remember.

My thoughts about the past often swirl around schools, probably because I have spent most of my life on one side of a desk or the other. For the last 13 or 14 years I have been working with people who educate teachers by using "cases" or slices of educational history from everyday lives. We have read, written, taught with, studied, and in all manner of ways used cases to try to help teachers learn from what they do. Despite George Santayana's admonition about being doomed to repeat the past if we fail to study it, we have been driven more by a vision of how educational life might be enhanced when teachers write and try to interpret histories of real-life educational events.

This collection contains stories written by teacher educators about how and why they use cases. It's really a kind of history about teaching teachers by using case methods. As I read, I noted some of the lessons the authors offer. Progress in teaching and learning can be measured in different ways. A good case capitalizes on the power of drama to help readers appreciate the richness of people's lives. Great teachers exist, and they need not be perfect people to do their jobs well. Teaching can mean making trade-offs, often unpleasant ones. Problems unsolved, deferred, ignored, or even solved can exhibit a long shelf-life. Teaching and learning with cases are not for the faint of heart.

As I enthusiastically recommend this volume to you, I respectfully suggest you recall one of the first lessons you learned when you entered the schoolhouse door: Stop, look, and listen. Not only are these behaviors likely to save you from peril, you might learn something from the people around you. Certainly I have learned from these writers.

Robert F. McNergney

PREFACE

MARY R. SUDZINA
UNIVERSITY OF DAYTON

Case-based teaching has captured the imagination of educators. Case studies, those "slices of life" that illustrate a myriad of dilemmas from moral issues to classroom management, are being increasingly integrated into teacher preparation programs. Although not a new idea in education, the explosion of case books since 1988 that chronicle behavioral, content area, and contemporary classroom dilemmas suggests that using cases fulfills a need in the way we prepare teachers and support professional development in in-service and graduate programs.

Research indicates that teaching with cases can offer teacher educators a variety of opportunities to expand and extend their teaching skills, problem solving abilities, and grasp of contemporary issues in classrooms today. Case discussions also offer a window into preservice, in-service, or graduate students' experiences, opinions, perceptions, or misconceptions of educational dilemmas. The benefits for students are also multiple: the development of higher-order thinking skills, and advanced research, problem solving, writing, and presentation skills. Students also report increased satisfaction with their grasp of issues and the range of strategies explored to cope with life in schools.

That all sounds fine. So, what's the big deal about teaching with cases? Don't cases teach themselves? Aren't they intuitively engaging to students? Many myths seem to abound about teaching with cases (see Chapter 2), particularly as they relate to applying cases to specific content areas and the goals of instruction.

A BOOK ABOUT CASE APPLICATIONS
AND CASE PRACTITIONERS

This is the book about teaching with cases that I have most wanted to read, the "missing link" between case texts and case research—the stories of those individuals who teach with cases. I've always been interested in what motivates individuals: *Why* people do *what* they do and *how* they do it. This natural curiosity extends itself to case applications and case practitioners: Who are the individuals who teach well with cases? What are their teaching experiences? Why did they decide to use cases? What works and *doesn't* work in their classes? What differences, if any, are exhibited by their students after using cases? In the past, simply hearing about someone's success stories and research hasn't been much help when I found myself at an impasse with a new teaching or counseling strategy. I wanted, and needed, to know more.

That is why this book is different. Not only will you meet 15 talented teacher educators through their photos and biographies, but you will share their personal stories of successes, shortcomings, and growing pains in learning to teach with cases in their particular content areas and teacher education programs. I am convinced that our experiences and choices with any teaching strategy are greatly influenced by who we are: our previous histories, teaching assignments, and experiences being a student, a teacher, an administrator, a parent, or all of the above. Because case outcomes are also influenced by the interactions and perspectives of the key players, there appears to be no "golden formula" that applies to all situations. However, there are strategies for teaching with cases that are more and less successful.

In essence, this book aspires to address "everything you wanted to know about case-based teaching, but were afraid (or didn't know) to ask." Although none of the authors would claim to know all the answers about teaching with cases, we've pooled our hard-won wisdom. And, the cumulative effect is stunning! Perhaps the biggest surprise is that teaching with cases has made us better listeners and better teachers.

What you will discover in this volume is that teaching with cases has been a challenging personal and professional journey for many of these teacher educators, and a journey that has been worth the trip for them and their students. Not only do they share their ideas and examples, but also their assignments, cases they have written, case texts, syllabi, assessment instruments, and resources. Much of this ancillary information can be found on our book Website:

<http://www.abacon.com/sudzina/>

The idea for this book grew out of my own search for how to teach effectively with cases. As you will read in the following chapters, many of the authors, including myself, were introduced to the case method at a conference or workshop. We were drawn to this idea as a way to enhance student learning and class participation, and to enliven our teaching as well. Generic case texts and guidelines, and even workshop leaders, can sometimes leave the impression that there is a straight-forward formula for teaching with cases and that's really all you need to know. As you will see, for most of us, that was just the beginning of learning to use cases effectively in our teaching.

This point became even clearer to me when after presenting my own research about teaching with cases at conferences, I was often approached by colleagues eager to begin teaching with cases who just wanted the essential facts. I found that I wasn't able to give them a 10-minute explanation, but needed to know something about their course and students. By the time I was finished asking nearly a dozen or so questions (see checklist, Chapter 2) about their particular teaching situation, discouragement had usually set in. I could empathize. So much of case teaching is trial and error learning and influenced by such things as time, case content, class size, room arrangement, course goals and assignments, and whether the students were preservice, graduate, or in-service teachers. One approach doesn't fit all.

Part of the magic about teaching with cases is that it is, by nature, interdisciplinary, just like the classroom, and life. No problem stands in isolation; it always bumps up against the social, emotional, contextual, intellectual, motivational, and even political agendas of the moment. Case issues and stories allow teacher educators to talk across content areas and levels of expertise with ease and familiarity with one another as they focus on a shared problem. However, many of us have observed over the years that even when teachers use similar problem solving models, or even the same cases, courses and case discussions can look very different. Although the content of the course drives the assignments and applications, the involvement of the participants and skill of the instructor as facilitator make a difference in the richness and quality of the discussions and the kinds of new learning that occurs. Our goal is to help make the transition to teaching with cases smoother and more successful for you.

TEACHING WITH CASES

The contributors to this volume present a wealth of experiences both as teacher educators and innovators in case-method teaching. They are in different stages of their careers, from several different geographic areas, and have adapted their teaching strategies with cases to fit their students and course goals. Cases are drawn from a variety of sources. Several of the contributors have authored or coauthored case study texts in their content areas. Several other contributors share their unpublished cases in their chapters. Still others offer samples of student case writing and case analyses that they use as part of their course content. All share their own stories of teaching and learning with cases.

Getting Ready to Teach with Cases

The first author you will meet is Hendrik Gideonse, Dean Emeritus at the University of Cincinnati. He discusses what a case is and what characterizes case instruction. This chapter succinctly captures the broad ideas embedded in case learning and enumerates five dimensions in case instruction: preparation, instruction, assessment, training, and resources.

In the next chapter, I outline some practical issues to consider when preparing to teach with cases. I discuss myths of case-based teaching and then offer some guidelines and a checklist of items to consider when teaching with cases.

Teaching with Cases in the Content Areas

This section is the heart of this text and presents 11 specific examples of teaching and learning with cases in the content areas:

- Amelia Klein from Wheelock College begins with a charming account of her early teaching experiences and their relationship to her current use of cases in early childhood teacher education programs. She also discusses using "live cases," and establishing collaborative communities among colleagues at her own institution, and internationally, for case-based teaching and professional development.
- Jim Allen, from the College of St. Rose and a fellow educational psychologist, offers us a spirited chapter of case "lessons" learned. Allen traces his journey from a neophyte to an experienced case facilitator with stops along the way to mentor students to national invitational team case competitions. Also included in this chapter are his student study guides for case analysis and case assessment.
- Debbie Libby teaches elementary language arts at Slippery Rock State University. Her chapter includes suggestions and questions to facilitate case discussion, as well as a list of case topics that she has written about to complement the primary language arts text. Libby concludes with excerpts from her students' writing that reflect the positive changes in their responses to case dilemmas from the beginning to the end of the semester.

- Steve Koziol, Brad Minnick, and Kim Riddell chronicle the layered effect of using case applications from a casebook, with student-written cases, to discuss student teaching dilemmas in the secondary English education program at the University of Pittsburgh. Their chapter also includes a case typography for selecting and using casebook cases, a case preparation guide for students, and *The Pittsburgh Reflection about Teaching Scale.*

- Joanne Herbert of the University of Virginia writes about her experiences videotaping cases of classroom interactions and the effects these videos had on her students and her teaching. She also provides an example of a teaching note and critical perspectives that were developed to accompany a series of videocases. Herbert concludes by describing a Web-based course that she codesigned using multimedia cases of contemporary classroom issues, the content of which is applicable to preservice, in-service and graduate teacher preparation programs.

- Todd Kent, now at Princeton University, was a doctoral student at the University of Virginia when the first draft of this chapter was written. He has been an innovator in supporting and transforming teaching and learning with cases through multimedia, Internet, Web, and CU-SeeMe technology. Kent describes his involvement with virtual case competitions, the use of telecommunications to enhance distance learning, and the technical and design issues associated with case-based courses on the World Wide Web.

- Tom Peacock at the University of Minnesota–Duluth has been greatly influenced by his Anishinabe heritage. His chapter describes the evolution of a multicultural studies course he teaches on the American Indian pupil to include cases as story. Peacock has melded his knowledge of the rich Anishinabe storytelling tradition to create a cycle of cases that illuminate tribal culture, traditions, and values, and their implications for schools and the students who attend them.

- Mark Mostert from Moorhead State shares his experiences as an undergraduate student in South Africa through the roles of teacher, principal, and associate professor in the United States. He suggests that personal experiences can have a profound effect on professional perspectives, judgments, and actions, and draws cases from a variety of sources, including his own text and a coauthored case text, in a capstone course on consultation and collaboration in special education.

- Bill Losito from the University of Dayton uses examples from classic and contemporary novels and short stories to invite critical engagement in moral issues as he and his students discuss the complexity of professional ethical decision making in this graduate-level course. Losito also presents a model for a moral view as well as criteria for objective reasoning and includes a case that he has written about an ethical reward system in an urban school.

- Bill Hunter teaches on the "hard" side of education at the University of Calgary—statistics and technology—and his sense of humor and gentle irreverence are infectious. He recounts his serendipitous exposure to cases through a case competition and the subsequent integration of cases into all courses he now teaches. In this chapter he presents a case he has written for his computer applications course and includes his course Website.
- Ted Kowalski at Ball State University is a prolific case writer, the author and coauthor of several case study texts, and an insightful case facilitator. He discusses how and why he uses cases in his doctoral seminar in school administration and offers excerpts from student evaluations to illustrate the power and value of case analysis for future administrators.
- The final chapter is again by Hendrik Gideonse, who shares his own story of becoming acquainted with case-based instruction. Gideonse then draws together the lessons learned in teaching with cases in the preceding chapters. With keen observation and insight he discusses both the positive and problematic issues in teaching with cases. He also offers some suggestions of his own, based on his years of facilitating cases in student teaching seminars.

A FINAL THOUGHT ABOUT TEACHING WITH CASES

Over the years, I've come to realize that, just as there are many excellent ways to teach, there are many excellent ways to teach with cases. We know that all excellent teachers do not look, act, think, or teach in the same way. However, we can observe the results of excellent teaching in the classroom by the quality of students' involvement and participation, knowledge of content, skills in analysis, reasoning, and research, as well as their written and oral presentations. Teaching is a craft that is ultimately learned by doing, and learned more effectively with constructive feedback and reflection. The following chapters are designed to give you a taste of what other teacher educators have experienced when teaching with cases and to "mentor" you as you embark on your own personal and professional journey with this exciting pedagogy.

ACKNOWLEDGMENTS

I have many people to thank for this book. This volume is dedicated to the many individuals who have made a difference in my life, and the lives of so many others, through their warmth and humor, high standards and desire for excellence, support, and personal and professional integrity.

My family has always been an important source of strength in my life. I'd like to acknowledge my mother, Ruth Jaqui Skudlarek, and my Godmother, Eileen Ann Dunne, for their gifts of golden summer days at the beach and an unquenchable zest for life. My six younger siblings have taught me a great deal about listening and compassion and will be my best friends for life. Love to Bill, Kate, Joe, Ann, Noel, and John. My husband of 28 years, Michael Sudzina, is a wonderful partner and a fabulous father and I'm grateful for his love and support. The ultimate joy in our lives comes from our daughters, Christine and Suzanne, who make us proud and keep us humble, alert, and entertained in the process. Nick, our beautiful Dalmatian, has been my constant companion these many long months of writing and rewriting. Love to all.

This book is also dedicated to all the chapter authors who gave so willingly and unselfishly of their time and expertise to share with others their hard-won lessons about teaching with cases. They have been a delight to work with and an inspiration for my own teaching and writing. Hendrik Gideonse has been especially generous and insightful in helping me shape and clarify the issues presented in this text. Mark Mostert, a treasured collaborator and friend, has been an ongoing resource in advancing my thinking, writing, and teaching with cases.

A special note of appreciation goes to Bob McNergney, and his talented colleagues from the Curry School, especially Joanne Herbert and Todd Kent, who have nurtured and supported my continuing work with cases. It was through Bob, and the University of Dayton's participation in the Commonwealth Center Team Case Competition at the University of Virginia in 1993, that I met several of the authors in this text and discovered the work of other excellent case practitioners. Appreciation also goes to Clare Kilbane, a former student of mine, now at the Curry School, who was there in the beginning and continues to enliven my work with cases.

Finally, thank you to Nancy Forsyth of Allyn and Bacon for her vision and encouragement of this project, and to Sean Wakely, my editor. Thanks, also, to my former chairman, Dan Raisch, for the secretarial assistance of Leah Durante and Joe Farrell. I couldn't have done this without all of you.

Mary R. Sudzina

Case Study Applications for Teacher Education

HENDRIK D. GIDEONSE

Hendrik Gideonse received his undergraduate degree in political science from Amherst College and his master's and doctorate degrees from Harvard University in the history and philosophy of education. He has been a college instructor, the director of program planning and evaluation for the research programs of the U.S. Office of Education, a professional staff member in the U.S. Senate, vice provost for academic planning, a professor, a dean, and a special assistant to the president of the University of Cincinnati. In 1996, Gideonse was named University of Cincinnati Professor Emeritus of Education and Policy Studies, and Dean Emeritus of Education.

The author of over eight books and monographs, as well as three dozen articles and book chapters, Gideonse has served on numerous national panels, task forces, and committees. He has accumulated over eight feet of data on students' responses to case studies from his own teaching. In 1998 he was the recipient of the AACTE Edward C. Pomeroy Award for Outstanding Contributions to Teacher Education. Gideonse currently divides his time between Cincinnati and Brooklin, Maine.

1

WHAT IS A CASE? WHAT DISTINGUISHES CASE INSTRUCTION?

HENDRIK D. GIDEONSE
UNIVERSITY OF CINCINNATI

One of the irresistible challenges in the community interested in using, in studying, and in improving the efficacy of case instruction in teacher education is to define what a case is and what case instruction means. I will not resist that challenge any more than those who have gone before me, but my answer, as you will see, is both fluid and open-ended. Certainly the following chapters suggest a very broad array of meanings people bring to the dialog. The authors talk of cases that are either open-ended (resolution left to the reader or analyst) or closed (resolution provided as part of the text). Cases are sometimes long and elaborate or only the fewest sentences needed to outline a predicament. Sometimes they are videoclips or films of "real life" in a classroom setting. They can be predicaments presented orally to a group. They can be stories. They can be generated professionally (by someone trained to prepare cases) or by teacher education students themselves and practitioners. Despite attempts by the cognoscenti (e.g., Shulman, Sykes, Merseth, etc.) to establish limits to what constitutes a case in their parlance, it seems clear that those engaged in what they think of as case instruction will continue to use the terms expansively.

But let's look at labeling for a moment. Is varied use of the terms *case* and *case instruction* a problem? Is it something important to quarrel over? Is orthodoxy necessary here?

CASE DEFINITIONS

I would suggest that looking across all the different meanings the authors subscribe to as they talk about these matters may offer some useful clues. For example, cases are about practice, imagined or real. While it is always possible to analyze a case in the abstract, doing so sooner or later would make one question why one took the trouble to start with a case if more or less pure ideation was the intent. Being about practice, cases are not about theory, although theory may be a powerful explanatory tool and instrumental in suggesting useful action as well.

Being about practice, cases of whatever kind are about specifics. They are almost inevitably about the context in which the specifics are embedded or which the student assumes/constructs for purposes of analysis. Cases are about action, intent, and obligation. Even when stated with the utmost parsimony (i.e., only two or three sentences to define a predicament), cases are about a multiplicity of variables, meanings, and theoretical perspectives that are present or might be brought to bear. Cases entail complexity and problematics. They invite controversy and debate about the circumstances, the issues, the purposes of the several stakeholders, and the actions that might be taken by them or on their behalf.

CASE LEARNING

Case learning, however presented, tends to be holistic. The boundaries between the otherwise discrete domains of our professional crafts and understanding blur or break down in the presence of the practical and the problematic. As academics and as specialists we see the world in terms of the scholarly categories or domains of practice in which we have invested ourselves. We may make distinctions between epistemic and axiological grounds for practice, between what we know and what we may value morally in our professional principles. These categories of professional discourse, while useful for intellectual purposes, do not stand still in case learning; instead, they cry out to be linked and stitched together as the demands of action surface.

Cases oblige us to go beyond what we know. They demand we address, in addition, what we ought. They oblige consideration beyond the technical and the theoretical to embrace the moral dimensions of teaching.

Furthermore, case instruction is quintessentially constructivist. Cases could, I suppose, be taught didactically, but what would be the point? The whole purpose behind case instruction is to engage the perceptual, problem identification and analysis, and decision taking capacities of students with the aim of honing those capacities to ever higher states of effectiveness.

Case learning is constructivist because it is active learning. Participants must engage with the material. They must work with and test their own understandings and perceptions. Furthermore, insofar as there is discussion in the pedagogical plan (and it is virtually impossible to imagine case learning without discussion), then social processes are engaged. From a pedagogical perspective, "where the learners are," what constructs are currently in operation in the learners, are readily apparent to instructors and learners alike, either in the form of their writing or their public dialog with one another. Moment by moment, in other words, in case learning instructors know far more about what is going on with their charges than in more traditional forms of didactic instruction.

It is important to note that case learning is constructivist for both student and instructor. In essence, in other words, case instruction is professional development for teacher educators. The majority of the authors affirm their conviction they are better teachers now after teaching with cases. For one thing, the instructor is always, often painfully, aware of what students are doing with the material, and the oft-expressed surprises found in the chapters of what instructors have encountered with their students attest to the instructor as learner.

There is a second sense of learning for instructors. It grows from the realization of the richness of the common ground they have gained as they engage instructional peers in dialogue about their experiences teaching from the same cases. When faculty members talk to a colleague about a course we teach in common, we can share content, our approach, the syllabus, maybe even our evaluation strategies, but it is almost always abstract and difficult, in the final analysis, to achieve close comparisons of the actual experience of teaching. When we talk to a colleague about teaching from the same case, however, the common ground of experience is remarkable, and the level of the conversation much deeper, more immediate, and much more intense. The interactions resulting are almost startling in their satisfaction and meaningfulness. When we talk about traditional courses, we can never be sure that the experience is the same. But when we talk about the instructional experiences arising from specific cases we have used in common, the social basis for a shared experience from which we can both learn is apparent.

CASE INSTRUCTION

Finally, whatever else case instruction may be, it is hard work. Far from being an "easy read" or being so forgiving because it is so highly motivating to students, case instruction is demanding. There are at least five senses in which that is so.

Preparation

Preparation for case instruction, for example, is at least the equal of other kinds of instruction. Some of the tasks are the same, of course. One must be clear about the purposes of the course, its goals, objectives, and articulation with other parts of the teacher education program. The case text or individual cases must be reviewed and selected, a syllabus prepared, and so on.

Before instructors teach a case, however, they must first do what they are going to ask their students to do, namely, analyze the cases themselves and undertake the same kinds of problem identification, review, consideration of alternative courses of action, the rationale for them, and the probable consequences of taking them. The instructor's analytic task, however, must be done from two points of view if the preparation is to be complete. The case must be explored from the vantage point of the instructor's knowledge and experience, but it must then also be imagined from the perspective of the students who will be exposed to the case, that is, their relative experience or naïveté.

Neither of these analytic tasks is particularly easy. For one thing, as instructors we must step back out of the particular specialization we have invested ourselves in an attempt to role play simultaneously all the specializations that might be appropriate given the specifics of the case. It helps if teacher educators have been teachers before they assume their role as teacher educators, because as practitioners they were obliged to be knowledgeable, if not expert, in all the technical and epistemological domains pertinent to their craft. (That is not to argue that there aren't other routes to developing this more comprehensive capacity, however.) Nonetheless, it is not easy to adopt the broad range of orientations beyond one's own specialty. Secondly, however, imagining what the responses of students might be is not a snap either. Evidence for that abounds in the chapters. Surely that is one explanation for the nearly universal expressions of surprise (sometimes bordering on dismay) at the responses students develop to cases presented to them.

A last part of the preparation has to do with anticipating the assessment strategies to be applied to case learning. Assessment, of course, flows from purpose, from objectives, and, indeed, from consideration of the best way of assuring your own accountability for what you intend for your students to learn through case instruction. What is assessed (for example, the discussion, written analyses of cases, or some other measure that may itself not be case-based) is as crucial a decision as how it will be assessed, and according to what criteria applied in what manner.

Delivery of Instruction

The delivery of the case learning experience is the second dimension of case instruction's demanding nature. Finding an appropriate meeting room, for example, is crucial. In too many institutions of higher education, sad to say, those who have had responsibility for designing, building, and furnishing the instructional spaces have assumed that teaching is telling. The spaces and the furniture virtually oblige all the students to face the one instructor, sometimes even to the point that the chairs and accompanying note-taking arms are bolted to the floors. Even where the chairs are movable, they are ill-suited to being arranged for small group work, especially where the acoustics of the room are hopeless in terms of dampening the commotion and energy of a half dozen or more small groups vigorously engaged in dialogue with one another.

Size of the class is crucial in this respect. Most of the classes discussed in the chapters seemed to range from the mid-teens to the mid-twenties. I myself had a class that ranged from mid-twenties at the low end, usually operated in the 40 to 60 range, but on one occasion went well over 100. Decisions need to be made about whether to do whole group or small group, or some combination, and how to arrange the class so that it can be done most efficiently. Consideration should even be given to setting up the class physically before meeting time, provided the classroom is not used immediately before the session, because individual groups of students can be almost marvelously ineffective in setting up small group configurations that are equidistant from one another to reduce noise pollution. (Please forgive the nuts and bolts here, but experience tells me that not to mention things like this is to fail to share hard-won learnings over time!) As several of the chapters note, attending to the physical configuration of space is crucial to advancing the social construction of learning.

Space and its arrangement are only one part of the delivery considerations. Facilitating case discussion is an art whose techniques can be learned, and they must be mastered if case instruction is to be successful. Achieving a balance among where the instructor thinks she wants to go, where students think they want to go, and where the instructor suddenly discovers she needs to go (i.e., the capacity for improvisation) means careful preparation, part of which grows out of the already mentioned preanalysis, but part of which attends more to the logic and flow of discussion. As several of the chapters suggest, worries about the management of case discussion frequently surface (e.g., Am I shaping it more heavily than I ought?). When the bulk of the conversation in cases takes place in small groups, only a portion of which the instructor witnesses while being a roving eavesdropper, working to secure accountability, thoroughness, and vigor in small group processes, it means attending very carefully to the operating instructions and developing feedback mechanisms that allow for needed adjustments from one class meeting to the next. In my own teaching, I addressed this by carefully specifying group leader and record keeper roles that rotated through the group and by eliciting weekly feedback from group members on their sense of the extent to which case discussions were doing what they thought they ought.

Assessment

The assessment of case learning is yet a third dimension of the demands of case instruction. As the following chapters attest, instructors can spend large amounts of time providing feedback to the students, for example, on their ability to apply appropriate educational psychology theory to cases. I asked students to do a half dozen or so cases in a 10-week quarter. It took me about 12 to 15 minutes per student per case, including preparation of a paragraph of feedback keyed to the published performance criteria. I read the student responses, discussion group by discussion group, after reviewing the recorder's record of their discussion together. As every teacher knows and appreciates, some student responses required much longer; where problems exist, figuring out their genesis and how to be constructive can be very trying! Of course, if summative judgment is the only objective, it can go a lot faster; when one hopes to teach through feedback, it always takes a lot longer.

The sheer volume of work in assessing case learning is not the only element in determining how demanding case instruction can be on the instructor. Conceptual puzzles also contribute. Specifying the desired or acceptable outcomes of case learning and devising measures to assess the degree of their presence is not easy. Because cases are so different, comparing performance across different cases raises obvious questions about reliability and validity of assessment. Further, performance on any given case or cases invites speculation about how good a predictor such performance is for assuring capacity to handle the next case, or more significantly, *de novo* problems arising in real practice.

Training

Several of the following chapters speak to the benefits received from having received formal training in the development and use of case instruction. Given the complexities and demands of case instruction, early exposure to such training is highly recommended. The training need not, however, be prior to first experimentation with case instruction; in fact, a good argument can be made that some prior experience will render the training that much more valuable. Faculty experimenting with case instruction should be urged to share that fact with their students, adopt an inquiry mode to their experimentation, and enlist students' feedback in both formal and informal ways.

Resources

It is important, finally, as part of this treatment of the particularly demanding nature of case instruction to say something about the resource implications of doing it properly, that is, assuring adequate instructional planning time, using pedagogical techniques dependent on discussion, and guaranteeing detailed and individualized feedback and assessment. Higher education increasingly uses various cost models to explain as well as justify the allocation of resources for instruction. While the use of cases on the surface may appear to be just a variant form of campus-based didactic instruction, for all the reasons sketched in this chapter, it needs to be understood as a variant of clinical instruction, labor intensive and decidedly dependent on reduced student–instructor ratios. Case instruction demands facilities suited to it and faculty resources greater than programs and institutions are used to expending.

SUMMARY

In sum, then, almost anything can be a case, so long as it presents a predicament from practice demanding some kind action. Even the briefest of cases will generate considerable discussion as antecedents and context are fleshed out and explored, alternative courses of action and their theoretical grounding developed, and the prospective consequences are imagined. Cases, even the most abbreviated, are complex and full of problematics. Case learning is holistic and constructivist. Cases engage practitioners' knowledge and the moral principles governing their practice. Finally, the preparation, delivery, assessment, training, and resource requirements of cases together help to explain the great demands of case instruction on the faculty who do it. But, for those who do choose to teach with cases, the benefits can far outweigh the demands.

MARY R. SUDZINA

Mary R. Sudzina is associate professor of educational psychology in the Department of Teacher Education at the University of Dayton. She earned a bachelor's degree in English and journalism from Virginia Commonwealth University, a master's in secondary guidance and counseling from Villanova University, a school psychology certification from Boston State, and a Ph.D. in educational psychology from Temple University. She is a former high school English teacher, guidance counselor, and college counseling psychologist.

Widely published, Sudzina won the University of Dayton's School of Education Research Award in 1994 and was honored as the first "star professor" for teaching by the school's undergraduate teacher education fraternity in 1997. She has been involved in case-based teaching as an instructor and facilitator, and in case competitions as a mentor, judge, and host. Research interests include: case-based teaching and learning, teaching with technology, current issues in teaching educational psychology, and school reform. Sudzina will assume the chair of the AERA special interest group for teaching educational psychology in 1999.

2

GUIDELINES FOR TEACHING WITH CASES

MARY R. SUDZINA
UNIVERSITY OF DAYTON

Teaching with cases can be an exhilarating teaching–learning experience. However, teaching with cases isn't for everyone. Although research suggests that teaching with cases offers multiple benefits to
both teacher educators and students that go beyond traditional teacher-
centered instruction, (see our chapter authors, and Sudzina, 1997), it is not
a panacea or a Band-Aid for poor teaching or unmotivated learners. It may
not be suitable for teachers who prefer to control and direct instruction
and discussions, and for students who have a strong preference to be told
the "right" answer. Case-based teaching seems to work most successfully
with teacher educators who are flexible and reflective and act as facilitators of knowledge with their students as together they co-construct knowledge and meaning from course content and case dilemmas.

With apologies to David Letterman, I'd like to offer some common
misconceptions about what case-based teaching is, and isn't!

DISMANTLING THE MYTHS

Although many students enjoy the challenge of discovering and uncovering case issues, some students just don't "get it." They may be holistic
thinkers who miss the nuances of interactions, or linear thinkers who
have problems looking at the whole picture before making judgments.

BOX 2.1   The Top Ten Reasons for *Not* Using Cases

(Myths of Case-based Teaching)

1. All students love analyzing cases.
2. Cases teach themselves; they are intuitively interesting.
3. Case issues are obvious and unidimensional.
4. Everyone sees case issues in a similar way.
5. Little or no preparation is necessary to teach with cases.
6. The quality of the case determines the success of the discussion.
7. There are no right answers; answers are relative.
8. Teaching cases takes about the same amount of time as lecturing.
9. Cases are adaptable to any situation.
10. Anyone can teach with cases.

Difficulty separating fact from emotion is an issue for some students who tend to go with what "feels right" in the short term rather than considering the long-term consequences of their actions. Many students have difficulty relating to issues or perspectives or contexts that are very different from their own experiences.

Cases don't teach themselves. *Instructors* are needed to facilitate case analysis and discussion. As illustrated later in this chapter, in the teaching strategies section, case issues are not always obvious, or even agreed on, in any given group of students. Prior student knowledge and experiences color the way a case is perceived and interpreted.

It can appear that teaching with cases requires less preparation on the part of the instructor, (after all, aren't the students doing most of the talking?), when, in reality, it may actually require *more* preparation than traditional teacher-centered instruction. Because teaching with cases is student-centered, instructors need to know their students, know the facts in the case, know the research, anticipate student responses, know how to give feedback, and when to redirect discussion, all without being controlling or authoritarian in manner.

There is no question that a fantastically written or presented case is preferable to a mediocre one. However, it is the interest that the case sparks, and the richness of the ensuing discussion, that determines the success of the case selected. From my own experiences, students have selected cases for analysis that I thought were only so-so, but because they were interested and invested in the topic, the discussions were among the best that we had that semester.

Case answers aren't all relative. Just because there usually isn't *one* right answer in dealing with an educational issue, it doesn't mean that anything goes. Often, one of the hardest jobs for case instructors is to point out to students why their answers may not work. Clearly, there are some actions and solutions that are preferable to others, and that can be supported with research and expert knowledge.

Cases aren't an economical way to communicate information. Lecture is perfect for that. However, learning with cases promotes a variety of ways to improve content comprehension, application, evaluation, and synthesis (see Sudzina & Kilbane, 1992) as well as long-term retention of information.

Cases are pretty adaptable, but, like many other teaching strategies, are not appropriate for any and all teaching situations. Common sense prevails. Dropping a generic case into a content-specific course, "just to teach a case," can be a very frustrating experience for students who may wonder what they are really learning. Also, cases are not the preferred mode for communicating basic information in a course.

Teaching with cases is hard work. Not everyone is cut out to teach with cases. I believe the most successful case instructors are those individuals who are *already* good teachers and are looking for other ways to enhance their teaching and their students' learning. You need to know your own style and educational philosophy and whether teaching with cases would work for you.

Are you still with me? Still interested in teaching with cases? Great! Then, let's read on.

A CHECKLIST FOR GETTING STARTED WITH CASES

There are many things to consider when organizing for case-based instruction: course content and setting, students, case sources, case selection, teaching strategies and assignments, and assessment (see Table 2.1).

Course Content and Setting Considerations

As with any new teaching strategy, it is important to consider whether integrating case studies and implementing case analysis will be compatible with, and enhance, your course goals and objectives. For example, course goals may include: increased student collaboration and class participation, increased reflection and problem solving skills, specific research and presentation skills, and/or the application of a particular body of knowledge to issues in classroom behavior, cultural diversity, or language arts. Some content areas have few appropriate cases readily available, which may discourage instructors from using them in their classes. Additionally, cases need to be integrated into the curriculum for a purpose and not tacked on as an interesting extra assignment.

Course organization and time constraints can also affect the ease with which cases are integrated into the curriculum. When planning to use cases

TABLE 2.1   A Checklist for Teaching with Cases

- Course content and setting considerations
  Course organization
  Course content
  Course goals and objectives
  Length of course
  Time and space considerations
  Field experience or lab requirements

- Student considerations
  Preservice
  Graduate
  In-service
  Novice or experienced
  Traditional or nontraditional
  Undergraduates, teachers, administrators, or support staff

- Case sources
  Case study texts
  Instructor-written cases
  Student-written cases
  Classroom-teacher written cases
  Cases included in content-area text books
  Short stories, novels, films, and media as cases
  Cases on the Internet and World Wide Web

- Case selection
  Format of cases (text, film, video, audio, multimedia)
  Generic or content-specific
  Context and complexity
  One issue or multilayered
  Length of cases
  Number of cases
  Purpose of cases

- Teaching strategies and assignments
  Case assignments (individual, small group, whole class)
  Kinds of case assignments
  When to assign cases
  The importance of a conceptual framework
  Strategies for case analysis
  Strategies for case discussion
  Integrating cases into the curriculum

- Assessment issues
  Criteria for grading cases
  Kinds of assessment measures
  Individual or group grades
  Instructor and/or peer review
  Format (oral, written, multimedia, Internet, Web)
  Access and familiarity with the literature

instructors need to consider the length of their term, the number of times their class meets per week, and the amount of time available in each class period in determining the number of cases to analyze. Field experiences and lab hours may be natural places where case studies can be integrated.

Several of the chapter authors also point out the importance of a classroom with flexible seating so that students can face each other when discussing a case, and create clusters for small group activities in class.

Student Considerations

The kinds of students that one has in class influences the choice and variety of the cases and assignments, as well as the breath and depth of discussions and analyses. Goals and objectives for case analysis should be adjusted to take into account students' learning sophistication levels and life experiences.

For example, traditional undergraduate students who test extremely well on objective tests may balk at the inexact and unpredictable nature of case analysis, and the teacher's new role as facilitator. They may feel frustrated as they are asked to shift their cognitive focus from a memorization to a problem solving orientation (Mostert & Sudzina, 1996), particularly when they are being evaluated for their efforts. Additionally, undergraduates tend to identify with the student or the teacher in most cases, as those are the roles with which they are most familiar, and often have difficulty taking on the perspectives of the principal, parents, or staff.

Older, nontraditional, and/or diverse students can offer insights into many case issues that traditional undergraduates may miss. It is generally advantageous to have diverse student viewpoints in any case discussion and group work. However, it is important not to call on individuals to always represent the "typical" or "average" viewpoint for the gender, cultural, or ethnic group to which they belong.

Other factors that will affect your choice of cases, discussions, and assignments include: whether your students are taking the course for university or in-service credit; if they are novice or experienced teachers, administrators, or support staff; and their previous experience with the case study method.

Case Sources

There are a wide variety of sources for cases. Case study texts highlighting common educational dilemmas (e.g., Kauffman, Mostert, Trent, & Hallahan, 1998; Kowalski, Weaver, & Henson, 1994; Silverman, Welty, & Lyon, 1992) are popular choices. Specific subject case books are making their appearance (e.g., Kowalski, 1995; Miller Cleary & Peacock, 1998; Mostert, 1998). Cases are also being integrated into some content-area texts, such as educational psychology, and include case supplements on video (Eggen & Kauchak, 1997) as well as a corresponding case study text (see Ormrod, 1998). Case resources and case studies can be found on the World Wide Web (see Chapters 7 and 8). Short stories, novels, films, and media also serve as cases of particular topics, issues, or dilemmas (see Chapters 3 and 11).

Several of the teacher educators in this volume have included cases they have written in their own content areas (see, e.g., Chapters 5, 7, 9, 11, and 12). Students can describe, as a case study, a classroom dilemma they have observed in the field, using the same format as the cases that they are studying in class (see Sudzina, 1993; Sudzina & Kilbane, 1992). I have students write their own case studies on pupils that they have observed and/or tutored in field placements, being careful to protect confidentiality. Students can also write cases about their experiences during student teaching (see Chapter 6). Classroom teachers, staff, and administrators may also write cases either as a topic for discussion in their courses or for their final exam. In these instances, the instructor and the students cocreate the curriculum.

Case Selection

The purpose for using cases should drive your case selection. Do you want to use generic or content-specific cases? Do you want your students to focus on one issue in a case or on multilayered cases? In what format do you want your students to access cases: text, film, video, audio, multimedia, or hypermedia? Is your course and case use going to be conducted in real time or in asynchronous time, as found in many distance learning initiatives?

Case content, length, and complexity also need to be considered in case selection, as well as the number of the cases to be discussed over the course of the quarter or semester. A quick rule of thumb is to teach no more than a case a class.

Teaching Strategies and Assignments

Teaching with cases requires time to analyze, discuss, reflect on, and debrief case issues. Instructors must also decide how and when to assign cases and how much time to allot to class discussion. Beware! Students can be masterful at sidetracking discussion and you may find yourself listening to everyone's personal experiences with a situation rather than focusing on the case at hand.

Assigning cases for research and analysis before class, and using one or more uninterrupted class periods for discussion and debriefing, seem to be more effective than analyzing cases "cold" in one or several brief time periods. When cases are assigned in advance, and with specific criteria to be covered, class discussion, interaction, and problem solving become more thoughtful (Sudzina, Kowalski, & Weaver, 1994). Similarly, instructors must prepare the case ahead of class and try to anticipate the kinds of responses their students may have. Teaching notes and instructor's manuals are helpful for that purpose although it really takes teaching a case several times to get the "hang" of it. Several texts offer helpful suggestions for teaching and learning with cases (e.g., Shulman, 1992; Wassermann, 1993; 1994).

When to assign cases also needs to be considered. Some instructors integrate and weave cases throughout the curriculum from the first day of class to illustrate salient issues and reinforce content, while other instructors cover much of the course content and then present cases as synthesizing experiences and a way to bridge theory to practice.

Many instructors generally assign the first several cases as an all-class activity and model the process of case analyses within the whole group. Individual written case assignments can also be used to measure students' growth and skill in case analysis but, because they are so time-consuming to grade, in-depth individual analyses are often reserved for a course project or final exam. One way around this time constraint is to assign cases for group analysis, presentation, and discussion.

Assignments can range from reading the case and preparing notes for class discussions to full-blown student case presentations including video, audio, PowerPoint, overheads, activities, handouts, reviews of the research, guest speakers, and role playing. Similarly, written analysis can range from a simple outline of the issues to an in-depth analysis complete with theoretical explanations and research citations. The teacher educators in Chapters 3 through 14 share their specific assignment and application ideas.

A special kind of case assignment and application is the case competition. This is where teams of students, usually from different institutions, engage in debate in person, or through telecommunications such as CU-SeeMe, Internet, and/or the Web, around a selected case issue and are rated by a panel of judges on their oral and/or written case analysis and presentations (see Chapters 4, 8, and 12; also Sudzina, 1995; Sudzina, 1994a, 1994b; Sudzina & Kilbane, 1994).

An important step in organizing for case-based teaching is having a set of unifying ideas, or a conceptual framework, to organize and facilitate case analysis, discussion, and assessment. I use the conceptual framework from McNergney, Herbert, & Ford (1994) that can be applied across content areas, educational issues, and levels of instruction (see also Chapters 5 and 7). The five steps include: (1) identifying the issues and facts in a case; (2) considering the different perspectives in a case; (3) identifying professional knowledge; (4) projecting actions that might be taken; and, (5) considering likely consequences, both positive and negative, of particular actions.

Early in the semester, I introduce this framework to my class through an overhead and direct their attention to my Webpage, where it is also found. I demonstrate how a framework can be used to shape thinking about educational dilemmas, from the identification of the issues through the possible consequences of particular actions. I often assign a short and controversial case for my students to read over the weekend prior to our first discussion. Embedded in this case are issues that I will discuss in my educational psychology class over the course of the semester in our primary content-area textbook. These can include: classroom management, discipline, motivation, diversity, teaching strategies, development issues, teacher expectations, gender bias, and cooperative learning. This sets up the relevance of the course content in dealing with "real life" educational problems.

As a warm-up to learning about case analysis, I ask each student to rank, in the assigned case, what they consider the top three issues, three most important perspectives, three most relevant areas of research needed, three most appropriate actions, and three possible outcomes as a consequence of their actions. Then, I go around the classroom and ask each student to share his or her perceptions. I list them on the chalkboard, along with frequency counts, to note the most common responses.

Assessing students' responses can be an enlightening experience! Even though all the students read the same case, they do not all see the issues and perspectives the same way. We often have 10 to 15 different responses for every item out of a class of 25 to 30 students. Such results surprise preservice teachers who assume their peers perceive classroom dilemmas in similar ways. I use this opportunity to reinforce the idea of multiple perspectives. I also like to see and hear what students think about certain issues, without the pressures of formal evaluation. These sessions help me to decipher student information gaps, disagreements, and misconceptions, and to make course adjustments.

My course assignments are posted to my Website. They explicitly state my expectations for the written analyses and oral presentations that students give toward the end of the semester. Using a required case study text, I have each class vote on the cases that they wish to analyze. Students then form into groups that range from two to five members depending on total class size and the number of cases to be presented. Additionally, I review the case analysis framework in class to make sure everyone understands what to look for in a case. The following suggestions are adapted from Sudzina (in press):

1. *Identifying the issues and facts in a case.* I ask students to brainstorm among themselves and to list all the issues they can identify. I also ask them to examine and list all the facts in the case and then to decide which facts are relevant, as well as irrelevant, to the case. Then they must decide among themselves which are the most important issues, and of those, which need immediate attention and which might be resolved at

a later date. Regarding those issues requiring immediate attention, students must decide if they would be willing and able to take action.

2. *Identifying perspectives and values.* Role plays can be very effective in helping students to recognize multiple points of view in a case. Many undergraduates initially tend to identify, and feel comfortable, with the perspectives of the student or the teacher in a case. They also tend to view situations in a very black or white manner and to see what is wrong, rather than what is right, in a situation. When students take the roles of nontraditional students, parents, or principals, they can often "hear" how the dialogue unfolds, and imagine the motivations, values, and perspectives behind the words of each of the players in the situation. This helps move students from a judgmental to a more compassionate and balanced interpretation of the facts and issues in a case.

3. *Identifying professional knowledge.* After identifying the case issues and perspectives, I encourage students to review the literature relevant to the case. Left to their own devices, most students tend to shoot from the hip, or limit themselves to the resources at hand. I want them to stretch themselves and to explore the extant knowledge on various issues within cases. I require an on-line review of the literature, using ERIC on the Internet or one of the Netscape search engines such as Infosearch, Altavista, or Yahoo. I caution students not to accept everything they read at face value but to weigh the evidence in light of the source, their own experiences, their peers' and others' expertise, and the circumstances of the case.

4. *Formulating actions.* Projected actions need to be realistic; that is, actions that students would be capable of undertaking as the teacher in the case. Again, role play can be a catalyst in helping students to see and hear how their proposed actions might be received by the other participants in a case. I often demonstrate how the style and phrasing of one's speech can be just as important as its substance. The reverse is also true—the "correct" words can be said, but if they are said insincerely or without conviction, the result can be a loss of credibility and capacity to effect change. Language, communication skills, and nonverbal behavior all need to be considered in terms of their effects on the choices of action, interpretation of such actions by others, and probable outcomes.

5. *Considering the consequences of actions.* I emphasize that even the most carefully reasoned actions may not have the desired consequences because of factors beyond the control of the teacher. In addition to offering their best solutions, students need to recognize that for every action there is always a "best case" and "worst case" scenario. The actual result may well lie somewhere in between, and might satisfy all involved. I encourage students to formulate contingency plans for a variety of responses in the case. What may seem obvious to one person may be totally overlooked by another. I caution students not to assume anything, but to clearly communicate and articulate the reasons for their particular choices and actions.

Assessment Issues

Assessment is an area that gives many case instructors a great deal of difficulty. Because there is no one right answer, a certain amount of latitude and flexibility in evaluating case analysis is needed. However, having a structure and criteria for evaluating cases (see Chapters 4, 6, 8, and 14), facilitates students' ability to look beyond the obvious and contributes to an enriched understanding of the issues as well as an informed class discussion. It also gives the instructor a basis for evaluating the quality of the analyses. The contributors in this volume tie their case evaluations to the research in some way to facilitate the connections between identifying problems and accessing the expert literature for lifelong learning and problem solving.

Case instructors need to decide the kinds of assessment measures needed to match their desired outcomes: a ranking, a rating, a formative or summative written or oral evaluation, and/or grades. Do you want to give individual or group grades, or both? Will your grades take into account instructor and/or peer review? There are many exciting possibilities. But any way you choose to assess cases, it isn't easy, and it is time-consuming. But to echo many of our contributors, it's worth the extra time and effort.

In my own classes, I have used evaluation criteria based on the five categories previously suggested as a conceptual framework for case analysis. A Likert scale, with scoring categories ranging from excellent to poor, was constructed for each item and distributed in class. I also add an additional item to assess case presentation skills. After each case presentation, the appropriate space was checked off by students and myself and scores tallied for each item. We then have the opportunity to discuss where we see things alike and differently. This approach has been effective in guiding preservice teachers to think critically about what constitutes excellent case analysis and to focus on how to communicate that information to others.

REFERENCES

Eggen, P., & Kauchak, D. (1997). *Educational psychology: Classroom connections* (3rd ed.). New York: Merrill/Prentice-Hall.

Kauffman, J., Mostert, M., Trent, S., & Hallahan, D. (1998). *Managing classroom behavior: A reflective case-based approach* (2nd ed.). Boston: Allyn & Bacon.

Kowalski, T. (1995). *Case studies in educational administration* (2nd ed.). New York: Longman.

Kowalski, T., Weaver, R., & Henson, K. (1994). *Case studies of beginning teachers*. New York: Longman.

McNergney, R., Herbert, J., & Ford, R. (1994). Cooperation and competition in case-based teacher education. *Journal of Teacher Education, 45*(5), 339–345.

Miller Cleary, L., & Peacock, T. (1998). *Collected wisdom: American Indian education*. Boston: Allyn & Bacon.

Mostert, M. P. (1998). *Interpersonal collaboration in schools.* Boston: Allyn & Bacon.

Mostert, M., & Sudzina. M. (1996, February). *Undergraduate case method teaching: Pedagogical assumptions vs. the real world.* Paper presented at the annual meeting of the Association of Teacher Educators, St. Louis.

Ormrod, J. E. (1998). *Educational psychology: Developing learners* (2nd ed.). New York: Merrill/Prentice-Hall.

Shulman, J. (Ed.). (1992). *Case methods in teacher education.* New York: Teachers College Press.

Silverman, R., Welty, W., & Lyon, S. (1992). *Case studies for teacher problem solving.* New York: McGraw-Hill.

Sudzina, M. (1993). *Dealing with diversity issues in the classroom: A case study approach.* Paper presented at the annual meeting of the Association of Teacher Educators, Los Angeles. (ERIC Document Reproduction Service No. ED 354 233)

Sudzina, M. (1994a, October). *Consequences of preservice participation in a national case competition.* Paper presented at the annual meeting of the Mid-Western Educational Research Association, Chicago. (ERIC Document Reproduction Service No. ED 376 161)

Sudzina, M. (1994b, February). *Mentoring and collaborating with cases: Developing the skills and resources to compete in a national case competition.* Paper presented at the annual meeting of the Association of Teacher Educators, Atlanta. (ERIC Document Reproduction Service No. ED 374 124)

Sudzina, M. (1995, April). *Case competition as a catalyst to restructure the teaching and learning of educational psychology.* Paper presented at the annual meeting of the American Educational Research Association, San Francisco. (ERIC Document Reproduction Service No. ED 382 683)

Sudzina, M. (1997). Case study as a constructivist pedagogy for teaching educational psychology. *Educational Psychology Review, 9*(2), 199–218.

Sudzina, M. (in press). Organizing instruction for case-based teaching. In R. F. McNergney, E. R., Ducharme, & M. K. Ducharme (Eds.), *Educating for democracy: Case-method teaching and learning.* Mahwah, NJ: Erlbaum.

Sudzina, M., & Kilbane, C. (1992). Applications of a case study text to undergraduate teacher preparation. In H. Klein (Ed.), *Forging new partnerships with cases, simulations, games, and other interactive methods.* Boston: World Association for Case Method Research & Application. (ERIC Document Reproduction Service No. ED 350 292)

Sudzina, M., & Kilbane, C. (1994). New contexts for educational case study application: From the classroom to competition and beyond. In H. E. Klein (Ed.), *Learning the doing—doing the learning: The art of interactive teaching.* Boston: World Association for Case Method Research & Application. (ERIC Document Reproduction Service No. ED 374 121)

Sudzina, M., Kowalski, T., & Weaver, R. (1994, June). *Case-based teaching: Reflecting on teacher education practices across content areas at two universities.* Symposium presentation at the annual meeting of the World Association for Case Method Research & Application, Montreal.

Wassermann, S. (1993). *Getting down to cases: Learning to teach with case studies.* New York: Teachers College Press.

Wassermann, S. (1994). *Introduction to case method teaching: A guide to the galaxy.* New York: Teachers College Press.

AMELIA KLEIN

Amelia Klein is an associate professor of education at Wheelock College in Boston, Massachusetts. She received her Ed.D. from Boston University in early childhood education. A recipient of her college's Cynthia Longfellow Teaching Award, she continues to search for innovative and effective teaching/learning approaches that will prepare her students to become competent (and blissful) teachers of young children.

Klein is a member of the executive board of WACRA™, the World Association for Case Method Research and Application. In her role as an active learner of case methodology, she has authored numerous papers, articles, and chapters on case teaching, and has organized and directed interactive symposia for educators in Eastern Europe. She is currently investigating cross-cultural applications of case-based teaching. Her interests include: travel (inspired by John Steinbeck's *Travels with Charlie* in high school), hosting international conferences, the study of humor, and young children everywhere.

3

"ALL I NEEDED TO KNOW I LEARNED IN KINDERGARTEN": APPLYING CASES TO EARLY CHILDHOOD TEACHER EDUCATION PROGRAMS

AMELIA KLEIN
WHEELOCK COLLEGE

My success as a case teacher can be attributed to skills I developed in an early childhood classroom, or, as Robert Fulghum stated: "All I ever really need to know I learned in kindergarten" (1988). For those who venture into the domain of five-year-olds (as I did in my first career) life is filled with challenges and adventure. In order to survive as a kindergarten teacher, I acquired skills and dispositions that not only enhanced my mental well-being, but also my effectiveness as a lifelong educator! Let me provide an example of one such adventure.

My kindergartners were looking forward to an excursion to O'Hare airport near Chicago. Feeling confident that I had thoroughly planned for any unforeseen events, I was astonished to discover the morning of the trip that none of the 10 adults who had volunteered to accompany me showed up. As I looked into the eyes of my children (all 40 pairs) I decided to avert (or perhaps confront) disaster by announcing that our plans would be carried out. However, certain restrictions would be applied. Each child would have to use the toilet *at least twice* before boarding the bus that was to carry us on our long and bumpy journey to the airport. (Visiting airport restrooms was no longer on the itinerary because I could only supervise activities in *one* of these environments.)

With my confidence and determination restored, we proceeded to the world's busiest airport. On arriving and entering the terminal, one little boy eagerly announced, "I have to go to the bathroom." Decisiveness was becoming my strength. I instructed another boy to accompany him and to "be back out here in one minute." Five minutes passed. I sent two more boys into the restroom. Five more long minutes elapsed before three of the boys rushed out and exclaimed "He's stuck in that thing and he won't come out!" My imagination was in overdrive as I contemplated my next action. I considered two possibilities: First, I could walk into the busiest men's room in the world with 39 children at my side (who at this point huddled around me in a state of anxiety); or second, I could send in the most articulate five-year-old (male) child in the class who *might* provide a more detailed explanation of the situation. As I reluctantly pondered my options a security guard came to the rescue. On returning from the scene with the missing (and mischievous) child in hand, he informed us that (1) an electric hand dryer apparently got "stuck" and not the child, and (2) the child was reluctant to come out of the restroom because he feared his actions would have negative consequences (he had never used an electric dryer before).

At this point, I sensed that other children were about to make "urgent" requests to use the restroom (their sense of curiosity and playfulness now aroused) and that I had to redirect their attention quickly. I needed to keep the group focused on the purpose of the excursion. I announced: "Does anyone know if airplanes have toilets?" After taking a poll (an opportunity to engage in mathematical thinking), the group was determined to find out "who won"! We made a graph on a paper towel (confiscated from the men's room) and proceeded to board an airplane for a tour. Thanks to an alert tour guide, we were whisked off to the cockpit, guided through the cabin, provided firsthand experiences to examine food and safety equipment, and, most importantly, each child was given a set of "wings" (pin) and a coloring book to take home. When I suggested that we verify answers to my question about toilets, the children were not in the least bit interested. Confirming the results of our poll now became a drudgery that we quickly calculated by using literacy skills and reading the labels on the restroom doors. (The "yes" group won.) Although requests to use the toilet were now to be honored, none were made. The children were eager to return to school to use their crayons in their coloring books.

Life experiences such as these provide opportunities to develop survival skills, build character, and enhance one's professional development. I learned as a kindergarten teacher that one must be prepared for the unexpected, take (calculated) risks, establish goals and pursue them, engage in creative problem solving, persevere, and maintain a positive and constructive attitude when confronted with new situations. I also discovered that teachers are active learners, that is, they "learn by doing." These skills and dispositions, together with my personal teaching philosophy (and, I must admit, a sense of humor) have guided my practice with adult learners.

A DEVELOPMENTAL JOURNEY

Before I elaborate on how kindergarten prepared me to become a case teacher, let me describe the developmental journey I have taken in my pursuit of knowledge about the case method. My first exposure to case-based teaching occurred when I accompanied my husband to an academic conference for business educators. The focus of the conference was on interactive teaching and the "case method." I had never heard of case method, this was seven years before Katherine Merseth published her classic *The Case for Cases in Teacher Education* (1991), and I assumed that it was an educational program tailored for another discipline. What could the Harvard Business School (which developed the case method for teaching business administration) tell me about preparing early childhood teachers to work with five-year-olds?

During the conference, I reluctantly attended sessions given by accounting, marketing, and business management professors. My initial attitude was one of indifference (a little learning is a dangerous thing). What happened during the sessions precipitated an educational voyage that continues in my career as a teacher educator. My state of indifference became a state of cognitive dissonance and curiosity when my teaching practice, the lecture method, was challenged. I experienced a state of disequilibrium because I strongly believed the lecture method to be an efficient way to help students acquire a "body of knowledge" that will prepare them for the professional world. Advocates for discussion teaching, however, argued that students need more than factual knowledge, recipes, and "correct answers." Learning by the case method, they proposed, provided students with opportunities to think and act like professionals. Roland Christensen's (1987) words changed my notion of pedagogy:

> *Reading about problems or memorizing principles does little to prepare the practitioner—architect, doctor, or manager—to apply concepts and knowledge to the complexity of real-life problems. Discussion teaching achieves these objectives better than alternative pedagogies. It puts the students in an active learning mode, challenges*

them to accept substantial responsibility for their own education, and gives them firsthand appreciation of, and experience with, the application of knowledge to practice (p. 3).

Building Bridges

On reexamining my notion of pedagogy, I made an important link to previously held knowledge. I discovered that the case method reflected early childhood education principles that I could apply to my work with adult learners.

A background in cognitive psychology, human development, and early childhood education shaped my philosophy of teaching and learning. As an early childhood educator, I was influenced by the theories of Dewey, Piaget, and Vygotsky. John Dewey, for example, believed that "teaching" was most effective when the student was engaged in inquiry learning, collaborative problem solving, and reflective thinking. The aim of education should be to promote a democratic process that fosters autonomy and responsibility on the part of students. He emphasized that learning experiences should represent *real-life situations,* be practical, and personally meaningful. (Education should be a preparation for *life.*) Piaget theorized that knowledge is constructed when a person experiences cognitive dissonance and seeks to resolve that dissonance. The aim of education, for Piagetian theorists, is to create *cognitive conflict* and to nurture critical, independent thinking that leads to qualitative as well as quantitative changes in thought. Vygotsky emphasized *collaboration* as a source of cognitive development. In his view, dialogue plays a crucial role in the learning process. For Vygotsky, cognition is socially constructed through interactions with adults and more knowledgeable peers.

Early childhood education philosophy provided me with a rationale and a theoretical framework for adult learning by the case method. I asked myself: Would my students acquire the basic knowledge necessary to become effective teachers of young children through case discussion? Would the case method provide a broader and more in-depth learning experience for them, as Christensen argued? Do all learners, regardless of age, need to be *actively* involved in the learning process? I reflected on these ideas by writing about them (Klein, 1989) and examining the work of experts in the field of case method (e.g., Christensen, 1987; Erskine, Leenders, & Mauffette-Leenders, 1981).

The Road To Discovery

The more I read about case method, the more questions I had. I was eager to discuss case methodology with teacher educators, but little was known about it in my field. I decided to investigate discussion teaching as it was used in other disciplines. I became a member of the international organization World Association for Case Method Research and Application (WACRA), which was founded in 1984. In the early years, members of the organization were primarily leaders in the field of business education. When attending WACRA conferences and listening to business educators, I discovered that we shared the same educational goals; we wanted our students to:

- apply theory to practice
- develop critical thinking skills
- engage in collaborative problem solving
- reflect on practice
- gain competency as decision makers
- be creative, innovative thinkers

These experienced case teachers became my first models. I was impressed by their general skills, practical wisdom, and level of confidence in using the case method. They had acquired a knowledge base that allowed them to experiment with innovative uses of cases. They were not just case teachers, but case writers and case researchers. I learned that case method was an art in itself, crafted to provide optimal learning experiences for soon-to-be professionals. The annual WACRA conferences became a source of information and training. One particular conference workshop, conducted by a faculty member from the Harvard Business School, provided an opportunity for me to be an active learner. For the first time, I became a participant in a case discussion. With the guidance of the discussion leader, I learned about case methodology from the inside out: I assumed the role of a student and experienced learning by the case method! The experience was exhilarating. The gifted case leader generated discussion that was thought-provoking and involved participants on both a cognitive and an emotional level. I was immersed in a process of intellectual stimulation and enlightenment. I wanted my students to have this same experience. I wanted to become a gifted case teacher.

The Journey Begins

My intellectual journey took several paths. I continued to be an active member of WACRA, attending conferences and corresponding with business case teachers about their work. I became a member of the executive board of the organization. My role was to explore case methodology in the field of teacher education and to encourage educators to join

WACRA, an interdisciplinary, international community of case teachers. This required that I establish contacts with teacher educators who were case users.

At this time, the education field was becoming informed about the case method. Publications focusing on case-based teaching were targeted for teacher educators (e.g., Kowalski, et al., 1990; Merseth, 1991; Shulman, 1992; Shulman & Colbert, 1987, 1988). The *Teacher Education Quarterly*, a leading journal for educators, devoted an entire issue in 1990 to "case methodology in the study and practice of teacher education." Professional organizations such as the American Educational Research Association (AERA) and the National Association of Early Childhood Teacher Educators (NAECTE) organized case colloquia at their annual conferences. Further support for the case method was given by national teacher education reform groups such as the Carnegie Forum on Education and the Economy, which recommended in its 1986 report that interactive approaches to instruction be incorporated in teacher training programs.

The education field was embracing the case method. My task of finding teacher educators who were case users became easier. I attended workshops at AERA annual conferences that provided hands-on experiences and put me in touch with experts as well as novices. Intensive workshop sessions were offered by leaders in the field such as Judith Shulman, Rita Silverman, and Bill Welty. I attended a two-day working conference on case-based teaching organized by Judy Shulman and the Far West Laboratory for Educational Research and Development. Presenting their views on case method were leaders in the field of educational research such as Carne Barnett, Judith Kleinfeld, Katherine Merseth, Rita Silverman, Lee Shulman, Gary Sykes, Selma Wassermann, and Bill Welty. The conference provided exciting opportunities for participants to interact with these outstanding scholars.

These experiences allowed me to become part of a network of case users in my field. We exchanged ideas, samples of our work, and resources. I developed other networks through WACRA and the teacher educators who became members of the organization. I coordinated the review process for papers presented at annual WACRA conferences and was able to learn more about innovative and diverse uses of cases in teacher education.

I became an avid reader. The wealth of publications available for "novices" provided me with theoretical perspectives and practical information. Particularly relevant for me were the writings of Christensen, Garvin, and Sweet (1991); Fosnot (1989); Jones, (1986); Kleinfeld (1988–1992); Shulman and Mesa-Bains (1993); Silverman, Welty, and Lyon (1991); and Wassermann (1993, 1994). By attending presentations at AERA conferences, I became familiar with the research and work of Harrington (1993) and Barnett and Sather (1992). The knowledge that I gained on my road to discovery provided an incentive (and a sense of courage) to experiment with case teaching.

Learning by Doing the Case Method

I began cautiously by presenting my first discussion case in a student teaching seminar. I chose an unpublished case that I obtained at an early childhood teacher educator's workshop. The case depicted a situation that was very familiar (and challenging) to my practicum students, guiding children's behavior. In the case, a teacher is confronted with the antisocial actions of kindergartners: A timid child is ridiculed and emotionally hurt by classmates who label the child a "cry baby." The case provided important variables for students to consider in developing a positive resolution of the problem situation.

I was surprised by the students' high level of enthusiasm and involvement in the case discussion. They were eager to apply their professional knowledge and to engage in collaborative problem solving. They appeared comfortable and confident as they explored innovative and effective approaches to classroom management. For the first time in my seminar, I observed my students as reflective practitioners. They were thinking and acting like teachers, confronting the unexpected challenges which they would face in their own classrooms one day. Their knowledge showed. Their maturity showed. And their readiness to assume teaching responsibilities showed. The case discussion provided me with a global view of my students' professional development. What went right? Why was I successful in my first attempt at case-based teaching?

I realized that the case that I used provided a personally meaningful and challenging learning situation that matched the interests and needs of my preservice teachers. Students were highly motivated and eager participants in the case discussion because they wanted to develop competency as classroom "managers," an area of expertise that is crucial for beginning teachers. The case discussion allowed students to exercise their newly gained knowledge in a low-risk situation. They engaged in collaborative problem solving with their peers and developed competency as problem solvers in the context of a "learning community."

The search for effective teaching cases now became my major goal. I tested cases from unpublished college "casebooks" and commercial textbooks. Although I carefully selected cases that contained relevant subject matter for my students, the cases did not generate the same degree of excitement and involvement as the first case I used. I concluded that the cases were somewhat generic and did not depict the intense "reality" my students encountered in their daily lives in school communities. I also found the textbook cases I used to be too narrow and "right-answer" oriented. My goals were to: (1) search for stimulating cases that were open-ended and closely related to the experiences of my student teachers, and (2) experiment with other (nonnarrative) forms of cases.

Selecting the "Right" Case

I chose a television documentary as a "case." The documentary portrayed daily life experiences of individuals living in a poor urban community (Klein, 1991). The documentary revealed the harsh realities of poverty and its effects on children and families. Scenes and personal accounts of suffering and anguish were powerful components of the documentary and stimulated intense discussions about issues of poverty, racism, ethics, and social/moral responsibility. The documentary was an effective teaching/learning tool that helped my middle-class students construct knowledge about the diverse school communities in which they would one day practice.

Another format that I used to facilitate interactive learning was the "live" or "living" case. A live case is an actual, ongoing situation that exists in a professional environment. I learned about the "live case" from business educators who placed students in corporate settings to investigate problems that were emerging in an organization. Case-based learning occurred as students solved problems together with field personnel. The live case allowed students to make decisions in the "real world," outside of the context of the college classroom. This approach appealed to me when teaching students who were not having concurrent field-based experiences, such as a practicum.

I provided a "live case" (Klein, 1992) to my students by inviting a guest from a correctional facility to speak about problems the facility was having in providing an appropriate play setting for visiting children. Several students went to the facility to investigate the situation, and then reported their findings to the entire class. This information (and that provided by the guest speaker) became the basis for the case discussion. The case fostered critical analysis and collaborative problem solving (which included staff and inmates at the correctional facility). The students were highly motivated not only because they could exercise their professional knowledge, but because they had a stake in the problem-solving process. Their solutions really mattered because they were making a contribution to the real world!

Although these approaches met my goals of providing stimulating, personally meaningful, thought-provoking case discussions, they presented challenges for me as a case leader. For example, "open-ended" cases provided a wealth of information that seemed overwhelming for the students who had to determine: *What is this a case of? What is the focal point of the case?* As a facilitator of learning, I needed to have a clear understanding of the purposes of the case I was presenting: (1) the knowledge to be developed, (2) how students' professional development would be enhanced, and (3) how course objectives would be met. I needed to formulate general as well as specific questions that would guide students through a discovery learning process. Finally, I needed to assess student performance carefully in light of the purposes for the case study. I discovered limitations as well as benefits of various case study formats. I concluded that a case discussion is not an end in itself, but is a means to an end. Careful evaluation of case discussions required that I establish further goals. I had to determine what remained to be done in terms of completing "unfinished business" (goals not achieved) or pursuing new goals constructed by the students. My practical experience provided a springboard as I made a transition from being a case experimenter to becoming a case *teacher* and *researcher.*

HOW MY TEACHING HAS CHANGED

Case method and other forms of interactive learning have become an integral part of my teaching. Through the process of case discussion I attempt to integrate the subject matter to be covered during particular course sessions. My goal and challenge as a case leader, therefore, is to design questions that facilitate investigation of relevant subject matter. The case serves as a nucleus around which students broaden their knowledge, enhance their practical wisdom, and think like professionals. Although my pedagogy has changed, my goals for the students have not. What has remained the same has been: content to be covered; knowledge, dispositions, and skills to be developed; preparation for the "world of work"; and reflective practice.

Setting the Stage

Prior to presenting cases for discussion, I have found it useful to "set the stage" or create a climate for learning that emphasizes active involvement. I explain to students that participation in course sessions is required. This is an external means of promoting active involvement. In order to motivate students intrinsically, I provide early childhood education principles as a framework and a rationale to define students' roles as learners. My expectations of students are transformed into responsibilities.

Involving students as active learners begins early in the semester. This process is initiated by asking students to describe, at the beginning of class, a problem situation that they have encountered at their field site. (These "problems" actually serve as mini cases.) I then ask the class to collaborate in assessing and exploring resolutions to the problem situations. Students are eagerly responsive because the situations presented are personally meaningful to them. (*This might happen to me tomorrow!*) After several sessions, students feel comfortable participating in an open forum. A sense of community, shared meaning, and camaraderie is also established. These sessions set the tone for the semester.

To further the spirit of interaction, I use games and simulations. These approaches present low-risk, nonthreatening "exercises" that engage students as creative thinkers and problem solvers. An example of a game, taken from a book on strategies for teacher training (Carter & Curtis, 1994), requires students to construct informed opinions using a "TV game show" format. Small groups of students collaborate as they respond to questions from the audience (other students in the class) such as, "What does my child learn by cooking?" or "Why doesn't the teacher use worksheets?"

Simulations require students to engage in role-playing. One example of a simulation I use, developed by a colleague (Phillips, 1995), provides opportunities for students to develop interprofessional team-building skills associated with inclusive practice. A professional team meeting is simulated in which students assume various roles and engage in collaborative decision making. The purpose of the meeting is to develop collaboratively an educational plan for a particular child with special learning needs.

One further strategy for facilitating interaction involves the physical arrangement of the classroom. Students must be able to have eye contact with all members of the group. I use a U-shaped configuration of tables as advocated by Silverman and Welty (1995). These authors also emphasize using visually accessible chalkboards to provide a means of recording and organizing information being presented during a case discussion.

Challenges

In developing knowledge about case-based teaching and learning, I have primarily focused on the intellectual needs of students. My emphasis has been on the process of learning. I have discovered that students have other needs that, if not met, can affect that process. *Emotional* and *physical needs* are important factors to consider in providing optimal learning experiences for students. For example, I observed that my students were more actively involved in case discussions when certain variables were met. First, they needed time to make a transition to the seminar. Prior to attending an early afternoon session at the college, the students have spent a full morning (four hours) in a classroom working with children. This is both physically and emotionally challenging. In order to help the student teachers make a transition from their work environments to the seminar (a three-hour meeting period), I allow a brief period of time for students to share their experiences. Talking about anxiety-producing events is therapeutic. As students present their problems to others, they receive empathy, support, and constructive advice. Students appear more relaxed and ready to focus on seminar activities.

Next, students performed better in a physical environment that was comfortable and conducive to learning. To combat physical fatigue, I have found it beneficial to select meeting areas that have adequate lighting, ventilation, acoustics, and comfortable chairs. (This requires extra effort on my part in reserving a classroom before rooms are assigned.) Providing simple refreshments, a task shared by the students and the instructor, satisfies the most basic need of all and replenishes students' energy levels. Scheduling a refreshment break at key periods in the seminar is also important in maintaining students' energy levels.

Finding a sufficient number of cases that relate to course topics and concepts has been another major challenge. One solution to this problem has been to write my own cases. Engaging in the process of researching, writing, testing, and revising a case is quite time-consuming. The degree of effort to write a quality case equals that of preparing a written document for publication. Obtaining release time from my teaching schedule and budgeting existing work time remain difficult tasks. One solution has been to collaborate with colleagues in the writing and/or editing of cases in progress.

Collaborating with Colleagues

Collaborative learning is a method that I applied to my *own* development as a case teacher. One approach I took was to organize case method workshops at my college for interested faculty members. Leaders in the field of case teaching (Rita Silverman and Bill Welty from Pace University, New York), and case writing (Joëlle Piffault from École de Hautes Études Commerciales, Montréal, Québec) were invited to conduct several training sessions. As a result of the workshops, my colleagues and I became a community of learners with common goals and objectives. We gave feedback to each other as we shared experiences applying the case method in our respective classes. For example, some of us used the same case and assessed its effectiveness as a teaching tool with different instructors and student populations. We discussed the challenges we faced as case facilitators and engaged in collaborative problem solving. We also talked about ways that cases could be adapted or extended to meet particular course requirements and the learning needs of students. Through this process we were introduced to new cases and increased our "supply" of case materials. We also became mentors to each other and developed a support system as we ventured into the "unknown" world of case teaching.

As a member of a special interest group on children's play at my college, I introduced the idea of developing cases to promote play education (Klein, 1996). The mission of the special interest group was to inform and educate those who work with young children about the nature and functions of play in children's development. I provided a rationale (or *made a case*) for cases in play education. As a result, designing cases to be instructional devices became a goal of the collaboration. Members are currently developing cases to be published in a case book on play. In their efforts to do so, they have become learners themselves. Workshops on case writing and editing have provided guidelines and support for the work of the play group.

I have also sought opportunities to exchange ideas with members of my profession outside of the college community. For example, in my travels to other institutions, I have initiated conversations and have learned more about case method through the experiences of others. This information has provided innovative models for my faculty and myself and has enhanced our expertise on effective use of case methodology.

NEW HORIZONS

As my developmental journey continues, I have sought new horizons in which to broaden and deepen my knowledge of case-based teaching. Collaborative projects developed with educators in other countries have provided an international scope to my study of case methodology.

One undertaking has been a cross-cultural research project. Together with Dr. Magorzata Karwowska-Struczyk, a teacher educator at Warsaw University in Poland, I am designing an ethnographic study that will investigate case teaching in two cultural settings (Karwowska-Struczyk, 1995; Klein, 1995). The goals are threefold: (1) to learn about my own teaching style and techniques in applying case methodology, (2) to relate these variables to student learning, and (3) to examine case teaching in an early childhood teacher education program in the United States and in Poland.

The study has required a great deal of preparation and collaboration. First, my colleague and I have had to develop a shared meaning by reading selected works on ethnographic research, case method, and the process of case writing (e.g., Leenders & Erskine, 1989). Next, we have attended workshops on case method, and have organized case workshops for colleagues at our respective institutions. Furthermore, we practice the art of case teaching in our respective courses, and are developing skills as case writers by writing cases for our current research project.

The ethnographic study will also involve researchers and educators from other countries (e.g., Denmark, Sweden) who will contribute their expertise and knowledge of case method research to the project. Together, investigators of the study will form an international community of learners that will explore the adaptability, resourcefulness, and universality of case method as a teaching tool.

WHAT I LEARNED IN KINDERGARTEN

My experiences in a kindergarten classroom have provided me with a foundation for lifelong learning. As I reflected on my early stages of development as a teacher, I realized that the dispositions, skills, and philosophical perspectives I hold today were constructed as a result of visits to an airport, reflective practice, and a sense of adventure and curiosity. Case teachers must be *learners, researchers,* and *risk takers.* They must have a passion for teaching that will motivate them to consistently seek innovative, creative approaches to teaching and learning. Acquiring pedagogical knowledge is an evolutionary process. There is no "level" at which one stops, because there is always something new to explore and discover in the realm of knowledge acquisition.

Case teachers must be *student-oriented.* They must be prepared to adapt their teaching to satisfy the needs of learners. Case teachers must trust and respect their students' ability to construct knowledge through self-directed learning experiences such as case discussions. They must be willing to share power and to nurture student autonomy as they engage in interactive dialogues with students.

Case teachers must be *teacher-oriented.* They must be aware of their own strengths and mindful that they must seek opportunities to enhance their effectiveness as educators continually. They must nurture their self-confidence by trusting and respecting *themselves* as learners. They must be patient and persevering. Finally, case teachers must maintain a positive, constructive attitude as they confront the challenges inherent in teaching and learning.

REFERENCES

Barnett, C., & Sather, S. (1992, April). *Using case discussions to promote changes in beliefs among mathematics teachers.* Paper presented at the annual meeting of the American Educational Research Association, San Francisco.

California Council on the Education of Teachers. (1990). Case methodology [Theme issue]. *Teacher Education Quarterly, 17* (1).

Carnegie Forum on Education and the Economy—Task Force on Teaching as a Profession (1986). *A nation prepared: Teachers for the 21st century.* Washington, DC: Carnegie Corporation.

Carter, M., & Curtis, D. (1994). *Training teachers: A harvest of theory and practice.* St. Paul, MN: Redleaf Press.

Christensen, C. R. (1987). *Teaching and the case method.* Boston: Harvard Business School.

Christensen, C. R., Garvin, D. A., & Sweet, A. (1991). *Education for judgement: The artistry of discussion leadership.* Boston: Harvard Business School Press.

Erskine, J. A., Leenders, M. R., & Mauffette-Leenders, L. A. (1981). *Teaching with cases.* London, Ontario, Canada: University of Western Ontario.

Fulghum, R. (1988). *All I really need to know I learned in kindergarten: Uncommon thoughts on common things.* New York: Villard.

Fosnot, C. T. (1989). *Enquiring teachers, enquiring learners: A constructivist approach for teaching.* New York: Teachers College Press.

Harrington, H. L. (1993, April). *Cases and teacher development.* Paper presented at the annual meeting of the American Educational Research Association, Atlanta.

Jones, E. (1986). *Teaching adults: An active learning approach.* Washington, DC: National Association for the Education of Young Children.

Karwowska-Struczyk, M. (1995). Introductory steps in implementing the case method at the Early Childhood Education Department of Warsaw University. In H. Klein (Ed.), *Teaching and interactive methods with cases, simulations and games* (pp. 417–420). Boston: World Association for Case Method Research & Application.

Klein, A. (1989). The case method approach and adult education. In H. Klein (Ed.), *Case method research and application: New vistas* (pp. 43–50). Boston: World Association for Case Method Research & Application.

Klein, A. (1991). Changing social values: Innovative use of TV documentaries. In H. Klein (Ed.), *Managing change with cases, simulations, games and other interactive methods* (pp. 393–398). Boston: World Association for Case Method Research & Application.

Klein, A. (1992). Beyond classroom instruction: Student learning in a social context. In H. Klein (Ed.), *Forging new partnerships with cases, simulations, games and other interactive methods* (pp. 141–148). Boston: World Association for Case Method Research & Application.

Klein, A. (1995). Case methodology and teacher education: An American perspective. In H. Klein (Ed.), *Teaching and interactive methods with cases, simulations and games* (pp. 409–416). Boston: World Association for Case Method Research & Application.

Klein, A. (1996). Constructing knowledge about play: Case method and teacher education. In A. L. Phillips (Ed.), *Topics in early childhood education series, Topics 2: Playing for keeps* (pp. 57–66). St. Paul, MN: Redleaf Press.

Kleinfeld, J. (1988–1992). *Case series in cross-cultural education.* Fairbanks, AK: University of Alaska, Center for Cross-Cultural Studies.

Kowalski, T. J., Weaver, R. A., & Henson, K. T. (1990). *Case studies on teaching.* New York: Longman.

Leenders, M. R., & Erskine, J. A. (1989). *Case research: The case writing process.* London, Ontario, Canada: School of Business Administration, The University of Western Ontario.

Merseth, K. (1991). *The case for cases in teacher education.* Washington, DC: American Association of Colleges for Teacher Education.

Phillips, A. L. (1995, April). *Inclusive support teams: Lessons for interprofessional educators.* Paper presented at the annual meeting of the American Educational Research Association, San Francisco.

Shulman, J. H. (Ed.) (1992). *Case methods in teacher education.* New York: Teachers College Press.

Shulman, J. H., & Colbert, J. A. (1987). *The mentor teacher casebook.* San Francisco, CA: Far West Laboratory for Educational Research and Development.

Shulman, J. H., & Colbert, J. A. (1988). *The intern teacher casebook.* San Francisco, CA: Far West Laboratory for Educational Research and Development.

Shulman, J. H., & Mesa-Bains, A. (Eds.) (1993). *Diversity in the classroom: A casebook for teachers and teacher educators.* Hillsdale, NJ: Lawrence Erlbaum.

Silverman, R., Welty, W. M., & Lyon, S. (1991). *Case studies for teacher problem solving.* New York: McGraw-Hill.

Silverman, R., & Welty, W. M. (1995, December). *Case method teaching.* Professional development workshop, Wheelock College, Boston.

Wassermann, S. (1993). *Getting down to cases: Learning to teach with case studies.* New York: Teachers College Press.

Wassermann, S. (1994). *Introduction to case method teaching: A guide to the galaxy.* New York: Teachers College Press.

JAMES D. ALLEN

James D. Allen ("Jim" to his friends) is currently associate professor of educational psychology at the College of Saint Rose in Albany, New York. He received his Ph.D. in educational psychology from the University of California–Santa Barbara (1982). For the past six years he has taught at least two, sometimes as many as four, sections of educational psychology courses utilizing case-method instruction.

Allen taught at Jilian Teachers College in the Peoples Republic of China in 1997. He also taught at Penn State University–Altoona, UCLA, and for California State University–Northridge. Allen also taught mathematics in public schools from 1972 to 1977. His research interests include case-method instruction, motivation and mastery learning, and classroom management.

4

TEACHING WITH CASES AND LESSONS LEARNED: THE JOURNEY OF AN EDUCATIONAL PSYCHOLOGIST

JAMES D. ALLEN
COLLEGE OF ST. ROSE

I graduated with a degree in teaching in June, 1973, (B. S., secondary education; B. A., mathematics) without having to take an educational psychology course. I assume that in some of my education methods courses principles of educational psychology were discussed, but I have absolutely no recollection of it. What I can recall vividly is my first teaching job, which started the Tuesday after Labor Day, 1973. I discovered quickly that almost everything that I had learned, or at least thought that I had learned, in my education courses seemed irrelevant. The actual practice of teaching was very different from the theories of education that had been abstractly discussed in my undergraduate classes.

MY JOURNEY BEGINS

After many different academic and career excursions, including completion of a Ph.D. in educational psychology, I taught my first educational psychology course in 1982, and became a full-fledged, tenure-track, college faculty member in 1984. I knew that I wanted to teach in a way that connected educational psychology theory to the actual realities of class-room conditions. This became the major criterion for me in structuring my courses and selecting texts. I used the Biehler and Snowman (1993) text because the authors used a significant portion of the text to illustrate theory applied to classroom practice. I was feeling pretty good about my teaching, thinking that I was, or at least Biehler and Snowman were, helping my students learn how to bridge the gap between theory and practice. But after a few years, I started to have doubts.

I had begun reading the literature on reflection, reflective teaching, and teacher education practices to promote the development of teachers as "reflective practitioners" (e.g., Ross, 1989; Schon, 1983, 1987; Shulman, 1986; Sparks-Langer et al., 1990; Zeichner & Tabachnick, 1990). This literature seemed to fit well with the cognitive and constructivist perspectives on learning that I used as the basis of my classroom instruction. Then, just before attending the American Educational Research Association (AERA) conference in 1991, I read Richert's (1990) "Case Methods and Teacher Education: Using Cases to Teach Teacher Reflection," which, for me, was the first detailed description of using cases to help promote the reflective thinking abilities of preservice teachers. This prompted me to attend several of the AERA sessions devoted to case methods where I was further convinced that the use of cases in my undergraduate educational psychology courses might help, not only to develop the reflective abilities of my students, but prove to be an excellent way to relate theory to practice. I decided that during the remaining semester and summer I would educate myself about using cases as a pedagogy to use in my fall, 1991 courses. I knew I could review the literature and read about using cases, but how was I going to develop my case method pedagogical skills?

CROSSING THE RIVER

In talking with several people at AERA, I found out about a conference on case methods that was to be held that June at James Madison University in Virginia. It was at that conference that I first saw a demonstration of the pedagogy of conducting a case and had my first opportunity to practice actually organizing and leading a discussion of a case. What I experienced as a case discussant (taking on the student role) is still vivid to me. I was excited, and so was everyone else. Cognitively the discussion was stimulating. Different aspects of the case were clearly more important and relevant to each of us and even common concerns were often viewed from very different perspectives. Some of us analyzed the case based on principles of motivation. Others focused on the dynamics of the student–teacher relationship. Still others on the ethical–moral dimensions of the case.

Affectively, I felt more energized than I had in any education course that I had ever taken. There was never a moment that I didn't feel excited and at the edge of my seat. It was clear that when it was time to bring the discussion to a close, many of us were disappointed; so afterwards, on our own, we continued to talk about the issues in the cases and the case method. From this experience, I learned my first lesson:

LESSON 1 *Careful selection of cases is important in order to match one's instructional goals and to stimulate vigorous discussions.*

The cases we used were well written with enough ambiguity to provoke discussion with multiple layers of interpretation. Equally important to the quality of the case discussions was the manner in which the cases were facilitated. Although the discussions seemed to proceed smoothly, but randomly, they were, in fact, not random at all. During the debriefing after each case discussion, case facilitators Rita Silverman and Bill Welty explained the strategies and rationale for their methods of leading a case discussion. It became clear that teaching by the case method required a lot of preplanning if the discussion was going to produce "reflective" thinkers who could integrate and apply educational theory to practical classroom problems. It was important to know what questions to ask; what points to emphasize by writing them on the board; when to let a discussion wander, and how to refocus it; how to respond to illogical connections as well as how to respond to brilliant insights; how to get students talking to students in challenging, but respectful ways. These were just some of the elements that needed to be considered before, during, and after a case discussion by the facilitator.

Luckily, I had the opportunity to work with a group of three other people at the conference to prepare a case for discussion, and I was chosen to be the case facilitator and enjoyed it tremendously. I found the give and take of each person's perspective stimulating, responding to unanticipated aspects of the case challenging, and came to the realization that almost everyone in the discussion, including myself, learned something new about teaching and the relevance of multiple theoretical perspectives to classroom dilemmas. I feel that without the dual experiences of being a case discussant and case facilitator, I would have had a discouraging experience trying to teach with cases. Thus, I learned my second and third lessons about the case method.

LESSON 2 *Experiencing a case as a discussant (i.e., as a student) before leading a case discussion as a facilitator (i.e., as the teacher) provides a perspective that helps one to appreciate the cognitive and affective impact that cases can have on students.*

LESSON 3   *Going through a case method training session to learn how to lead a case discussion before doing it "for real" can help to develop new pedagogical skills benefiting both the teacher and the students.*

However, there were still many aspects to case method teaching I needed to learn.

EXPLORING NEW ROADS: CASES AND EDUCATIONAL PSYCHOLOGY

During the next semester I introduced the use of cases into my undergraduate (*EPY 350*) and graduate (*EPY 502*) educational psychology survey courses. The case text that I used for these educational psychology survey courses was the one edited by Silverman, Welty, and Lyon (1992). I began using these cases because I received my initial case facilitation training from Silverman and Welty at the Virginia Conference.

The *EPY 350* course is the only common core course that all educational majors take at the College of Saint Rose. It is usually taken during the junior year after having completed a separate developmental course in the sophomore year. Students come into the class with diverse academic preparations and aspirations. Many also come into the class with unique life and schooling experiences, because the approximately 25 percent are nontraditional students returning to school. Class size is typically 20 to 25 students. The major purpose of this course is to provide students with the psychological foundations for learning and teaching. Cases are primarily used to help preservice teachers apply educational psychology principles to realistic learning situations and dilemmas that occur daily in classrooms. A second purpose is to help students become more reflective and better decision makers. A third purpose is for students to realize that there is no one right teaching method that can be applied to the dynamic atmosphere of the classroom.

The *EPY 502* course is primarily for graduate education students who have no previous academic background in education. Most of the students in the class have undergraduate degrees in disciplines other than education and many are making midlife career changes. The content coverage includes development as well as general educational psychology topics, but includes more depth and provides a greater research basis than the undergraduate *EPY 350* course. The text I use in this class provides depth and has a strong research base (see Ormrod, 1998; Woolfolk, 1998). Class size typically ranges from 15 to 25 students. Again, the major purposes for the course are to provide a psychological foundation for future graduate education courses and to help students to begin thinking like teachers. Cases are used to help achieve both these goals.

LESSON 4   *The use of case studies needs to match course goals and objectives.*

When I first began using cases I integrated them into the course as a companion to each of the major topics of the course. For example, one case would address the topic of behavioral learning theory. Another case would address information processing theory. Yet another case would focus on motivation issues. This meant discussing approximately 10 to 12 cases a semester. The general format of the class was to discuss the text readings over the topic for two to three hours and then focus on a case related to that educational psychology topic for one to one and a half hours. Students were required to bring a one-page typed outline of the case to class the day of discussion to be used for their reference during the discussion. After the discussion students were required to write a two-page analysis that was to be turned in the next class meeting.

The outline that students prepared for the class discussion seemed to be working well. Putting it together required students to analyze the case in reference to the course topics rather than just reading the case as an interesting story (see Appendix A). The outline also seemed to facilitate the quality of the discussion because each and every student had several ideas written down, which increased the number of students who voluntarily participated and allowed me to call on the nonvolunteers as well. By the middle of the semester, typically 90 percent of the students contributed to the discussion and often it was 100 percent.

Although the oral class discussions of the case were very stimulating and seemed to help provide a context for students to see how educational psychology principles could be used in classroom situations, I was not very satisfied with the two-page written analyses. These analyses were, for the most part, extremely fragmented and superficial. I began to think that due to the complexity of the cases and because of the high level of analysis and synthesis I was looking for from the students, two pages was an unrealistic expectation. Some of the more conscientious students began to turn in four- to five-page analyses for each of the cases that were more in line with what I was hoping for. This prompted a change in future semesters of what I expected from students (see Appendix B) and how I evaluated their understanding of educational psychology principles through the written case analyses (see Appendix C).

LESSON 5   *Having students prepare a short (one- to two-page) written outline of the case to bring to class helps to promote more effective and stimulating discussions.*

LESSON 6   *Having students write an analysis of the case after discussion helps them to develop a deeper understanding of educational psychology* *principles and how they can be applied in educational situations, but they need to be of sufficient length (five to seven pages) to address the complexity of factors interacting in a case.*

In addition to focusing students' attention on the issues in a case, I believe there are several other reasons the class discussions proceeded so well. The first was the physical arrangement of the class. I always requested a room that had tables and chairs (rather than the arm-desk/chairs), which could be configured in a U-shaped arrangement with the opening of the U toward a blackboard and overhead screen. In this arrangement I can see every student and see those who are following along, those who have facial expressions that indicate that they have a different perspective, or those who have an immediate reaction to what another student has just said. This arrangement also allows each student to see every other student and to respond face-to-face with whomever they agree or disagree with. I also have each student create a name card to place in front of them so that they call each other by name. One of the great benefits of this is that students get to know almost all of the other students in the class by name, which is unusual in most classes. Students have often commented on how a certain camaraderie seems to develop throughout the class, which is a unique experience for many. Another great benefit for me is that this allows me to learn the students' names very quickly. I have found during my 20 years of teaching that knowing and calling a student by name helps to build respect and rapport that is invaluable.

LESSON 7 *Developing a classroom atmosphere in which good rapport exists between class members helps to develop a "community of learners" that encourages open discussion, friendly disagreements, and cooperation in the study of cases. The physical arrangement of the class and the ability to know one another by name helps to build this rapport and sense of community and promotes active participation by students.*

Another factor that contributes to lively discussions is my own case preparation. After I read a case, I create my own outline of the major dilemmas of the case and note those passages in the case description that are especially illustrative. I concurrently refer to the educational psychology text and note the text references that provide theoretical explanations. I then create a list of possible solutions, supported by theoretical principles, to each of the listed dilemmas along with possible consequences, both positive and negative, that might result from initiating the listed solutions. In other words, I create an outline similar to what I expect each student to prepare except mine is more extensive both in depth and breadth. Next, and what I believe to be the most important preparation for a facilitator, I prepare a set of questions that I will ask sometime during the discussion. Questions for each of the case discussions are similar in intent but vary by the content of the case. The intent is to help students develop application, analysis, synthesis, and evaluation skills. Box 4.1 lists some questions that I ask students to consider in facilitating a case discussion.

I also develop a set of specific case questions that I call my "Devil's Advocate" questions. These are questions that I know will be counter to the viewpoints held by many students in the class. I do this to encourage students to question and challenge my perspectives (and eventually other student's perspectives) by providing an alternative explanation based on logical reasoning. For example, when discussing a behavioral management problem, I might quickly suggest corporal punishment to control pupil misbehavior. My expectation is that many students will offer more positive and effective solutions. In addition, I raise questions that challenge viewpoints and beliefs that have long been held by students and that coincide with the actions of the teacher in the case, but are poor pedagogical practices. Students who have experienced poor pedagogy by their teachers often fail to realize this and assume certain strategies are good practice. For example, one of the major issues I raise in every case, and throughout the course, is the issue of teacher responsibility for what occurs in the classroom. I tell students up front that my bias is that the only behavior one always has control over is one's own and therefore placing the blame for problems on others doesn't solve classroom problems. Consequently, class discussion focuses on how the teachers in the cases can change their behaviors, which might change the behaviors of others. Preservice teachers often have trouble with placing the responsibility of classroom conditions

---

BOX 4.1   Questions to Facilitate Case Discussions

- How would (a particular action by a teacher in the case) affect other actions, perhaps by a student or a parent?

- Which specific educational psychology principles apply to (an issue that has just been pointed out in the case)?

- What do you think about (a comment that another student just made)?

- Why is (whatever the student suggested was a problem) a problem and what are the consequences?

- How does (a point that a student is making) relate to (a point that someone else has previously made)?

- How would you evaluate the likely success and possible consequences of (your solution) compared to (a solution suggested by someone else)?

primarily with the teacher; they often initially blame the students in the case for all the problems.

Thus, I continually ask my preservice teachers what the teachers in the cases are doing that creates the particular classroom or school environment in the case. Once the preservice teachers begin to focus on the teacher's actions, I begin to raise questions regarding teaching practices that are commonly accepted by preservice teachers but are, in fact, not based on sound educational and psychological principles. For example, college students often do not have a clear understanding that for grades to be valid they need to be as accurate and objective as possible a measure of one's academic knowledge or ability, and not based on a subjective evaluation of one's effort. Thus, when in a case a teacher lowers a student's math grade to a "B" (even though the student has a 98 percent test average, is a peer tutor, and in the teacher's own words "the best student in the class") because of his failure to do ungraded homework, many college students believe the teacher is right in assigning the "B" even through it is not a true reflection of his academic ability. In other words, I try to ask questions that force preservice teachers to reflect on how they will deal with learning situations by challenging the beliefs they currently hold by finding sound reasons to support these beliefs or to begin adjusting them.

LESSON 8   *The amount of preparation for a case by the facilitator–instructor can have a major impact on the quality of the discussion of the case. Preparing an organized set of challenging, stimulating questions is particularly helpful in improving the content and quality of the case discussion by the facilitator.*

Preservice teacher assessment of these courses at the end of the semester overwhelmingly favored the use of cases. A few of the major reasons students endorsed a case-based course include: learning to appreciate "many perspectives on a case" other than their own; learning "educational psychology principles and how they apply to actual situations in a fun (intrinsically motivating) way"; finding case discussions "stimulating" and allowing them to "communicate freely and easily with other students and the teacher"; and gaining an understanding of the "teacher's responsibility" in solving classroom problems (see Website for additional comments by students).

LESSON 9   *Preservice teachers almost universally endorsed the use of case studies in educational psychology classes for a variety of cognitive and affective benefits.*

Since I began using cases in 1991, I have reviewed a number of the educational case books published in the last 10 years, and continue to use the Silverman, Welty, and Lyon (1996) cases for several reasons. First, the cases have an authentic feel to them because they are based on real experiences that teachers have encountered. Second, they are dilemma-based, or problem solving, cases. There is always a surface problem as usually described by the teacher/narrator, and then there are more subtle and "under the surface" problems that encourage thoughtful analyses of the complex environments of classroom and schools. Third, they are edited by Silverman, who also teaches educational psychology courses, so the cases are structured to allow for application of educational and psychological principles. Fourth, I can choose from a data bank of approximately 60 cases those cases that I wish to use for a particular class. This allows flexibility on my part in choosing cases that best fit with my objectives and the variety also helps me from being bored from facilitating the same cases repetitively.

LESSON 10   *Being able to select from a large number of cases is helpful in making a closer match between course objectives and case content and provides for instructor interest and flexibility in leading case discussions.*

RECORDING A JOURNEY: PRESERVICE TEACHERS WRITING CASES ON CLASSROOM MANAGEMENT PROBLEMS

One of the difficulties that students sometimes have in discussing a case is their lack of experience on "the other side of the desk." That is, they have viewed classrooms as students all their lives, but almost never as a teacher. Therefore I began looking for a way to integrate students' experiences as a teacher with using cases. That opportunity developed when I taught a one-credit elective course on classroom management (*EPY 351*) for senior students who were currently student teaching, or who had student taught during the previous semester. Because students in this course either were experiencing the classroom from the perspective of a teacher, or recently had the experience, I thought this would be a good course to integrate the use of cases in a different way. I had each student write a case dealing with a classroom management issue that they were either dealing with currently or had dealt with during the previous semester as a student teacher. Students working in groups of three to four acted as peer critics and editors to help one another in formulating a case "problem" and then in writing a case analysis to solve the problem.

The class met for two and a half hours for five evenings during the semester, every third week. During the first class students were introduced to major classroom management issues, assigned a concise text on classroom management (see Evertson et al., 1994; Emmer et al., 1994), taken through a case discussion, and formed into groups to begin brainstorming themes for their cases.

For the second class, students were to bring an outline related to the case that they planned to write and to discuss it with their small group members to obtain feedback and direction. Then, during the third session, the students brought in a rough draft of their case study for additional feedback. By the fourth session, students had their "case" problem well formulated and their group discussion turned to finding solutions to their dilemmas (although this has been going on in most groups already). Then, during the final session, students brought in their completed case with an attached analysis for solving their case problems, and presented it to the entire class.

My major responsibilities included floating around to each group and facilitating the group process and encouraging students to relate their problems and solutions to the classroom management themes of the class text(s) and related educational psychology principles. The dynamics of the groups work especially well when there is a mix of students, some who are presently student teaching and some who have completed their student teaching, but grouped by common majors (i.e., elementary education majors grouped together, secondary education together, special education together, etc.). The students who had completed student teaching seemed to benefit the most from the actual writing of the case (and it showed in the quality of the final submission) by reflecting on what they encountered, how they dealt with it, and what they might do differently in the future. The students who were currently student teaching struggled more with the writing of the case, but seemed to gain great benefits from the class discussions with their peers who had already student taught. Listening to their peers discuss the classroom management problems that they had to deal with seemed to add a more "real" dimension to the problems the current student teachers were encountering. Many also expressed feelings of empathy with peers with whom they had had classes during their teacher education programs. Often, student teachers will actually have the opportunity to "try out" some of their solutions to the classroom management problems they are experiencing, which allows them to have a more meaningful student teaching experience.

LESSON 11   *Students who generate and write their own cases based on actual classroom experiences have the opportunity to reflect "in-practice" as well as "on-practice" (Schon, 1987) and to relate principles of educational psychology to classroom practices.*

DRAG RACING IN VIRGINIA

Early during the spring 1992 semester, I came across an announcement for the 1992 Commonwealth Center Invitational Team Case Competition to be held at the University of Virginia during Memorial Day weekend. I had just finished my first semester teaching with cases and was enthused by the students' positive comments regarding their classroom experience discussing cases. This, along with my own excitement about how much more students seemed to learn in the process, resulted in my forming a team of students and submitting an application. The Commonwealth Center was looking for diversity among team members so that was a major criterion I used in considering which students to approach, along with my knowledge of their abilities to orally discuss and write about cases. The first five students I asked were excited about the possibility of participating in a case competition (and I think a little surprised that I thought so highly of their abilities). Of course, I told them that there was no guarantee that our team would be chosen because the competition was being advertised nationally. It turned out that we were, in fact, chosen to be one of five teams to compete out of 26 team proposals submitted, and the only non-university institution.

Once chosen, students began to prepare for the competition. Students voluntarily met to discuss a variety of cases and engage in mock presentations. I often took on the role of evaluator, judge, and critic. The team also openly discussed the strengths and weaknesses of one another, and then chose a team captain, a person to act as editor for the written document that was to be judged, a discussion facilitator, and also decided among themselves who would be the "expert" and take primary responsibilities for certain educational and psychological concepts. The benefits of working as a team on a professionally relevant and "real" project was an experience these students had that was uncommon for most students at this stage of their learning, especially because none had engaged in student teaching yet. The team members made reference to this fact several times in the following months.

Once the team arrived for the case competition at the University of Virginia, they experienced being treated as professional educators whose ideas were listened to with respect, challenged, and evaluated by experts in the field of education and other disciplines. Again, this experience allowed students to gain an appreciation for their skills not only as outstanding students, but as entry professionals into their teaching careers. The competition was structured to bring out the best in students without denigrating the other competing teams and was intensive. Our team arrived late Friday afternoon, attended a competition orientation early Saturday morning, were handed the case to analyze at about 10:00 A.M., spent the next six to seven hours discussing the case, and turned in a typed case analysis at 5:00 P.M. for evaluation. On Saturday evening, teams organized themselves for the oral competition the next day. On Sunday from 8:00 A.M. to 1:00 P.M. each team had approximately one hour to defend its analysis before a panel of judges and an invited audience.

During the oral competition, when each team was responsible for responding to unrehearsed questions about the case from a panel of provocateurs, our team demonstrated the ability to respond to some very tough questions. I believe that this was partly due to their extensive preparation and ability to think on their feet quickly, but also to the manner in which they had experienced case questions during the previous semester. Many of the questions were of the "Devil's Advocate" variety or asked for concrete solutions to difficult situations. The team demonstrated their particular skill in relating educational and psychological principles and theories to the issues in the case.

During the preparation and competition phases, I was impressed at how well the students met the challenge of the rigor of the competition and performed in a professional manner. It gave me insight on how much students are capable of if given opportunities and experiences to demonstrate their knowledge and abilities.

After the case competition, several students wrote about the benefits they derived from the experience. They found the chance to work professionally with peers as a team on a common and real educational endeavor an opportunity they had seldom experienced and one from which they derived great satisfaction. They found that the diversity and uniqueness of perspectives among the team members, and learning to listen and respond to these various perspectives, contributed to their professional and personal growth. They felt pride in their ability to actually demonstrate their professional knowledge before a group of experts. One student recounted that her feelings of intimidation at the beginning of the oral defense of the case analysis were transformed into feelings of exuberance by the end of the hour due to her self-awareness of how well she and her team were responding to some tough questions by the provocateurs. Overall, the team members found their participation in the competition to be one of the major personal and professional experiences in their lives.

LESSON 12   *Students experience advanced growth in their personal and professional development and a sense of accomplishment when given challenging and realistic opportunities (such as case competitions) to demonstrate their knowledge and intellectual skills.*

REFUELING

After teaching with cases for one and a half years, I was starting to feel pretty comfortable with the pedagogy in general, but there were some specific concerns that I had regarding my ability to facilitate discussions.

I was particularly concerned with how to take advantage of the powerful dynamics that emerge during the case discussions between students. I felt that I was being too dominant when I was the facilitator and that the discussions often turned into a series of dialogues (teacher–student 1; teacher–student 2; teacher–student 3, etc.) rather than students dialoguing with one another. This lead me to take a week long seminar on teaching by the case method at Harvard University in January, 1993. At the seminar I saw several different methods of case facilitation demonstrated, each of which was analyzed and discussed regarding strengths and weaknesses. For me, one of the most useful demonstrations was by Chris Christensen, a master at getting students to respond to one another instead of addressing all their comments to the teacher. He demonstrated how, by preparing key questions, laying the groundwork for having students respond to one another, and using nonverbal messages and gestures, he was able to get students to quickly begin talking to, challenging, agreeing, and building on other students' perspectives and ideas. Again, I also had multiple opportunities to participate as a discussant (rather than a facilitator) in case discussions and was reminded of the affective motivating power that well-planned case discussions have. I also began to question more seriously the quantity of cases that I was having students prepare for discussion and writing analyses on. I became convinced that having students discuss 10 cases a semester was not realistic if I wanted them to analyze them in any depth.

LESSON 13   *Developing the pedagogical skills to teach with cases is an ongoing process that can be enhanced by observing other case facilitators.*

When I returned to campus from the Harvard seminar, I started to make adjustments in my teaching with cases. I reduced the number of cases discussed during the semester from ten to seven and eventually to six. This forced me to be more selective of which cases I thought would work best for specific educational psychology topics. I found that I could find cases that would allow integration of several educational psychological topics at one time (e.g., a case that dealt with both motivation principles and multicultural issues). I found that by having students prepare outlines for all the case discussions, but only requiring them to write five to seven page analyses on any four of the six cases increased the quality of their analyses.

LESSON 14   *Case study analyses written by students improved in quality when the quantity of cases allowed sufficient time to write thoughtful analyses and when the guidelines for required content of the analyses matched course expectations.*

CHECKING THE MILEAGE

After teaching with cases for almost three years I had very strong feelings about how helpful cases were in getting students to integrate educational psychology principles into practical applications and how students demonstrated a higher level of cognition through their analysis, synthesis, and evaluation of case studies. I also had lots of student testimonials, via end-of-course evaluations, that students thought they learned more through a case method and enjoyed it more. (The strongest testimonials were from the students who stated that they actually looked forward to attending the 8:00 A.M. *EPY 350* class.) However, I was feeling uneasy about the lack of empirical research studies demonstrating significant differences in students' academic and professional performance if they took a case-based versus a noncase-based educational psychology course. There are a lot of theoretical, philosophical, and personal testimonial justifications for the value of cases, but where is the empirical research that as an educational psychologist I've been trained to seek out? It is scant.

During the past four years, I have been conducting a group of related research studies to investigate the effectiveness of case studies in educational psychology survey courses. The findings clearly demonstrate that students in a case-based educational psychology course learned significantly more than students in a noncase-based section of the same course, made advances in their moral–ethical reasoning abilities and levels of reflective thinking about educational issues, had higher levels of in-class motivation, and were rated by cooperating and supervising teachers as being more "reflective" during their student teaching experiences (Allen, 1994; 1995).

LESSON 15   *Research findings that support the effectiveness of case pedagogy enable educational psychologists to provide a scientific rationale for teaching with cases and proceed with more confidence in using them.*

CRUISING ALONG: OLD BYWAYS AND NEW HIGHWAYS

I am convinced, by both personal experience and research, that teaching educational psychology courses, in which the objective is to connect theory to practice, is enhanced by using case studies as part of the instructional pedagogy. I also firmly believe that I am a better educational psychology teacher by using cases, and that students are better prepared in a teacher education program that includes case methods. As an instructor I benefit by knowing that students are more knowledgeable regarding educational psychology principles and their ability to apply them to educational situations, as well as being able to demonstrate analytic, evaluative, and reflective thinking. I also find teaching more en-joyable when dialoguing with students rather than being a dispenser of knowledge. Students are more motivated to learn, learn more educa-tional psychology content, and say that they enjoy the learning process more when cases are used. In short, by being generators and construc-tors of their own understanding, students learn more.

Although I have learned many lessons on my journey with cases, there are still some lessons I need to learn and additional directions I hope to travel regarding case methods. A major lesson I am still trying to learn is to figure out the most effective and efficient manner to pro-vide students with meaningful evaluative feedback about their cases that allows me time for other endeavors. In a typical semester I may teach three classes using cases, with each class having 20 to 25 students, each student writing six or seven one- to two-page case outlines, and four five to seven page case analyses. Because it takes me approximately five min-utes to evaluate an outline and 30 minutes for a case analysis, I spend between 150 and 185 hours a semester (10–12 hours per week) provid-ing written feedback to students about their ability to apply appropriate educational psychology theory to the cases. This task can be the best of times; it can also be the worst of times. It provides me with a great deal of satisfaction when students "get it" and write an analysis that is logi-cal and insightful. It is disheartening when students demonstrate lack of clear and logical thinking, do not have a clear understanding of the prin-ciples, and write poorly. However, every semester the majority of stu-dents show progress in their abilities from the beginning of the semester to the end, and that's what encourages me to continue to provide the quantity of feedback that I provide.

I have experimented with having students only write two case analy-ses a semester and the amount of progress was noticeably less than when students write four analyses during the semester. So, perhaps the lesson I need to learn is that good case method instruction requires a commit-ment to teaching that reduces involvement in other endeavors, but that it is worth it if one believes in the importance of providing feedback that contributes to students' professional growth.

LESSON 16   *To teach effectively with the case method one must be prepared for the time commitment involved in preparing for a case discussion and pro-viding students with meaningful and useful evaluative feedback.*

I believe that the power and benefits of cases for students' professional growth would increase greatly if placed in a developmental sequence of professional teacher training rather than in isolation in individual courses. However, for this to occur requires extensive collaboration between edu-cational psychology faculty and faculty in teacher education departments.

I know that in the foreseeable future I will continue to travel the case method highway as a way to teach many of the educational psychology courses that I teach, but I will also try to encourage a more systematic and developmental approach for using cases in our teacher education program. The lessons that I have learned on my journey have been valuable ones for me; perhaps they can serve as a road map for other travelers.

REFERENCES

Allen, J. D. (1994). A research study to investigate the development of reflective thought processes of preservice teachers through the use of case studies in educational psychology courses. In H. E. Klein (Ed.), *Learning the doing—doing the learning: The art of interactive teaching* (pp. 3–14). Boston: World Association for Case Method Research & Application.

Allen, J. D. (April, 1995). *The use of case studies to teach educational psychology: A comparison with traditional instruction.* Paper presented at the annual meeting of the American Educational Research Association, San Francisco.

Biehler, R. F., & Snowman, J. (1993). *Psychology applied to teaching* (7th ed.). Boston: Houghton Mifflin.

Emmer, E. T., Evertson, C. M., Clements, B. S., & Worsham, M. E. (1994). *Classroom management for secondary teachers* (3rd ed.). Boston: Allyn & Bacon.

Evertson, C. M., Emmer, E. T., Clements, B. S., & Worsham, M. E. (1994). *Classroom management for elementary teachers* (3rd ed.). Boston: Allyn & Bacon.

Ormrod, J. E. (1998). *Educational psychology: Developing learners* (2nd ed.). Englewood Cliffs, NJ: Merrill/Prentice-Hall.

Richert, A. E. (1990). Case methods and teacher education: Using cases to teach teacher reflection. In B. R. Tabachnick & K. M. Zeichner (Eds.), *Issues and practices in inquiry-oriented teacher education* (pp. 130–150). London: Falmer Press.

Ross, D. D. (1989). First steps in developing a reflective approach. *Journal of Teacher Education, 40*(2), 22–30.

Schon, D. A. (1983). *The reflective practitioner.* San Francisco: Jossey-Bass.

Schon, D. A. (1987). *Educating the reflective practitioner.* San Francisco: Jossey-Bass.

Shulman, L. (1986). Those who understand: Knowledge growth in teaching. *Educational Researcher, 15,* 4–14.

Silverman, R., Welty, W., & Lyon, S. (1992). *Case studies for teacher problem solving.* New York: McGraw-Hill.

Silverman, R., Welty, W., & Lyon, S. (1996). *Case studies for teacher problem solving.* New York: McGraw-Hill, Primis. (Data bank of cases)

Sparks-Langer, G. M., Simmons, J. M., Pasch, M., Colton, A., & Starko, A. (1990). Reflective pedagogical thinking: How can we promote it and measure it? *Journal of Teacher Education, 41*(4), 23–32.

Woolfolk, A. E. (1998). *Educational psychology* (7th ed.). Boston: Allyn & Bacon.

Zeichner, K. M, & Tabachnick, B. R. (1990). Reflections on reflective teaching. In B. R. Tabachnick & K. M. Zeichner (Eds.), *Issues and practices in inquiry-oriented teacher education* (pp. 1–21). London: Falmer Press.

APPENDIX A
CASE STUDY OUTLINE GUIDE

Problems & Related Ed. Psych. Principles*   Supportive Evidence from Case

Teacher's Perspective

—

—

—

—

My Perspective

—

—

—

Solutions & Related Ed. Psych. Principles*   Possible Consequences

—

—

—

—

*Ed. Psych. Principles (Note: These should be related to the most re-cent readings from our educational psychology text).

APPENDIX B
CASE STUDY ANALYSIS GUIDE

A written analysis will be required for several of the case studies discussed. The analysis is to be typed, double-spaced, and approximately 5–7 pages long. It should minimally contain the following information:

1. A clear statement of the problems in the case that the teacher must resolve. Both the teacher's perspective of the problems and your perspective should be identified. Often these two perspectives will not be the same. You need to state *why* these problems are important and cite specific evidence in the case that illustrates that these, in fact, are problems. You must *support* your perspective based on the theory and principles of educational psychology presented in the assigned readings and discussed in class. Your thinking regarding the problem should reflect what you are learning from educational theory and research.

2. Some possible solutions to the problems. Try to be as specific as possible, citing a specific "plan of action" for the teacher to solve the problems. Your solution should be written clearly enough so that the teacher in the case study could read your solution and begin trying it in his or her classroom tomorrow to solve the problems. Also address possible consequences for your suggested solutions. Be sure to relate your solution directly to the readings assigned in class, primarily those under present consideration and any appropriate readings done earlier in this course or another course.

APPENDIX C
CASE STUDY ANALYSIS EVALUATION CHECKLIST

1. _____ A clear statement of the problem(s) in the case that the teacher must solve.

    _____ teacher's perspective
    _____ supportive evidence from case
    _____ relation to principles and theories of educational psychology*
    _____ your perspective
    _____ supportive evidence from case
    _____ relation to principles and theories of educational psychology*

2. _____ Possible solutions to problem(s) addressed in (1) above.

    _____ specific "plan of action" that the teacher could initiate to solve problem(s)
    _____ integration of appropriate educational psychology principles* to support your "plan"
    _____ possible consequences that could result from the suggested solutions

3. _____ Reference page (references are listed on a separate page)

    _____ APA style

4. _____ Correct use of grammar, spelling, sentence structure, and so on.

5. _____ Social Security number (no name on papers)

* (Principles from most current readings required; principles from previous readings optional as appropriate and desired.)

DEBORAH SHARP LIBBY

Deborah Sharp Libby is an assistant professor in the Elementary Education and Early Childhood Department at Slippery Rock State University, Slippery Rock, Pennsylvania. Libby teaches several courses in reading, language arts, and assessment in early childhood and elementary education. She also supervises students in field experiences and student teaching.

Libby earned her doctorate in reading and language arts at the University of Pittsburgh and was introduced to the use of teaching cases by her advisor, Stephen Koziol. With case-integrated instruction, Libby has found that students are more likely to find multiple solutions to problems and support their reasoning in a professional and comprehensive manner. Although case-integrated instruction is definitely more time-consuming, Libby believes the rewards at the end of each discussion are worth it.

5

CASE-INTEGRATED INSTRUCTION FOR TEACHING ELEMENTARY LANGUAGE ARTS: A TEACHER EDUCATOR'S DISCOVERIES

DEBORAH SHARP LIBBY
SLIPPERY ROCK STATE UNIVERSITY

I was first exposed to case-based teaching early on in my experience as a teaching assistant and doctoral student at the University of Pittsburgh. My advisor, Stephen Koziol, was exploring the use of cases in English education and encouraged me to try them out in an elementary education course that I was teaching. The notion of using cases, problem-centered narratives describing a teaching event or series of events, to fuel class discussion intrigued me. Having spent seven years teaching in an elementary school, I felt that it was imperative to expose my elementary education preservice teachers to real-life teaching experiences in an effort to help them see the connections between theory and practice in the elementary classroom.

I also felt compelled to help these students understand "what" actions they may take in the classroom; "how" those actions could be carried out; and "why" those actions would be appropriate. I thought that by finding a teaching methodology and materials that required preservice teachers to think critically and reflectively about teaching in this way would help them become more aware of the complex role that teachers play in elementary classrooms. I had strong feelings about this because it seems that, all too often, teachers teach skills, concepts, and content simply because they are required to, and give little or no thought to varied approaches, the unique needs of the individuals that they are working with, and underlying reasons for "why" they are teaching various lessons.

Case-based teaching seemed to serve as a natural bridge allowing me to accomplish my desired goals and to bring my students one step closer to the classroom. I was excited to try it because I believed that it would provide my students with many opportunities to think aloud, discuss, vicariously experience, and respond to authentic issues that teachers encounter in the classroom. I also felt that it would allow them to better see the connections between the theory discussed in our class and the practice that occurred out in the field. This approach seemed as if it might make the kinds of critical and reflective thinking connections about teaching that I was trying to foster in my students a more natural and automatic process.

Helping teachers to think critically and reflectively about their practice and role as teacher in the classroom is difficult. The teacher is no longer seen as only a "narrow transmitter of knowledge" (Merseth, 1991, p. 12), but is viewed as an individual who has the power to influence and interact with learners within multiple contexts and in multiple ways. A number of categories have been identified to characterize essential and influential components of a teacher's knowledge, including: a person's orientation, prior knowledge and experience, personal and social values, content knowledge, knowledge of students, and pedagogical knowledge (Shulman, 1986; Van Mannen, 1977; Zeichner & Liston 1987). Thus, helping prospective teachers to think in a more strategic and pedagogical fashion is no easy undertaking. It requires that teacher educators understand something about preservice teachers' attitudes and conceptualizations of education, teaching, and learning.

As a result, I began to explore the influences that may shape preservice teachers' attitudes and conceptions about teaching. Teachers' early experiences as pupils appear to be related to their expectations about teaching, the role of the teacher, teaching behavior, and ultimately the choice of entering the career of teaching (Fuller & Bown, 1975). A number of research studies support the idea that individuals enter teacher education programs holding some conceptualization of teaching (Griffey & Housner, 1991; LaBoskey, 1993; Swanson, O'Connor, & Cooney, 1990). More specifically, these studies suggest that preservice teachers do not enter teacher education programs as blank slates.

In my experiences in teacher education, I have found that preservice teachers appear to draw on their own experiences as students in the classroom, creating a picture of what they believe constitutes the role and life of a teacher. Yet, it is important to keep in mind that these representations evolved from a student's perspective and, consequently, may result in inaccurate, incomplete, and possibly inappropriate representations of teaching. In light of this knowledge, it is really important for teacher educators to find approaches to help bring students' views to the surface. I thought that using cases in my class would help me achieve this by exposing students' thoughts regarding teaching practices and issues that present themselves in the elementary classroom. In turn, I also felt that this would allow my class to examine more closely the role of the teacher and begin to eliminate their misunderstandings and misconceptions about teaching and learning.

Thus, I had a strong commitment to integrating cases into course readings, discussions, and activities. As I began exploring the use of cases, I found myself thinking about John Dewey's writing that emphasized the value and importance of knowledge and reflection. Dewey reasoned that conditions need to be created to engage teachers in "reflective action," which he broadly described as "active, persistent, and careful consideration of any belief or supposed form of knowledge in light of the grounds that support it and the further consequences to which it leads" (Dewey, 1933, p. 9). This belief aligned itself with my vision and goals for case teaching and, based on this belief, a colleague and I began to use the term "case-integrated instruction." I felt this term better defined how I viewed the use of cases in teacher education, as an educational tool that was specifically and meaningfully embedded in the course content for the purpose of enhancing students' understanding of educational practices, techniques, strategies, scenarios, and the complex role of being a teacher.

MY INITIAL EXPERIENCES

I was eager to begin using cases in my course, *Introduction to Elementary Education.* Merseth's (1991) monograph, *The Case for Cases in Teacher Education,* influenced my thinking and helped me to prepare to use cases. Merseth viewed cases as a type of hands-on/minds-on activity that allowed students to encounter and think through a variety of classroom teaching situations, problems, and roles. Using these ideas, my colleagues and I adapted several cases from *A Casebook for English Teachers: Dilemmas and Decisions* (Small and Strzepek, 1988) that dealt with situations that related to management, literacy, and language arts issues in the elementary classroom. For example, one case dealt with the child of a migrant farmworker whose dialect, grooming, manners, and background were very different from that of his peers. The case focused on issues of acceptance during this child's first few days of school and be-havior management problems that present themselves as a result of other students struggling with this child's differences. The teacher not only has to deal with classroom management, but also cultural appreci-ation, dialect differences, and literacy issues.

I built in time to work with cases in my course syllabus so the stu-dents would see the cases as an integral part of the course, taking up ap-proximately 25 percent of class time over the course of the semester. Because work with cases was a significant part of this course, I carefully selected and strategically placed particular cases throughout the semes-ter and closely tied them to assigned readings from our text, *Learning To Teach* (Arends, 1991), and resultant class discussions. My aim was to help the students reach a greater understanding of the topics and concepts covered in the course through discussion of realistic cases that were linked to the course content.

Students were required to respond to each case in an essay format as homework. I assigned this as homework because I believed that this would allow the students to think through the case on their own more carefully. Their responses were guided by a writing prompt shaped by the work of Judith Shulman (1992) and by John Dewey's five steps of reflec-tion (Dewey, 1933, p. 72): (1) recognizing that there is a problem or issue; (2) locating and defining the problem; (3) identifying possible solutions; (4) supporting those solutions with sound reasoning; and (5) close ob-servation and consideration of the solution to determine if it is success-ful or if another course of action should be considered. In their written responses to each case, the students were to analyze the situation by identifying the facts and issues present in the case, outlining possible op-tions and alternative solutions that they might recommend to this teacher, and offering an explanation supporting why they made partic-ular recommendations. The students' written responses then served as one basis for their participation in class discussions, because students could refer to their written responses throughout class discussions.

Discussion of the cases took place for approximately an hour and a half of class once every two weeks. I hoped that class case discussions would provide preservice teachers with opportunities to engage in colle-gial talk about teaching practices drawing on skills of critical analysis, reasoning, problem solving, perspective-taking, and decision making. I also hoped that the discussions would serve as another source for me, as instructor, to learn about my students' depth of knowledge and under-standing of course content.

Unfortunately, my initial experiences with cases were not what I had anticipated. In the beginning, I had naively thought that simply providing students with the opportunity to respond in writing as homework and to engage in classroom discussion where they could identify the facts, issues, and solutions of the case would result in rich, insightful, and enlightening written responses and discussions. However, even though the students' involvement was quantitatively high, (they were writing responses and eagerly getting involved in our discussions), their responses were qualitatively mediocre. This behavior concerned me.

My students seemed simply to throw out solutions without any consideration given to how and why they might be carried out, what the consequences of those actions might entail, and what the students' thoughts, reactions, and educational needs might be. The problem was seen in a very unitary way, it was "the issue" and "the problem." I had really expected the students to think through the cases in a more broad, methodical, and precise fashion. I found myself beginning to question my teaching practices more and more. Something was missing.

WRITING MY OWN CASES

I approached my third semester of using cases and decided to use cases in a reading and language arts methods course for elementary education preservice teachers that I taught. As I started to think about integrating cases into this course, I found myself searching for cases that would deal with particular management and pedagogical strategies relevant to the teaching of reading and language arts. Those available in most casebooks (Greenwood & Parkay, 1989; Shulman & Colbert, 1987; Silverman, Welty, & Lyon, 1992) only provided general cases of teaching that tended to minimize the role of subject content and most often focused on management and interpersonal issues in teaching rather than on specific instructional and/or pedagogical issues.

My search for meaningful cases to use in conjunction with my course was frustrating. Work with cases is believed to have broad implications in the field of education, yet in order to accomplish curricular goals, such as helping students examine, analyze, and make critical judgments about the nature of students' learning and teachers' practice, requires that the cases have strong connections to course content. In my search for cases that would tie in to my course, I kept coming up empty-handed. I knew that it was believed that the discussion of a case itself is one of the key processes in the case method (Merseth, 1991) and, after my first few semesters of working with cases in elementary preservice teacher education courses, I found that the discussion of cases will only be valuable if the cases have a purpose and are clearly related to the curriculum. This led me to begin to write my own series of cases to meet my overall content needs and the specific goals and focuses of my courses, which are:

- Literature-based instruction
- Classroom discussion focused on children's literature
- Whole language
- Reading workshop
- Grouping children for success
- Writer's workshop and the writing process
- Alternative forms of assessment

As I began to write my own cases, I found my writing being influenced by my own numerous educational experiences. Specifically, the content of each case evolved from several sources: (a) my own experiences as an elementary teacher, (b) my experiences as a student teaching supervisor when I observed the initial challenges confronting novice elementary student teachers, and (c) the course texts from which I identified specific areas and current issues that are important for elementary teachers to be knowledgeable about in the fields of reading and language arts. One of the main goals was to tailor each case in a way so that it would match up with assigned course readings from *Teaching Reading with Children's Literature* (Cox & Zarillo, 1993) and *Invitations: Changing as Teachers and Learners K–12* (Routman, 1994). The cases would address salient issues and topics that would promote the kinds of discussion, thinking, and reasoning within the reading and language arts curriculum that I thought prospective teachers should know how to address and think through.

I crafted the cases for my course so they were rich in detail in order to situate the students' thinking and help them understand the classroom context. For example, one of the cases deals with multiage groupings, assessment, and reading instruction in an innovative elementary school. Students are provided with the philosophy behind this school's classrooms to understand further the perspective of the administration, teacher, and students. The following is an excerpt from that case:

> *Our educational philosophy embraces the notion that children need to be viewed by teachers as "active, unique, and whole." This philosophy has evolved out of the work of developmental psychologists such as Jean Piaget. A growing amount of support for our program has also emerged in a great deal of the research dealing with language development. This literature emphasizes that learning best occurs in a setting where discussion and sharing of knowledge and ideas is valued; where choices are viewed as essential elements of learning; where errors are*

viewed as natural and expected components of the learning process; and where "whole language" activities are valued that find children immersed in functional and purposeful language experiences.

Yet, in each case, the problems were intentionally structured to be somewhat vague in definition, so that there were no simple, clear-cut, right or wrong answers. My intent was to create contextually rich cases that were both oriented around problems faced by elementary teachers and linked to the course content and concepts emphasized in the assigned course reading and course texts (see Table 5.1). More than one dilemma or issue was present in each case, a common occurrence in elementary classrooms.

I began my third semester teaching by using cases in my reading and language arts methods course for elementary education preservice teachers. However, as more case discussions took place, I found myself increasingly concerned about the level and intensity of the students' responses. Unfortunately, I found no change in the students' quality of responses over the first few discussions. As in past semesters, they still tended to view the cases from a right/wrong orientation, finding the cases to have a simple problem and solution; there was little recognition that the learners' needs, feelings, and reactions were distinct from those of the teacher, and they included little or no support for their analyses of the situations present in the cases. I had hoped that the new cases I had developed might make a difference. Although I still felt that the cases were good, I was disappointed with the quality of my students' responses and our class discussions.

This continued to surprise me because everything I had read concerning case-based teaching had led me to believe that cases were more engaging and intellectually stimulating than basic classroom discussions, helping to bring a sense of reality about teaching practice and pedagogy to the university classroom, and exposing students to settings otherwise unavailable to them (Merseth, 1991; Shulman, J., 1992; Shulman, L., 1992). I had expected thoughtful, detailed responses from my students; however, their responses still seemed overly simplistic and lacked consideration of critical issues, such as the multiple points of view present in the case, support for decisions made, and the consideration of multiple approaches and solutions to the problems that should be considered by competent classroom teachers who thinks about their practice in a critical and reflective manner. I began to question whether this could be attributed to the fact that they simply were not attending to the issues embedded in the case, or, perhaps, they simply did not know what to focus on and how to think through it.

On further observation, I noted four specific problematic patterns that seemed to surface in my students' oral and written responses to the

TABLE 5.1   Reading and Language Arts Cases and Assignments

Case	Problem	Setting	Teacher Gender	Focus of Problem	Final Question	Related Text
#1—Equal Opportunity	Gender bias issue as teacher calls on boys more. Leading and facilitating a discussion.	3rd grade	Female	Teacher behavior	I guess I am just not sure of what I can do to get all of my students involved. What should be my next course of action?	Cox, Chapters 1,2,5,6 Routman, Chapters 5,6 Share: Runaway to Freedom.
#2—A Tale of Survival	Planning issues, lacking prewriting activity, teachers' response to student questions, grammar problem in written directions	suburban central Ohio, 2nd grade	Female	Teacher behavior	What could I do to make this assignment work?	Cox, Chapters 1,2 Routman, Chapters, 7,8 Share: The True Story of the Three Little Pigs
#3—Ability Grouping	Struggle with ability grouping and management of reading workshop	1st/2nd grade multigroup classroom	Male	Teacher behavior	The main issue troubling me is how can I best organize my time and energies during D. E. A. R. time to meet with all my children and monitor their progress.	Cox, Chapter 6 Routman, Chapter 4
#4—Our E-Mail Pen Pals	Technology, E-Mail, concern with content and quality of pen pal letters	5th grade	Female	Teacher behavior	What can I do to encourage my students to send meaningful messages?	Cox, Chapter 8 Routman, Chapter 8
#5—The Cooperative Challenge	Cooperative writing activity, unruly students, management	Urban Pittsburgh, 4th grade	Female	Teacher behavior	Do you have any suggestions?	Cox, Chapters 8, 10 Routman, Chapter 3 Share: Wizard of Earthsea and Jackdaw
# 6—Glimmer of Hope	Students draw a creative writing blank, time issue, whole language versus basal issue.	Rural Pennsylvania, 1st grade	Female	Teacher behavior Student behavior	Is there a glimmer of hope? Is it realistic to think that I can integrate some whole language activities into my classroom?	Cox, Chapters 4, 6 Routman, Chapter 2
#7—The Art of Discussion	Small group of students dominate a whole class discussion	3rd grade	Female	Teacher behavior	I feel like my literature discussions are lacking depth of thought and full participation from my students. How can I change this pattern?	Cox, Chapters 1,2,5,6 Routman, Chapter 6 Share: Ramona Quimby, Age 8, Chapter 1

cases used as part of class. First, I noted that the preservice teachers avoided or simply did not consider attending to the multiple perspectives and points of view of those individuals involved in the case, such as those of the learners, parents, and teachers. Second, the students rarely grounded their suggestions, solutions, and recommendations in any type of personal and/or professional knowledge, experience, and/or philosophy. Third, students tended to view the cases narrowly as involving one problem and one solution, and expressed at the end of each of the first several discussions their surprise at the numerous issues and solutions that had been identified by their peers when they discussed the cases as a group. Fourth, our discussions tended to be very choppy, because the participants seemed somewhat timid about sharing their ideas.

As a result of these initial discoveries, I began to reflect on my role as the instructor and facilitator of the class case experience. Case-integrated instruction was a methodology that I felt could really help preservice teachers explore their role as teachers in the classroom, but obviously there was more involved in the approach than what I had been doing up to this point. One of the main challenges that surfaced throughout my work with cases over the past two semesters was finding ways to provide the types of scaffolding and support that would help the students develop their professional voices and evoke critical analysis and thoughtful responses. I had a strong feeling that I needed to take a more active role in helping the students begin to think like teachers, but I wasn't really sure what that role should entail. This led me to formally revisit and continue to closely explore what others in the field of education were doing with cases (Grant, 1992; Kagan, 1993; McNergney, Herbert, & Ford 1993; Merseth, 1991; Shulman, & Colbert, 1989; Shulman, J., 1992; Shulman, L., 1992; Silverman, Welty, & Lyon, 1992; Sykes & Bird, 1992). I also began to keep a reflective journal regarding case discussions in my class. My journal served as an additional source of evidence to help me better understand and illuminate what was or was not taking place during class case discussions. I wrote in my journal for 30 to 40 minutes following each class session that involved cases. My intent was to summarize what took place, highlighting what went well, noting problems encountered, and exploring possible solutions that might prove helpful.

THREE ELEMENTS OF CASE DISCUSSION

From this close examination of others' work and my journal, I identified three elements of case discussions, (see Table 5.2), that I felt would help me provide a scaffold to facilitate and enhance preservice teachers'

TABLE 5.2   Three Elements of Case Discussions

1. Questioning techniques and prompts that:
   a. encourage careful analysis of the case.
   b. encourage students to make connections between texts and materials exemplified by the case.
2. A case analysis grid to record and organize discussions
3. The application of verbal assists to:
   a. encourage better student involvement.
   b. help students to synthesize key ideas, clarify ideas, and bring closure to discussions.

learning. In addition, I started to respond to the students' written responses in writing after our case discussion. Ultimately, my goal was fourfold: (1) I wanted to keep our discussions focused and on track; (2) I wanted to keep some sort of record of our discussions for all to see; (3) I wanted to make sure the students' ideas were listened to and discussed; (4) I wanted to make sure the issues and concepts embedded in the cases were fully explored and discussed.

First, I found that I needed to ask a wide range and variety of questions to prompt and guide students' thinking. The purpose of posing questions was to focus our discussions clearly and keep them to the point. The types of questions that I decided to pose fell into two overall pedagogical categories. First, I asked a series of questions that encouraged the students to: (a) identify facts and issues present in the case; (b) attend to the multiple perspectives of the individuals addressed in the case; (c) identify possible solutions; and, (d) provide information to substantiate the analysis offered. Second, I posed a series of questions that required the students to reflect on the supporting classroom texts and materials related to issues and concepts in the cases. Some of the questions I developed prior to our class discussions. However, I also noted that there were many times when I needed to develop questions on the spot in response to something that students said or omitted saying. This required that I become an active and careful listener during our case discussions. As I closely listened to and monitored my students' questions and comments, I found that many "teachable moments" presented themselves. This is especially significant because students' comments are often shaped and greatly influenced by their own personal experiences, which may prove to be very different from the case and one another.

The first type of question allowed me to initiate, guide, and facilitate our discussions. Each questioning area of focus was meant to encourage the students to contribute and allowed me to redirect those who drifted off task tactfully. I also posed questions and made comments to prompt the preservice teachers to examine the cases' issues in a way they may not have considered. Prompts included such questions as: "How might the students perceive the teachers' actions? What might the student(s) be thinking? How might a parent respond to this situation? What perspectives do we need to consider when working through this case? Why is your solution(s) reasonable and appropriate? Provide me with the reasoning to support your recommendations. What else could you do in this situation? What do you see as the facts and issues in this case? What evidence do you have to support this?"

It was also important to help the students see the relationships between the case issues, the supporting classroom texts, and materials that explained the general principles and concepts exemplified by the case. This led me to develop a second series of questioning prompts, such as: "How does your solution relate to the discussion strategies that experts in our texts recommend? What makes you think that including some type of prewriting activity would be appropriate? What knowledge and experience do you have that tells you that these solutions are reasonable and appropriate?"

The need to develop questions to prompt preservice teachers' thinking is not surprising considering the work done by Fuller (1969, 1974) and Fuller and Bown (1975) suggesting that beginning teachers are very egocentric in orientation. Fuller and Bown (1975) note that many teachers move through a basic survival stage, working to develop some sense of their role as teacher, and during that time appear to be preoccupied with themselves, showing little if any concern for their students' needs, interests, and attitudes. These findings mirrored what I was observing in my students' oral and written responses to cases. These preservice teachers tended to focus on the teacher in the case and spent little time discussing the needs of the other participants, such as the students or parents. A questioning technique was needed to encourage these students to think about other perspectives as well as a range of pertinent issues and solutions related to the case, rather than one issue and one solution.

Second, I introduced a case analysis grid, (see Figure 5.1), adapted from a grid that Joanne Herbert presented at the annual meeting of the American Educational Research Association (see McNergney, Herbert, & Ford, 1993). I thought that this grid would serve as an excellent visual graphic organizer for students to view what was discussed. In this way, we would have a framework and reference point for organizing the main ideas and concepts in a logical order. I used this particular grid in conjunction with the questions that I posed to record the students' comments and thoughts, cueing and encouraging them to attend to specific issues in the case. Specifically, I hoped that this would help the students

Facts & Issues	Perspectives	Relevant Knowledge (Personal & Professional)	Solutions

FIGURE 5.1   Case Analysis Grid to Organize and Record Students' Comments

see how much they contributed to our discussions as well as the multiple issues, perspectives, and solutions that could be offered. I also believed that the grid would expose the students to each other's thinking and emphasize that teachers need to reflect on their practice because there are usually numerous issues to consider and various ways to handle a situation in the classroom.

Third, I found that I needed to use a series of verbal assists that fell into two overall categories: (a) those that encourage better student involvement, and (b) those that help students synthesize keys Ideas, clarify Ideas, and bring closure to our discussions. The need for verbal assists was very much the same as the need for good questions: to keep our discussions to the point and maintain their focus. In respect to encouraging student involvement, I found that I needed to ensure that everyone who wanted to share in case discussions had a chance to participate. This role required that I at times provide the participants with verbal assists to encourage them to tell more, to make connections to others' responses, to substantiate responses with personal and professional knowledge, and to entertain multiple solutions. Verbal assists included such comments and questions as: "Are there any relationships between the solutions you have proposed? How could we handle this situation? Which of these proposed actions would you use, and why?"

It was also necessary to synthesize key ideas, clarify ideas that were clouded or misunderstood, and bring closure to our discussions; however, I tried to avoid being seen as the individual with all the answers. Once again, this required me to develop a series of verbal assists to prompt and refocus students' thinking. Sometimes, in order to encourage students to revisit and to continue to think about ideas that were clouded or misunderstood, I played the role of "devil's advocate" by posing a contrary or overlooked perspective. For example, I might ask, "How might the student's parents feel about how you chose to discipline their child?" Additionally, I would usually build on this question by providing the students with a hypothetical situation in which I spelled out the parents' past interactions with teachers in the school, the child's home life, and the parents' views on discipline. In both of the above examples, I believed that the verbal assists and prompts that I presented would help expose students to the kind of thinking that teachers need to engage in when various issues and scenarios like these present themselves in the classroom.

I also began to explore various ways to bring our discussions to closure in order to ensure that the students were aware of key ideas and notions. The following response is an example if how I would bring our discussion to closure through summarizing what had been said in an attempt to tie the students' ideas to those highlighted in our text. "You have proposed that the teacher has multiple options to explore in order to address the issues present in the problem, such as restructuring reading time to include silent reading, buddy reading, conferencing, and journaling. It appears to me that you have all been communicating the importance of literacy, stressing the importance of maximizing the amount of time children spend reading and responding to quality children's literature. Your solutions are appropriate, especially when we consider the points stressed in the assigned chapters read for today's class." However, there were other times when I felt that our discussions would benefit from finishing the case discussion with a question. For example: "What do you think was the most salient point made during our discussion today? What was the main point(s) that you should take away from our discussion today?"

Finally, I also began to respond to each individual's written response in writing. I thought that by collecting and reading the students' written responses I would be able to learn more about each individual student's thoughts regarding the case, what these preservice teachers knew and understood, as well as what additional information they needed to be exposed to. I also believed that this provided me with an additional opportunity to respond to the students' comments on an individual basis. After we had discussed each case, the students' written case responses were collected and I provided written feedback to the students the week following each case discussion. Thus, through written feedback and interaction during class discussions, I encouraged students to think about the salient issues in the case.

OUTCOMES OF CASE-INTEGRATED INSTRUCTION

I believe that the instructor's role and strategies are very important in case-integrated instruction. I'm pleased to report that the quality of subsequent case responses and discussions improved in four significant ways. I believe the positive changes can be attributed to the modifications I made in my instructional approach as well as to the cases that I crafted to use for my classes. Specifically, students spent more time attending to the perspectives of the different individuals addressed in the case. They also became better at supporting their recommendations with professional and personal knowledge and experiences. Additionally, students identified more appropriate solutions. I also noticed that the flow of class discussions improved and became conversations, as students' level of participation reached a deeper and more comprehensive level. It seems clear to me that case-integrated instruction can be a valuable pedagogy for exposing students to classroom issues and situations as well as helping them to learn to think through those to explore a variety of options to solve problems.

The first change noted in the students' responses showed that they began to spend more time attending to the multiple perspectives of the individuals addressed in the case. Initially, the students' responses indicated that they were basically concerned with the teacher and the content of the case, rather than the learner. There was little recognition that the learners' needs and feelings were distinct from those of the teacher. For instance, the following excerpt from a student's written response to one of the first cases is typical. The case dealt with a classroom situation in which boys dominated the class discussion. This preservice teacher did not respond to the needs, interests, and/or abilities of the student(s), but, rather, tended to focus on the teacher, the teacher's sense of power and control, and her own thinking as evidenced in the "I" statements throughout in the following response:

> I think that Rebecca Stein needs to set the rules for discussion. Students should not call out. I am not saying they shouldn't be able to give input into the discussion, but a more structured discussion might be more appropriate for the third grade.

I found that this response lacks explicit references to learners' needs and feelings and seems to view learners' needs and feelings as synonymous with the teacher's. It also makes no mention of learners' potential reactions to ideas and/or issues. For example, this participant could have offered an explanation for why a more structured discussion might be more appropriate for third graders and discussed learners' feelings and responses to this type of format. Instead, the point of view is focused on what the teacher needs to do and how the teacher needs to control both the talk and the content.

In later case discussions that occurred in connection with my new instructional approach, the students still did not attend as extensively to the multiple perspectives present in the cases as I would have liked. However, they did begin to respond to the learners' needs, even though they still had the tendency to focus primarily on their own perspectives. For example, one student offered several solutions, but was only responsive to learners' needs in relation to one solution; she made no explicit references to how the other solutions offered might impact or influence learners. She said:

> *The students could write in a journal after every reading. They could write about what they want or be given a prompt. This would allow every student to respond to the reading. The girls may feel more comfortable and not so overwhelmed by the boys' assertiveness. Another solution could be to reinforce classroom rules. Another solution could be to offer different activities.*

In this response, the student offers a number of solutions but only begins to consider the learners' perspectives in relation to one solution, i.e., that in this case the girls may feel more comfortable if they write in a journal, even then this consideration seems somewhat shallow. This is not surprising given the studies that suggest that seeing learners' needs, feelings, and perspectives as distinct from a teacher's needs, feelings, and perspectives can be a challenging undertaking for preservice teachers at this stage in their career (Carter, Cushing, Sabers, Pinnegar, & Berliner, 1987; Fuller & Bown, 1975). Even though I would like to see greater growth and development in this area, I do feel that the students did become somewhat more sensitized to, and aware of, the need to attend to others' perspectives. Yet, as an instructor who continues to use cases, I wonder if there is a type of technique or scaffold that I can use to help my students begin to consider the needs of the individuals involved in a case more thoroughly. I am continuing to pursue a range of discussion and questioning techniques that may assist me in accomplishing this goal.

The second significant change I noted was that the students showed growth in their ability to identify the complexity of the problem(s) in the case, and to explain and support their recommendations with professional and personal knowledge and experiences. In their initial experiences with cases, students tended to simply restate details in the case and offered little or no application of personal ideas, theories, or attitudes in support of their analyses of the situation. The following excerpt illustrates a typical early response to a case that dealt with a small group of boys dominating a class discussion:

> *The issue is that a pattern of class participation has been dominant. The boys demand more attention than the girls and call out answers*

*without being called on. The problem is how to get the rest of the class
involved. One way is to get "all" the students involved. Another solution might be to give a class participation grade. A third option is to
do a combination of things.*

In this response a number of solutions are offered; however, no personal or professional knowledge and or experience is offered to explain
the solutions offered. The solutions seemed to be thrown out without
any consideration given to how they might be carried out. The problem
is seen in a very unitary way, it is "the issue" and "the problem."

By the end of the semester, after I had used my revised instructional
format, students were explaining and justifying their analyses by refer-
ring to their personal experiences as well as their professional knowledge
as was evident in the following typical response:

*In this situation, Ms. Stein has many factors that are really working
very favorably. In her third grade classroom the students are accustomed to using a whole language approach in which curriculum information is taught through the use of trade books and children's
literature. As Yopp and Yopp pointed out, this type of instruction provides a wider and richer exposure to language and often results in increased reading comprehension. Students become accustomed to
using higher order thinking skills and move into the analysis, synthesis, and evaluation levels of Bloom's taxonomy. Have the teacher
take a more active role in the discussion. As shown in a "Literate
Voices" study by Villaume and Worden, students benefited greatly by
the modeling and facilitation provided by the teacher leaders.*

In this response the student went to great lengths to ground and substantiate her recommendations in theory by making reference to a number of professional resources. There is at least an implicit recognition of
the variety of issues and problems. I found that students also began to
think about accountability and started to make an effort to substantiate
the recommendations offered. Additionally, many of the students began
to make comments about the need to analyze carefully cases of teaching
in order to make sense of what they were learning throughout the course
and to be accountable for the solutions they recommended. These types
of responses seem to suggest that the students were gaining an awareness
of the importance of thorough analyses and that their attitudes and levels of analyses were becoming more sophisticated (see Swanson, O'Connor, & Cooney, 1990).

The third significant change I noted was that students identified a
greater number of appropriate facts, issues, and solutions as we pro-

gressed through the semester using the revised case format. In their early responses, the students tended to approach the case from a one-dimensional perspective, working from a right–wrong orientation, stating that there was basically one problem and one solution. The following is another student example from an earlier case in which the student identified the problem as the boys dominating the discussion. She proposed that the way to handle this issue was to provide the children with a point system for participation:

> *The boys seem to dominate the discussion. If this is a very serious problem and it is disrupting the classroom then there needs to be a visual aid where children can see they get points for participation.*

However, after employing the revised instructional format, I found that my students approached the cases from a very different angle. In their later responses, it is evident that the preservice teachers became willing to deal with the ambiguities in the problems and solutions. They became appropriately tentative in setting priorities for solutions. They also considered multiple approaches and/or solutions to a problem as is evidenced in the following response:

> *There are a number of alternatives Mary could follow. To begin with, Mary could evaluate how "talk" is used in her classroom overall. In "Developing Literate Voices" the authors indicate that literate voices and high student engagement occur more frequently in classrooms where talk is used for active inquiry rather than for recitation and review. In addition, Mary should recognize the value of her students' comments and stories about themselves. It's great that the students saw a bit of themselves in Ramona.*
>
> *[In my] student teaching in kindergarten, I constantly have students starting to go off on a tangent during class discussions. My cooperating teacher showed me a great way to let students know their ideas are valuable while directing the conversation back to where it should be. For example, when Mary's students said, "I always feel nervous the first day of school," Mary could have asked a few questions. "I'll bet that is scary for you. How did Ramona feel on the first day of school? How is that like or different from your feelings." Mary could also develop the students' literate voices. She could invite others to share their thoughts. A combination of these alternatives should help Mary with her problem.*

This later response sounds quite different from the earlier response shared. It illustrates the kinds of changes that tended to take place over the semester in the students' abilities to think with flexibility about educational issues and problems as evidenced by their oral and written responses. In this response the student has not only considered multiple approaches and solutions, but she begins to see the multiple aspects of the problem.

What I learned about using cases in teacher education has strongly influenced the level and way in which my students interacted with each other and responded to the cases. The way that I engaged and prompted students throughout case discussions and commented on their written responses seemed to influence how they analyzed the issues and problems in the cases. As noted earlier, I found that I needed to prompt the students repeatedly in order to fully encourage consideration of the complex issues, perspectives, and solutions of the case as well as to elicit the type of support (i.e., personal and professional knowledge and experience) that would explain and justify their analyses and encourage them to consider the larger social, cultural, and/or ethical issues involved in the case.

I believe that the prompting that occurred during our class discussions, as well as the individual comments and prompts that I wrote on the students' written responses, resulted in the students considering a broader range of issues and solutions and providing more personal and professional knowledge and experience to substantiate the issues that they identified and the recommendations proposed. I think that the prompts I provided may have emphasized the importance of being prepared to explain, justify, and substantiate ones' teaching techniques and decisions and suggest that the instructors' role is important in case discussions.

Given my experiences with cases over the past five years, it appears that the benefits of case-integrated instruction for preservice teachers may be far-reaching and deserve future exploration. The materials and strategies associated with case-integrated instruction are well suited, in my opinion and experience, to help preservice teachers understand information and apply what they are learning in a meaningful context. They help students get one step closer to the classroom practice by helping them to think through situations that they may encounter and ways that they, as teachers, could respond. Ultimately, case-integrated instruction seems to help students become reflective practitioners (Schon, 1987), preparing them to think like teachers, through framing and analyzing problems, and using their professional knowledge and training to make well-informed decisions.

SUMMARY AND CONCLUSIONS

I am convinced that case-integrated instruction is an important component of teacher preparation, helping preservice teachers to explore and understand the role of the classroom teacher in a more comprehensive manner. A question that may be posed is whether the results that I have found can be attributed to the effectiveness of cases and case-integrated instruction or simply to good instruction that involves asking well-thought-out prompts and questions. I believe that the combination of cases and the practices used to discuss those cases creates a powerful educational tool that promotes critical thinking, reflection, and discussions that expose preservice teachers to a wide range of issues that classroom teachers must think about.

I also believe that this approach has made me a better teacher educator because it requires that I be reflective about my own teaching practices. I find myself paying close attention to new and current teaching techniques, practices, issues, and scenarios that unfold in the elementary classroom when I am out in the public schools. Thus, teaching with cases helps me to stay up-to-date, not only on educational research, but also with what is currently taking place in area school districts and classrooms.

Teaching with cases also helps me merge theory and practice by allowing my students to see how various interventions may play out in the classroom setting. Additionally, I find that my students tend to be more enthusiastic about using cases as an instructional mode. They like having the opportunity to serve as an "Ann Landers" consultant, offering advice to a beginning teacher who needs assistance. I believe that they are more willing to discuss cases in relation to assigned readings because the cases are less theoretical in nature and provide the students with a situation in which theory is being played out in practice. The level and quality of our discussions really begins to grow after a few case discussions because the students learn that there is usually more than one "right way" to handle any given situation and that helps them to feel more comfortable responding to the cases. It has been my experience that the preservice teachers I work with find this form of instruction meaningful, insightful, and applicable to their future lives as teachers in elementary school settings.

REFERENCES

Arends, R. (1991). *Learning to teach.* New York: McGraw-Hill.

Carter, K., Cushing, K., Sabers, D., Pinnegar, S., & Berliner, D. (1987). Processing and using information about students: A study of expert, novice, and postulant teachers. *Teaching and Teacher Education, 3,* 147–157.

Cox, C., & Zarillo, J. (1993). *Teaching reading with children's literature.* New York: Macmillan.

Dewey, J. (1933). *How we think*. Boston: D.C. Heath & Co.

Fuller, F. (1969). Concerns of teachers: A developmental conceptualization. *American Educational Research Journal, 6*(2), 207–227.

Fuller, F. (1974). *The experience of teacher education: An empirical review and conceptualization*. Austin,TX: Research and Development Center for Teacher Education, University of Texas.

Fuller, F., & Bown, O. (1975). Becoming a teacher. In K. Ryan (Ed.), *Teacher education* (74th Yearbook of the National Society for the Study of Education, Pt. 2, pp. 25–52). Chicago: University of Chicago Press.

Grant, G. (1992). Using cases to develop teacher knowledge: A cautionary tale. In J. Shulman (Ed.), *Case methods in teacher education* (pp. 211–226). New York: Teachers College Press.

Greenwood, G. E., & Parkay, F. W. (1989). *Case studies for teacher decision making*. New York: Random House.

Griffey, D., & Housner, L. (1991). Differences between experienced and inexperienced teachers' planning decisions, interactions, student engagement, and instructional climate. *Research Quarterly for Exercise and Sport,* 196–204.

Kagan, D. (1993). Contexts for the use of classroom cases. *American Educational Research Journal, 30*(4), 117–129.

LaBoskey, V. K. (1993). A conceptual framework for reflection in preservice teacher education. In J. Calderhead & P. Gates (Eds.), *Conceptualizing reflection in teacher development* (pp. 23–28). Bristol, PA: Falmer Press.

McNergney, R., Herbert, J., & Ford, R., (1993, April). *Anatomy of a team case competition*. Paper presented at the annual meeting of the American Educational Research Association, Atlanta, GA.

Merseth, K. (1991). *The case for cases in teacher education*. Washington, DC: American Association of Colleges for Teacher Education.

Routman, R. (1994). *Invitations: Changing as teachers and learners K–12*. Portsmouth, NH: Heinemann.

Schon, D. (1987). *Educating the reflective practitioner*. San Francisco: Jossey-Bass.

Schulman, L. (1986). Those who understand: Knowledge growth in teaching. *Educational Researcher, 15*(2), 4–14.

Schulman, J., & Colbert, J. (1987). *The mentor teacher casebook*. San Francisco, CA: Far West Laboratory for Educational Research & Development.

Shulman, J., & Colbert, J. A. (1989). Cases as catalysts for cases: Inducing reflection in teacher education. *Action in Teacher Education, 11*(1), 44–52.

Shulman, J. (Ed.) (1992). *Case methods in teacher education*. New York: Teachers College Press.

Shulman, L. (1992). Toward a pedagogy of cases. In J. H. Shulman (Ed.), *Case methods in teacher education*. New York: Teachers College Press.

Silverman, R., Welty, W., & Lyon, S. (1992). *Case studies for teacher problem solving*. New York: McGraw-Hill.

Small, R., & Strzepek, J. (1988). *A casebook for English teachers: Dilemmas and decisions*. Belmont, CA: Wadsworth Publishing Company.

Swanson, H., O'Connor, J., & Cooney, J. (1990). An information processing analysis of expert and novice teachers' problem solving. *American Educational Research Journal, 27*(3), 533–536.

Sykes, G., & Bird, T. (1992). Teacher education and the case idea. In C. Grant (Ed.), *Review of research in education* (Vol. 18, pp. 457–521). Washington, DC: American Educational Research Association.

Van Mannen, M. (1977). Linking ways of knowing with ways of being practical. *Curriculum Inquiry, 6,* 205–228.

Vygotksy, L. S. (1975). *Mind in society.* Cambridge, MA: Harvard University Press.

Zeichner, K., & Liston, D. (1987). Teaching students to reflect. *Harvard Educational Review, 57*(1), 23–48.

STEPHEN M. KOZIOL, JR.

Steve Koziol is chair of the Department of Teacher Education at Michigan State University. Prior to this appointment, he was a professor of English education at the University of Pittsburgh, where he also served as director of secondary and art education programs and chair of the Department of Instruction and Learning. He was born and brought up in New England and was an English teacher in upstate New York before heading to the West Coast to complete his doctorate at Stanford University.

Koziol has recently been part of a UNICEF effort to introduce primary grade teachers and teacher educators in Bosnia–Herzegovina to the uses of informal drama as active learning pedagogy. He has published widely and is a regular presenter at national meetings of the National Council of Teachers of English and the American Education Research Association.

J. BRADLEY MINNICK

J. Bradley Minnick is a clinical instructor in English education at the University of Pittsburgh. He attended Dickinson College and earned both his bachelor's and master's degrees at the University of Pittsburgh. He formerly taught English at several high schools in Pennsylvania.

In the English Education Program at the University of Pittsburgh, Minnick has been responsible for designing and implementing writing courses. He has created assessment tools to facilitate supervision and has worked with student teachers and interns to help them create student-generated written and videotaped teaching cases.

KIM RIDDELL

Kim Riddell is an instructor in English education at the University of Pittsburgh. She received her B.A. in elementary education and an M.A. in English/creative writing from San Diego State University. She is also certified to teach English as a Second Language and secondary English.

In addition to her work teaching methods courses at the University of Pittsburgh, Riddell has taught writing and literature to college students and worked as an instructor in prison and community literacy programs. She has also conducted active learning workshops in using classroom journals and informal drama for teachers in Bosnia. Riddell is currently completing her dissertation research on the collaboration of three teacher educators conducting an English methods course at the University of Pittsburgh.

6

CASES AND CLINICAL FIELD EXPERIENCES IN SECONDARY ENGLISH EDUCATION

STEPHEN M. KOZIOL, JR.
MICHIGAN STATE UNIVERSITY

J. BRADLEY MINNICK AND KIM RIDDELL
UNIVERSITY OF PITTSBURGH

A t the University of Pittsburgh, we have been exploring the use of cases in conjunction with preservice teachers' clinical field experiences for almost 10 years. Since 1986, all of our teacher education programs have been offered at the graduate level only. Although we have worked with cases in conjunction with the clinical field experiences in both our Master of Arts in Teaching (MAT) and our Professional Year (PY) options, this chapter will focus on our work in the PY option.

After completing four years of undergraduate education, our students typically come to us for their fifth year, enthusiastic and passionate about their futures as teachers of English in middle and secondary classrooms. But we find that most of our students also tend to think about teaching situations in terms of how they were taught. Because of this, they often have clear-cut ideas about what works and doesn't work pedagogically. For instance, early in the professional year, we find that our students are often quick to judge the teacher portrayed. They tend to be very prescriptive and offer oversimplified solutions to the case problems posed. Here is an excerpt from Lori, a recent participant in the program, in response to a case of a teacher introducing a poetry unit to eighth graders:

> *The major problem presented in this particular case is the fact that this is a traditional teacher who is having difficulties breaking out of that mold. This causes her to immediately give up on trying something new and creative as soon as it backfires even the slightest. She needs to focus on how she is teaching poetry. The students will respond the way she wants once she allows them an opportunity to truly express how they feel.*

Lori went on to identify several alternative poems that *would* have been better choices for the case teacher to have used and to describe a procedure that the case teacher *should* follow to give students time to discuss their feelings and reactions to these new poems. Lori's response was marked by a prescriptive tone and a belief that good content selections will "naturally" spark interest in students.

However, at the end of the professional year, after experiences in methods classes, teaching laboratory, student teaching, and a student teaching seminar, including experiences in analyzing and responding to other cases, Lori's response to the same case had changed to a more constructive and reflective position:

> *From the standpoint of a future teacher, I believe that the teacher in this case is approaching the subject of poetry in a difficult manner and with a hopeful frame of mind. His or her ideas about helping students see how thought-provoking poetry can be, and reading nursery rhymes as an introduction, seem to be reasonable for starters. However, this teacher sets himself or herself up for a bad answer by asking a question like "What is poetry?" without a motivating introduction. Students will most likely have a preconceived notion of poetry as difficult, boring, and abstract, since most teachers don't work at making poetry something that they can understand—almost a game for the students. Students usually have the belief that poetry is too hard to understand. Thus, teachers must try to spark students' interest by focusing it towards something that holds personal interest for them and engaging them actively in responding.*

Lori went on to propose an array of poems to *consider* as alternatives to the ones mentioned in the case, identified some features of them that might be relevant in making decisions about selection, and identified several specific strategies. These strategies included using imagery and choral reading exercises, free writing, and response journal writing as *possibilities* for use, depending on the students and the goals. In context, this is a rather sophisticated response for an advanced novice. This excerpt shows Lori's growth in being able to analyze multiple facets of events in instruction, see the problems and issues from learner as well as teacher or curriculum perspectives, propose a variety of instructional options for consideration, and overall maintain a tentativeness rather than prescriptiveness in reflecting about the situation and possible courses of action. We think the difference evident in these excerpts reflects the kinds of changes in being able to think carefully and creatively about instruction that we want to take place during professional preparation. We believe that connecting case investigations with clinical experiences contributes directly to supporting those changes.

BEGINNING CASE USE

We began using cases in the student teaching seminar in 1987 as part of our continuing effort to encourage our preservice teachers to be thoughtful and reflective about what they were doing as they learned to be teachers. We had been using response and dialogue journals in methods courses, and as a requirement during student teaching, since the early 1970s. Through modeling and discussion in our coursework, laboratories, and practicums, we emphasized the importance of our students being able to analyze their own and others' teaching. In the teaching laboratory, students were videotaped teaching a variety of lessons that they planned themselves, and then engaged in the analysis of those lessons through self and peer evaluations. In the fall term practicum, journaling was used to highlight the importance of reflecting on what they had observed. During student teaching, supervisors emphasized a clinical supervision model that accented the student teachers' abilities to describe and explain teacher and student actions in and behind classroom events. The student teachers continued their reflective journaling. In order to provide a collegial supportive environment and encourage collaborative problem solving, student teachers were asked to share and discuss problems and success experiences in their student teaching seminars.

In that context, we had two principle purposes for introducing case responses and discussions initially in the student teaching seminar and then in the teaching laboratory and the practicum. First, we wanted to extend, and to some extent formalize, our students' consideration of problems and issues beyond their own immediate context. Like most beginning teachers (Fuller & Bown, 1975; Leithwood, 1992), our students were very concerned about their own behavior and their own success; they focused on their knowledge of the content they had to teach, about what they were doing and saying, about what they saw as logical in a lesson design, and about what they were comfortable in doing or in allowing to be done in a classroom. We saw that our efforts to promote reflection on their own actions were helpful, yet we were not satisfied by the extent to which we were able to get many of them to think beyond their own situations or unique experiences as examples of some larger construct or type of event, and to relate these individual experiences to broader principles and theories.

Shulman (1986) described cases as examples of "specific, well-documented, and richly described events" and suggested that case investigations might be a way to encourage in student teachers the development of "strategic knowledge—the wisdom of practice that is necessary when more than one principle applies, when principles oppose each other, when no simple solution is evident but a decision must be made." In this way students could consider experiences beyond their own and connect these shared experiences with the theories presented in methods classes.

Our second reason for using cases was to deepen our understanding of how well our students were able to reflect on and reason about their own and others' instruction, and we wanted to be able to document more clearly how their attitudes and abilities changed as they progressed through the professional preparation program. Responding to the same or similar cases seemed to us to be a way in which we could monitor those changes as we introduced new and modified existing features and experiences in the program. Cases provided a shared set of conditions and circumstances situated in a classroom or school experience that could be addressed at the same time by our preservice teachers. Their responses provided us with a means to look at their differences in progress at any point in the program as well as the differences across time for each of them.

SELECTING AND USING CASEBOOK CASES

When we decided to introduce cases as part of the student teaching seminar, we started small by using cases from available casebooks to supplement the discussion of student-generated problems. Available casebooks for education (e.g., Kowalski, Weaver, & Henson, 1990; Shulman & Colbert, 1988; Silverman, Welty, & Lyon, 1992; Tripp, 1993; Wassermann, 1993) seemed aimed at providing something for everyone; there were cases involving a kindergarten teacher, a third grade teacher, a reading specialist, a special education teacher, a seventh grade social studies teacher, a tenth grade English or math teacher, and so on. We also noticed that cases in casebooks addressed a wide range of problems and issues, although we found that these rarely addressed issues of the teacher as teacher, that is, of the teacher engaging in instruction and having to make pedagogical decisions in response to events occurring in and as part of that instruction. While we understood and supported the notion of cases as "richly described events," we were looking for examples of cases that most directly addressed problems of a teacher teaching something to someone. To help us in identifying and selecting cases to use, we developed the following case typology to categorize the focus of a case (see Table 6.1).

Applying a Case Typology

We found this case typology useful in making the decisions about the focus and sequence of cases to introduce in the student teaching seminar. It helped us get beyond selecting cases to use because they looked interesting or provocative, and instead pushed us to think about how our selection of cases related to the goals of the seminar and the needs of our students, and how the cases themselves interconnected. However, we also want to note that the categories are not tight and exclusive. Many cases address issues that cut across the categories, and this seems to be especially evident with cases in more recently published casebooks in which lengthy, detailed cases often take on a soap-opera quality. In addition, what has struck us most clearly when we have examined cases from different casebooks is that, except for some cases in the curriculum and instructional decision-making category, most available casebook cases are not anchored in the particular context of a teacher trying to teach something to someone. In many instances, the teacher's primary responsibility as "teacher" seems to be incidental. This proved to be a very important issue that influenced our selection and use of cases in the context of the subject-specific student teaching seminar, and in the practicum and microteaching laboratory.

Initially, we tried to select cases representative of the different types of problems that we felt the student teachers might encounter either in their student teaching or in the beginning years of teaching. We selected cases that addressed management problems, interpersonal/intercultural issues, professionalism, and parent/community relations to complement our attention to the English curriculum and instruction issues through peer discussions of student teaching experiences. In postprogram evaluations, our students told us that the cases we used were interesting, but they wished that the issues were more directly relevant to their situations. In particular, our secondary English student teachers said that they were not especially interested in considering a case if it dealt with a grade level or subject matter that was different from their own situation, and they saw little applicability to cases that dealt with unique social and interpersonal problems of elementary, math, or special education teachers in settings vastly different from in their own experiences. In short, they

TABLE 6.1   Case Typology

Category	Description
Discipline/ Management Focus:	• focus appears to be on matters such as a child acting out in the classroom, a student using foul language in the classroom, several children talking back to the teacher either in the classroom or somewhere in the school, students getting into arguments with each other in the classroom, and children becoming angry at the teacher because of some perceived unfair action • often embedded are issues of interpersonal or intercultural differences that make the situation more complicated • what the teacher was trying to teach, or how, or why, or how effectively receives little attention
Interpersonal/ Intercultural Focus:	• usually identify some open conflict between the teacher and one or more students or among several students, at least part of which is attributed to personal, gender, or intercultural misunderstandings • included teachers' dilemmas evolving from encounters with students who are "different": come from a strange area, have handicaps, speak funny, look different, etc. • rarely in these cases does pedagogy, content area, instructional level, or curriculum seem to be at all important; if mentioned, they exist only as general background information not pertinent to the dilemma
School Politics/ Professionalism:	• focus on the actions and dilemmas teachers face in their overall professional duties and roles in a school • may deal with interactions and conflicts with other teachers, school administrators, and staff, or they may relate to problems with school rules and policies • problems may include such things as having another teacher interrupt a class, having a specialist in who doesn't do anything but blames the teacher for not accommodating students who need help, interacting with the department chair or principal over an issue of grading or curriculum, being evaluated by an administrator who holds different views about instruction, having to deal with censorship, dress and appearance, room appearance, or nonteaching responsibilities, and deciding on joining or supporting local, regional, or national professional groups • instructional elements related to learners, subject matter, pedagogical choices, etc. are generally peripheral to the main dilemma

TABLE 6.1   Continued

Category	Description
Teacher/Parent/ Community Relationships:	• usually focus on tensions between the teacher and others outside of the school itself • dilemmas may focus on interactions with parents who object to what the teacher is trying to do and want him or her to return to doing the "old" things, who object to a child's treatment, or who don't like the teacher and communicate that to their children or they may address issues of community censorship, including community efforts to impose particular standards about curriculum inclusion, teacher morality, where the teacher lives, or what the teacher may do in aspects of his or her private life • instructional elements related to learners, subject matter, pedagogical choices are generally peripheral to the main dilemma
Curriculum/ Instructional Decision Making:	• most address issues of curriculum choice such as children wanting to study things that the teacher does not want to include, the school wanting to adopt a text or curriculum approach that the teacher doesn't agree with, the teacher wanting to teach something that doesn't fit in the curriculum, and the teacher having to make difficult content selections • few address issues or dilemmas in the actual design of specific lessons for identified learners in a given subject and school context • some address examples of instructional implementation, e.g., how to get reluctant children to participate in a discussion, how to engage disinterested students in their learning, how to select from among competing options for student assessment, or how or whether to implement a general response or reinforcement system • some focus on the teacher's attitudinal response to instruction, such as those in which the focus seems to be on the teacher's disappointment that students don't like or aren't responding to instruction that the teacher has spent considerable time, energy, and value in preparing

were telling us that they did not perceive the cases we were using to be "cases of something" but rather saw them as interesting but not particularly useful episodes to talk about.

Although there is much research about the needs and interests of beginning teachers (e.g., Veenman, 1984; Weinstein, 1988) to indicate that they are concerned about management and discipline issues and about working with students, other teachers, administrators, and parents as professionals, it also appeared that, at least in the context of the student teaching seminar, our student teachers wanted to deal with problems and issues that were more centered on the kinds of curriculum and instructional decisions they had to make and set in contexts somewhat similar to their own.

Selecting English Content Cases

In our second year, we began to concentrate on cases from *A Casebook for English Teachers* (Small & Strzepek, 1988). This casebook contained an array of cases addressing issues and problems specific to English language arts curriculum and instruction, and included many with management and interpersonal issues incorporated in a specific instructional context. Each case was written in a very personal style; readers were to imagine having the problem story told to them by a colleague or that the problem had happened to them. Most of the cases end at a dilemma point at which the speaker has to make a decision about what to do, and each case is accompanied by some questions to "ask yourself," some specific action steps to consider, and some recommendations for follow-up activities and professional readings. At first, we tried to select cases that mirrored an issue or problem that had come up in general seminar discussion, although we also included some cases intentionally to bring up a curriculum or pedagogical issue that we felt would push our students to think beyond their immediate circumstances.

CASE APPLICATIONS

Student Teaching Seminars

Initially, we used cases on a biweekly basis to stimulate group discussion in the English student teaching seminar. We shared a case, sometimes in writing and sometimes orally, for general discussion, expecting that the cases would be a safe way for student teachers to talk about instructional problems within the context of another teacher's story, to go beyond concentrating on their own personal experiences. Seminar discussions themselves were intentionally open-ended. The instructor asked questions such as: "What do you see as the main problem(s) in this case?" "What other issues or problems are there?" "What would or could you do in that situation?" and "Why?" Not surprisingly, these case discussions varied greatly in their apparent success. Some cases seemed to spark considerable discussion, especially if one or more of the students could identify with something that happened in them, while others seemed to approach it as simply another academic exercise.

Overall, our students responded positively to the use of cases as part of the student teaching seminar. They said that discussing the cases enabled them to have a better understanding of issues and problems that they were having or could anticipate in their teaching. In particular, they felt that the cases and the discussions helped them frame and better understand underlying issues that were occurring in their student teaching, what we observed as the "something like this is happening in one of my classes" phenomenon. Although our student teachers still thought some cases were artificial, they saw value in our emphasis on viewing the case situations from the different perspectives and weighing the benefits of multiple solutions during the discussions because it forced them to consider alternatives. In other comments, they said that the practice of considering cases helped them to avoid being reactive, and to learn to stop and think before jumping to conclusions about situations.

Focusing on curriculum and instruction-oriented cases set in the content and context of English instruction was more successful in stimulating thoughtful speculation among the English student teachers than were the more generic cases. Even with these cases, some students indicated that it was difficult for them to get very involved in a case that was not close to what they were experiencing in their student teaching. If they were teaching at the middle school level, a case that addressed the teaching problems of a 12th grade teacher seemed to be very distant for them. We see this as further testimony to the importance and immediacy of the student teaching experience; for most student teachers, success in their practicum was the center of their attention.

Finally, they consistently commented on how the discussion of cases helped them sustain a sense of the group and professionalism. Our student teachers are placed in a variety of school sites, and as valuable as the sharing and discussion of site-based problems are in the seminar, those discussions often resemble gossip about what they are doing at their individual school sites. Discussing a relevant English teaching case, as we did in the seminar, gave them the opportunity to work together at framing and developing solutions to a problem and contributed to sustaining feelings of a "community of English teachers" that had been developed during the previous semester.

As a staff, we perceived two other outcomes of the case discussions in the student teaching seminar. First, we saw that our student teachers increasingly began to frame their own sharing of problems and "stories" from their site experiences in language similar to those of the cases. They seemed better able to sequence events and to present them in a way that led up to, and sometimes through, their dilemma and invited questions and comments. They seemed to be thinking about episodes in their own student teaching as cases. Second, supervisors and some cooperating teachers began to comment that the student teachers seemed to be more "reflective" about their own teaching. In particular, near the end of their student teaching, university supervisors found the student teachers to be more able to generate and consider multiple options to curricular and instructional problems rather than to seek formulaic, quick solutions.

English Teaching Labs

From these initial experiences, we decided to extend our use of cases into other components of the program. Although we retained some casebook discussions during the student teaching seminar, allowing the instructor to select particular cases in response to student teachers' experiences and needs, we decided to be more specific about the cases used in the preceeding term's practicum and microteaching laboratory experiences. The cases selected for emphasis in the laboratory were related to the techniques and content topics that students were required to practice within the lab, their practicum observations, and, in some instances, what they were discussing in methods courses. As much as possible, we were seeking to use the cases to extend the interrelatedness of our students' experiences across these various components of the program.

In the English teaching lab, microteaching practice sessions offered students initial experiences with topics such as: expressive oral reading, presenting information and explaining concepts in literature, writing, and language, and directed and interpretive discussion. Case discussions were sequenced for alternating weeks beginning with week four. As part of their preparation for a case discussion, students were required to write an initial response to the case following general guidelines that asked them to identify and explain what they saw as the problem(s) and issue(s) in the case, and what they would consider as options to recommend to the teacher. Case discussions were generally open-ended, although the instructor often modeled the asking of probing or challenging questions and pushed students to support or explain the rationale for recommendations.

We used five cases in the teaching lab, each adapted from *A Casebook for English Teachers* (Small & Strzepek, 1988), and each related to a specific instructional technique or curriculum topic being addressed in the lab and in the practicum. The first case, for example, involved a teacher's attempted use of a guided imagery exercise with middle school students. This kind of technique had previously been modeled and explained in the creative drama methods course and discussed in the teaching of literature course; it builds on the oral reading and oral presentation practice lessons carried out during the first several weeks of the lab. Similarly, when students read and respond to the "Unread Story" case, they had already been designing and practicing leading directed discussions in the lab and observing literature discussions in their practicum, as well as motivating and implementing discussions of literature in their methods classes. In this way, our students saw that the cases build on and were related to their activities in the lab, in the practicum, and often in their specialized methods courses. The case discussions pushed them to use these experiences to frame and propose solutions to instructional problems *and* to explain and justify their ideas. Oftentimes, the case and the discussion brought up nuances of pedagogy or learning that had not been explicit in their earlier instruction. Thus, this expanded their understanding of both the use of a technique and the handling of content for adapting to different learners.

Over the past two years, as we have refined both our timing and our sequence in the use of cases, we have also noticed how the cases discussed in the lab have become referenced in the methods courses. The students themselves brought up the cases again in those courses, sometimes to get more or different opinions and sometimes to support their justifications for, or challenges to, theoretical positions.

USING STUDENT-GENERATED CASES

Calls for emphasis on student-generated cases as a basis for discussion and learning in teacher education programs (e.g., Shulman, J., 1987; Shulman & Colbert, 1989; Kagan & Tippins, 1991) make good sense to us. A major task in developing reflection in teachers is in helping them to learn how they can think about, understand, and improve their own teaching. Teachers need to be able to learn and grow from their own experiences (Shulman, L., 1987). Being able to analyze and reflect on someone else's teaching is not the same thing as being able to think about your own instruction. Working with casebook cases appeared to be helpful in promoting collaborative attitudes among Professional Year students and in developing their skills in analyzing instruction. Our study of cases also encouraged a general disposition to flexible thinking and seeing things from multiple perspectives; however, the task of writing and discussing in response to an existing case may be "too constraining to allow preservice and inservice teachers to express fundamental aspects of their teacher beliefs" (Kagan & Tippins, 1991). Using student-generated cases seemed to be the next logical step.

At the time we decided to expand our use of cases into the prestudent teaching clinical experiences, we also decided to build in opportunities for our student teachers to prepare their own cases as part of their requirements in the student teaching seminar. Our first approach was to mirror the kinds of cases that the students were working with from the casebook. From their experiences during their first 10 weeks of student teaching, student teachers were to identify and write about a particular problem or issue that they had encountered during their practicum. Their models were the casebook cases that they had been reading and responding to. During the last four weeks of the student teaching seminar, student teachers had opportunities to respond to and discuss the cases prepared by their peers. After the first year, which emphasized only the peer discussion of student-generated cases, we added the requirement that students prepare a written response to their own case as well as to one case prepared by a peer.

Our informal studies of differences in the written responses to a casebook case, a peer's case, and their own case by English student teachers (Sinning, 1992) supported the contention by Kagan and Tippins (1991) that responses to self-generated cases provoked less prescriptive language and fewer broad generalizations. The student teachers' responses to their own cases contained more descriptive detail overall than did their other responses; they were much more able to speak of particular students with specific backgrounds and how those backgrounds influenced both the problem(s) and the plausibility of different solutions. In addition, their responses to their own cases rarely contained phrases such as, "the teacher should," "the first mistake was," and "the teacher needs to. . . ." Rather, phrases such as, "I think . . . ," "I suspect . . . ," and "I hope that . . . " were more typical and reflect, we think, a higher degree of tentativeness usually associated with reflective experienced teachers. Given the experience of responding to external cases, writing and responding to their own case seemed to enable student teachers to elaborate on a situation that they knew better than anyone else and, at the same time, to achieve a degree of distance from a personal experience, a distance that encouraged depth in self-analysis.

Case Preparation Guides

Over the past several years, we have continued to explore the use and consequences of student-generated cases both in the student teaching seminar and in the teaching laboratory. Based on some of our experiences with the Assessment Development Laboratory Project for the National Board for Professional Teaching Standards (NBPTS), and with an interest in enhancing the depth of reflective responses to self-generated cases, we increased and made more specific our expectations for the student teacher's commentary about his or her case episode. The Case Preparation Guide (see Box 6.1), shows how we have tried to be more

BOX 6.1   Case Preparation Guide

Lee Shulman notes in "Toward a Pedagogy of Cases" (1992) that a case is not just an episode or incident put down on paper; a case must be a case of something, an "instance of a larger class, an example of a broader category." He goes on to identify five shared characteristics of the teaching narratives that are "cases":

- Narratives have a plot—a beginning, middle, and end—and they often include a dramatic tension that must be relieved in some fashion;
- They are particular and specific; they are not statements of what generally or for the most part has been;
- They place events in a frame of time and place; they are quite literally local and situated;
- They reveal the working of human hands, minds, motives, conceptions, needs, frustrations, misconceptions, jealousies, and faults; human agency and intention are central to those accounts;
- They reflect the social and cultural contexts within which the events occur.

For this student teaching seminar, I would like you to use the following guidelines to prepare and organize your "case." There are many types of cases— pedagogical, management, personal/ social relations, role definition, ethical action—and oftentimes a case reflects issues or problems that cut across these areas. You are not required to prepare a case of a certain type, but I do expect that your case: (1) relates to your work as a teacher of English/communications, (2) reflects your attempt to characterize a situation from your real experiences in the program, and (3) represents something that is or was meaningful to you.

Preparation Guidelines

1. Describe the context for the case episode: the nature of the school, the nature of the class situation, some sense of what has been going on relevant to the case. What's been studied? How have students responded to their instruction? What surrounding information like school policies or place in the curriculum is pertinent? Keep in mind that there is a reader who must try to understand this context. (1–2 pages)

2. Present the narrative that accounts for the events of your case. Consider Shulman's characteristics above to decide what will bring your case to life. Do you need to include examples of student comments or responses, class materials, pieces of dialogue between participants? Keep in mind that your case generally should lead to some point of "dramatic tension" or a "dilemma" point. (1–3 pages)

3. Commentary: In addition to presenting the details of the case itself, you should provide your own written response and analysis of the problem. In this commentary, you should be sure to indicate and explain your understanding/speculations of the problem(s) in the case, what you see as the alternative options available in moving toward resolution or decision, and your reasoning about those alternatives, including support from professional theoretical, research, experiential, and political/practical perspectives. How are the problems or issues understood and solutions/decisions given priority when the events are considered from different points of view, e.g., students, other teachers, parents, administrators, not just your or the "teacher's" own. (1–4 pages)

explicit both about characteristics of cases and about what we were expecting, especially in the commentary.

So far, we have been pleased with the results of having students use the Case Preparation Guide as a basis for their student teaching case preparation. During seminar discussions, students are encouraged to think of some of the problems and issues they share. However, what student teachers choose to write up as their cases is quite varied. One student teacher's case, "My Yarmulke and the Public School System," described his very troubling and emotional dilemma of what he could or should do when told by the principal that he was not permitted by school rules to wear his yarmulke as a teacher in a public high school. Some student teachers address specific instructional problems such as student grouping in relation to cultural sensitivity and making grading decisions. Others choose to focus on learning problems of individual students, e.g., how to work with a student who will not do oral report assignments, and how to understand and work with a student who probably has a learning disability. Not surprisingly, some also choose to focus on discipline issues, e.g., "She's a B____!" said by students to the student teacher about the mentor teacher, or "Coping with the Vocal Complainer."

It has been common for students to talk about their "case" issue for several weeks, and they seem comfortable in obtaining and integrating the evolving multiple perspectives that follow from the discussions. By the end of the seminar, everyone seems to have an investment of some kind in each of the cases, and the students themselves have insisted that they get final copies of the cases of their peers.

English Teaching Labs

In 1994 we intensified our work with student-generated cases by building that activity into the English teaching lab to encourage preservice English teachers to learn to problematize events in their own situations. For our preservice English teachers, writing cases based on their lab or program or invented school experiences seemed to be enjoyable, especially in that it gave them a chance to use their own experiences as both "teachers" and "writers." The freedom they were given also posed some dilemmas.

Many of the preservice teachers at this beginning stage of their professional preparation had difficulty grasping the idea of "problematizing" their teaching and other program experiences. Some, perhaps because they were themselves "writers," were more focused on the craft of fictionalizing, shaping the details of the case into an interesting story, than addressing pedagogical issues. Some were concerned with experimenting with the form, creating almost soap operas describing home as well as program events and developing "characters" resembling professors, instructors, and classmates. One case was presented from the point of a view of a semicolon! The cases that did focus on teaching events showed little beyond what would be expected of beginning novices; commentaries about their experiences tended to portray "problems" simply, explicitly, and as easily solvable. Most of the cases lacked depth—they were almost parables—and seemed intended to show a teacher in the process of committing pedagogical sins, obvious problems with obvious solutions or absolutions.

In the year following, we began studying the differences resulting from using self-generated cases in different ways. In one section of the teaching lab, the focus remained on student-generated cases. In that section, we required the students to prepare cases based on their teaching lab episodes. For each teaching lab episode, the preservice teacher planned and taped a practice lesson and participated in the postlesson discussion; afterwards, the preservice teacher wrote a description and self-assessment of the experience as a "case." These student-generated "cases" from the lab experiences rather than the casebook cases became the basis for later whole group discussions.

In a second section, the instructor continued using the casebook cases with the students being required to prepare written responses before participating in class discussions of the cases; in that section, students did not prepare their own cases based on teaching lab episodes.

In a third lab section, we asked students during the first 10 sessions to read and respond in writing and orally in class discussion to the set of casebook cases that we had selected because of their connections to topics in other courses and the lab practice assignments. In addition, each student was to prepare a case about any problem that they had encountered that related to their teaching, either in the lab, from prior teaching experiences, or from practicum observations. Each student prepared only one case, and they staggered due dates so that their cases could be distributed to peers at least a week before a scheduled discussion date. A peer, rather than the instructor or the case-writer, led the discussion of the case, again according to an appointed schedule.

Students' prior casebook discussion experiences and the time to consider and select the "case" they wanted to present to their peers seemed to have very positive effects on the quality and focus of these student-generated cases. These shared cases were in some ways more authentic and less artificial than those from textbooks. Perhaps because the teachers in these cases were no longer anonymous and/or because of the collaborative environment that had been created in this lab section, the preservice teachers were less interested in viewing the teachers described in the cases as "wrong." In particular, discussions centered more on help-ing the case teacher be more successful with the lesson than on diag-nosing and elaborating on their pedagogical sins, essentially redirecting the focus of the case discussions from the performance of the teacher to the objectives of the lesson and the relationship between pedagogical ac-tion and the effect on students. In practice, these preservice teachers were participating as "a community of teachers" (Sykes & Byrd, 1992).

RECOMMENDATIONS

We see our work with casebook and student-generated cases as continu-ing work in progress. Yet, we think our experiences in selecting and using cases in connection with student teaching and prestudent teaching lab-oratories and practicums suggest some general guidelines and directions for continuing exploration.

Case Selection

While many cases are intrinsically interesting and many cases in recent casebooks tell elaborate stories, we think that teacher educators need to be careful and considerate in selecting and sequencing the cases they use with preservice teachers. Our Case Typology has helped us categorize and organize the different types of cases in casebooks. Given the normal and understandable preoccupation of student teachers with their own success in their own placement(s), we have found it most useful to select cases that address instructional and curriculum issues faced by teachers in contexts reasonably like those of the student teachers themselves.

In Vygotskian terms, it would appear that student teachers during the beginning weeks of their site experiences are very fragile and self-concerned with "zones of proximal development" that do not extend widely from the immediacy of their particular site experiences. They do not appear to see the relevance of cases that address teachers in situa-tions very different from their own. In that context, we recommend be-ginning by selecting cases that promote reflection and application from within the boundaries—that is, that are close to the student teachers' own teaching and site context—before using cases that center around less immediately similar contexts.

Student-Generated Cases

We believe that moving students to create their own experience-based cases that become the basis for peer discussions encourages the development of analytic and reflective skills and attitudes important to sustain long-term professional development. Moreover, we see that creating cases and discussing peer cases has distinct advantages over working with cases involving anonymous teachers in unfamiliar environments, especially in building a sense of community. From our experience, however, responding to and discussing casebook cases before, and to some extent concurrently, with attempts to create their own cases is helpful to preservice teachers. This not only by gives them experience with models that they can use to understand what cases are but also provides them with opportunities to analyze and reflect about examples from some secure distance before they attempt to enter their own experiences into the case arena.

Program Connections

We have seen in our uses of cases the important role that cases can play in helping preservice teachers see connections among their professional experiences. The lack of perceived coherence in programs, as Goodlad (1990) has observed, is a major problem in teacher education. Although we had not begun our work with cases expecting them to be a factor in internal program coherence, we have found that cases can be ways that students make connections across professional experiences. In the teaching lab and prestudent teaching practicums, case selections related to practice sessions and observations encouraged students to connect what they were observing with what they were practicing within a context that also required them to use what they were learning about in methods courses. What has surprised us was the extent to which the cases then subsequently became common experience referent points in the methods courses as the students considered the practical implications of theoretical and philosophical perspectives.

That student teaching experiences have a dominating effect on student teachers' views and orientations to teaching, views and orientations often at odds with those in their university-based teacher education programs, is widely understood (Zeichner & Gore, 1990). We have found that both the discussions of carefully selected casebook cases and the preparation of self-generated cases as we have used them have encouraged our student teachers to reconnect experiences in their student teaching with the knowledge and perspectives they studied in earlier program components. In addition, we have come to realize that the portfolio samples we require as part of the documentation process in student teaching, samples adapted from NBPTS School Site exercises that include video examples and reflective commentaries, represent "cases" in themselves. These self-generated cases, built on instructional activities emphasized in the teaching lab and the specialized methods courses, further highlight the interconnectedness of program priorities and their importance as part of student teaching expectations for both student teachers and mentor teachers.

Assessment

Many writers (e.g., Merseth, 1991; Shulman, 1992; Sykes & Byrd, 1992) have noted that the array of benefits that occur from preservice teachers' participation in case investigations, assessing what they have learned or are able to do as a consequence of the use of cases in teacher education, is still an uncertain enterprise. Reflection and developing reflective abilities has been a major focus, and there are a number of different approaches to assessing the reflective abilities of preservice teachers (e.g., Van Mannen, 1977; Zeichner & Liston, 1987; Colton, et al., 1989; La-Boskey, 1994). We have ourselves conducted a number of investigations exploring the use of scoring rubrics based on expert-novice teacher characteristics to characterize differences among and changes in preservice teachers' written responses to cases (Koziol, et al., 1988; Canan, 1990; Shinling, 1992; Libby, 1994; Minnick, 1996). What has been effective for us at this point has been anchoring our formal assessments of progress in reflective thinking about instruction in rubrics that use Likert-type scales for rating students' written responses to cases on such dimensions as perspective taking, depth of analysis, and flexibility of thinking (see Box 6.2). Overall, however, there is no consensus in the profession on appropriate criteria or sets of procedures to guide assessment of the use of cases in various components of teacher education programs.

Teacher Development

Although many studies seeking to identify differences between expert or experienced teachers and novice teachers use protocols that in ways resemble cases, there is little information about how experienced teachers differ from novices in their response and interpretation of cases. Some casebooks (e.g., Shulman & Colbert, 1988; Shulman & Mesa-Bains, 1993) contain short reactive responses from experienced teachers and teacher educators to cases prepared by new teachers, but we have not found collections that include cases and case responses from the same teachers over time or that compare the responses of experienced teachers as well as beginning teachers.

Our own very preliminary investigations that involved having mentor teachers responding to the same pedagogical cases as their student teachers

BOX 6.2   The Pittsburgh Reflection about Teaching Scale

Deborah Sharp Libby & Stephen Koziol
University of Pittsburgh

1. Degree of perspective
   taking/empathizing

   low   1   2   3   4   *high*

low   • egocentric focus on one's
          own perspective/ feeling/
          actions
       • little attention to or re-
          gard for students' needs/
          feelings/ attitudes
       • imposes own position
          without consideration
          of individual
          differences
       • concern is with content,
          not learner; concern is
          with teacher, not with
          learner(s)

high   • makes explicit references
          to students' needs/feeling
          as distinct from teacher's
          feelings
       • considers students'
          and/or parents' potential
          reaction to idea and
          issues
       • refers to adapting lessons
          or techniques to suit the
          circumstances

2. Depth of Analysis

   low   1   2   3   4   *high*

low   • only restates or rehashes
          details in the prompt
       • no application of per-
          sonal ideas/ theories/ at-
          titudes to the experience
       • no application of theory,
          philosophy, or research
          to explain the analysis or
          recommendations

high   • explains or justifies
          choices/ analyses with
          reference to personal ex-
          periences or theories
       • explains or justifies
          choices/ analyses with
          reference to professional
          theories, philosophies, or
          research
       • considers large-scale cul-
          tural or ethical issues in
          analyses or
          recommendations
       • sees relationships
          among elements in the
          problem(s) and
          solutions(s)

3. Degree of Flexibility

   low   1   2   3   4   *high*

low   • rigid, absolutist,
          right–wrong orientation
       • no consideration of am-
          biguities in the problem
          or solutions
       • one-dimensional analysis
          of the problem with rigid
          solutions

high   • sees and is willing to deal
          with ambiguities in the
          problems and solutions
       • sees multiple aspects of
          the problem and issues in
          the prompt
       • considers multiple ap-
          proaches or solutions
       • is appropriately "tenta-
          tive" in setting priorities
          for solutions
       • options reasonably fit the
          problem

(Canan, 1990; Sinning, 1992) were not encouraging. There were few differences in the qualitative nature of the responses from each group, perhaps reflecting the lack of sensitivity in our evaluation rubric or the possibility that responding to cases masked the abilities of experienced teachers who were themselves unfamiliar with analyzing or reflecting on someone else's teaching. In any case, we think that there is a need to extend our studies of the use of cases beyond preservice education into in-service education by exploring more directly the nature of experienced/expert teacher responses to cases and the impact of case investigations on the continuing professional development of preservice teachers.

REFERENCES

Canan, J. E. (1990). *Reflective problem solving in teacher education.* Unpublished master's thesis, University of Pittsburgh, Pittsburgh, PA.

Colton, A. M., Sparks-Langer, G. M., Tripp-Opple, K., & Simmons, J. M. (1989). Collaborative inquiry into developing reflective pedagogical thinking. *Action in Teacher Education, 11*(3), 44–52.

Fuller, F., & Bown, O. (1975). Becoming a teacher. In K. Ryan (Ed.), *Teacher education* (74th yearbook of the National Society for the Study of Education, Pt. 2, pp. 25–52). Chicago: University of Chicago Press.

Goodlad, J. (1990). *Teachers for our nation's schools.* San Francisco: Jossey-Bass.

Kagan, D. M., & Tippins, D. J. (1991). How student teachers describe their pupils. *Teaching and Teacher Education, 7*(5/6), 455–456.

Kowalski, T., Weaver, R., & Henson, K. (1990). *Case studies on teaching.* New York: Longman.

Koziol, S., Burkette, G., & Norris, L. (1988). *Fifth year versus fourth year students profess in professional training.* Paper presented at the Conference on English Education, Louisville, Kentucky.

LaBoskey, V. K. (1994). *Development of reflective practice: A study of preservice teachers.* New York: Teachers College Press.

Leithwood, K. (1992). The principal's role in teacher development. In M. Fulan & A. Hargreaves (Eds.), *Teacher development and education change* (pp. 86–103). London: Falmer Press.

Libby, D. S. (1994). *Working to encourage reflection: Integrating cases into the curriculum of a reading and language arts methods course.* Unpublished doctoral dissertation, University of Pittsburgh, Pittsburgh, PA.

Merseth, K. (1991). *The case for cases in teacher education.* Washington, DC: American Association of Colleges for Teacher Education.

Minnick, J. B. (1996). *Textbook cases vs. student-generated cases: A performance study of preservice teachers.* Paper presented at NCTE spring conference on English Education, Boston, MA.

Shulman, J. (1987). From a veteran parent to novice teacher: A case study of a student teacher. *Teaching and Teacher Education, 3,* 319–331.

Shulman, J., & Colbert, J. (1988). *The intern teacher casebook.* San Francisco, CA: Far West Laboratory for Educational Research and Development.

Shulman, J., & Colbert, J. A. (1989). Cases as catalysts for cases: Inducting reflection in teacher education. *Action in Teacher Education, 11*(1), 44–52.

Shulman, J., & Mesa-Bains, A. (Eds.) (1993). *Diversity in the classroom: A casebook for teachers and teacher educators.* Hillsdale, NJ: Research for Better Schools and Lawrence Erlbaum Associates.

Shulman, L. (1986). Those who understand: Knowledge growth in teaching. *Educational Researcher, 15*(2), 4–14.

Shulman, L. (1987). Knowledge and teaching: Foundations of the new reform. *Harvard Educational Review, 57*(1), 1–22.

Shulman, L. (1992). Toward a pedagogy of cases. In J. H. Shulman (Ed.), *Case methods in teacher education.* New York: Teachers College Press.

Silverman, R., Welty, W., & Lyon, S. (1992). *Case studies for teacher problem solving.* New York: McGraw-Hill.

Sinning, K. (1992). *Some uses for case studies in the development of reflective problem solving among preservice teachers.* Unpublished master's thesis, University of Pittsburgh, Pittsburgh, PA.

Small, R., & Strzepek, J. (1988). *A casebook for English teachers: Dilemmas and decisions.* Belmont, CA: Wadsworth.

Sykes, G., & Bird, T. (1992). Teacher education and the case idea. In C. Grant (Ed.), *Review of research in education* (Vol. 18, pp. 457–521). Washington, DC: American Educational Research Association.

Tripp, D. (1993). *Critical incidents in teaching.* London: Routledge.

Van Mannen, M. (1977). Linking ways of knowing with ways of being practical. *Curriculum Inquiry, 6,* 205–228.

Veenman, S. (1984). Perceived problems of beginning teachers. *Review of Educational Research, 54*(2), 143–178.

Wassermann, S. (1993). *Getting down to cases.* New York: Teachers College Press.

Weinstein, C. S. (1988). Preservice teachers' expectations about the first year of teaching. *Teaching and Teacher Education, 4*(1), 31–40.

Zeichner, K., & Gore, J. (1990). Teacher socialization. In W. Robert Houston (Ed.), *Handbook of research on teacher education.* New York: Macmillan.

Zeichner, K., & Liston, D. (1987). Teaching students to reflect. *Harvard Educational Review, 57*(1), 23–48.

JOANNE MAY HERBERT

Joanne May Herbert is a faculty member in the Department of Curriculum, Instruction, and Special Education at the University of Virginia where she teaches courses in instruction, assessment, and educational research. Her recent research examines the effects of using text-based and videotaped cases with preservice teachers.

A former teacher in the Charlottesville Public Schools, Herbert has 15 years experience working with children in kindergarten through fourth grade. Much of her research has been conducted in elementary settings where she has examined teacher and student thinking, more and less effective ways to intervene with classroom teachers, and the effects of formative evaluation on teachers and students. Her writings have been published in a variety of professional journals and publications. She is also coauthor, with colleague Bob McNergney, of the text, *Foundations of Education,* (2nd ed., 1998).

7

ADDRESSING CONTEMPORARY ISSUES IN TEACHER EDUCATION: TEACHING WITH VIDEO, MULTIMEDIA, AND CASES ON THE WEB

JOANNE MAY HERBERT
UNIVERSITY OF VIRGINIA

As a faculty member in the Department of Curriculum, Instruction, and Special Education at the University of Virginia, I teach courses in instruction, assessment, and educational research. Since December 1995, I have also worked with several colleagues on the development and delivery of an Internet-based course funded, in part, by The Hitachi Foundation. The course is case-based and focuses on teachers, students, administrators, parents, and other people in school communities who are engaged in one way or another with integrating curriculum in elementary and secondary schools and offering instruction across content areas.

My initial exposure to cases came in 1987, my second semester of graduate study at the University of Virginia, when Daniel Hallahan (Curriculum, Instruction, and Special Education) and Robert McNergney (Educational Evaluation) invited me to participate in a study of teachers in mainstreamed classrooms. Working with another graduate student, (Clay Keller, now at the University of Minnesota–Duluth), I developed a "case" of a first-year teacher named Marcia. The case was designed as a piece of research, rather than as a teaching case. Data were collected through interviews, ethnographic notes, videotapes of teacher–student interactions, and stimulated-recall sessions conducted with Marcia and two of her students—a general education student and a student with learning disabilities—both in an inner-city school.

Stimulated-recall sessions involved showing portions of a videotaped lesson, first to Marcia and then to each of her students. During these sessions, I played videotapes and audio recorders simultaneously, stopping the videotapes at points of interest to ask specific questions about particular events. I also encouraged Marcia and her students to stop the videotape whenever they wished to make spontaneous comments about activities of interest (see Calderhead, 1981; Clark & Peterson, 1981). The completed case consisted of unedited videotapes, transcripts of stimulated-recall sessions, and a written document that described: (1) the teacher and the school community in which she worked, (2) teacher–student interactions during one hour of instruction, and (3) a description of patterns of thoughts and behaviors demonstrated by the teacher across time (Herbert & Keller, in press).

I used the case of Marcia as an instructional tool a year later with 15 individuals who were principals, in-service teachers, or full-time graduate students. At the time, I was a teaching assistant in a semester-long course on evaluation of teaching that met for three hours a week. The course concentrated on the practical implications of theory and research and encouraged enrollees to consider teachers' points of view, to observe classroom behavior of both teachers and students, and to provide feedback to teachers based on in-class observations.

On the evening I taught the case, I first showed class members a videotape of one of Marcia's lessons and asked them to describe what they saw and heard. I next had students read transcripts of Marcia's thoughts and those of her students about various events in the lesson; again I led a discussion, asking participants to consider similarities and differences in Marcia's and her students' interpretations of behavioral events (Gallagher, Tankersley, & Herbert, in press). Discussion was lively, and I was pleased that class members seemed eager to participate. At the same time, I was somewhat uncomfortable in my role as discussion leader, particularly when students made quick judgments about Marcia's teaching. They made many critical comments without fully considering the facts, the perspectives of stakeholders, and relevant readings. Although I had prepared questions in advance, I had not anticipated students' reactions. Sometimes I had difficulty formulating questions that encouraged students to think more deeply about issues of teaching and learning.

I knew that Marcia had been selected as a participant in the research program because she had been identified by her principal and a former university instructor as "an excellent first-year teacher." In my own work with her, I found Marcia to be extremely dedicated; perhaps *driven* would be a more appropriate word. She wanted the best for her students and demanded much from herself. The time I had spent with her both inside and outside her classroom had convinced me that she was not only a remarkable young teacher, but a nice person too. I liked her. For some reason, though, as my students watched Marcia on the videotape, they were very critical of what they saw and heard. They thought Marcia was too demanding, too severe. Had I read too much into Marcia's behavior, been too generous because of my closeness to her and my own experience in similar situations? Had my students given her too little credit?

Despite my disappointment with this class session, the videotape served as a "common" classroom experience that students referred to and raised questions about during the remainder of the semester. They commented that the case helped them to think about practical implications of the teaching strategies they were studying in class. I could not help but notice the power of videotape to bring people a step closer to the classroom. I also realized the need to improve my strategies for teaching the case. Over the next few years, I used the case of Marcia with pre-service and in-service teachers, stretching myself to ask better questions.

DEVELOPING VIDEOCASES, TEACHING NOTES, AND CRITICAL PERSPECTIVES

In 1991, my first year as a faculty member at the University of Virginia, The Hitachi Foundation funded a proposal that allowed a colleague and me to develop a series of videocases on teaching and learning in multicultural settings (Herbert & McNergney, 1995). These cases had three components: a videotape, a teaching note, and a set of critical perspectives (see Figure 7.1).

Videotapes consisted of "slices of life" from communities of learning in the United States where teachers, in one way or another, were addressing issues of multicultural education. The introduction on each videotape included a description of the classroom teacher who was the subject of the case, scenes from and information about the school and community in which he or she worked, and questions to consider while viewing the videotape. These include: (1) identifying educational issues and problems, (2) thinking about events from multiple points of view, (3) considering what a teacher might need to know to be successful in the situation depicted on film, (4) forecasting actions they might take if they were the classroom teacher, and (5) speculating about the consequences of such actions.

The introduction was followed by a series of unstaged classroom episodes, each followed by the teacher's reflections on practice. Teaching episodes were approximately three minutes long and represented a variety

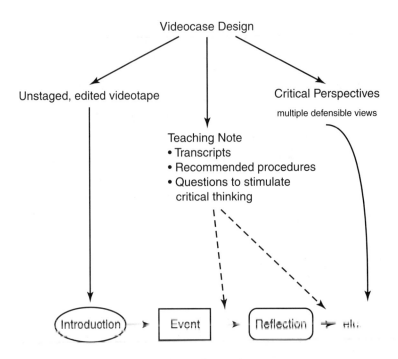

Videocase Design

Unstaged, edited videotape

Critical Perspectives

multiple defensible views

Teaching Note
• Transcripts
• Recommended procedures
• Questions to stimulate
  critical thinking

Introduction ▸ Event ▸ Reflection ➤ Hi.

FIGURE 7.1   **The Structure of a Videocase**

of teaching and learning activities occurring across time in a teacher's class-room. Reflections on each episode were two to three minutes in length.

The teaching note included transcripts of verbal interactions during videotaped events as well as teachers' thoughts about those events. The note also offered specific directions for organizing a class for teachers and using instructional time to discuss the case. Discussion questions in the note suggested specific ways an instructor might challenge viewers to think about facts and issues in the case, relevant perspectives, relevant knowledge, possible actions, and consequences of those actions as part of a reflection process of case analysis.

An Example of a Teaching Note

The following teaching note for the videocase of *Mary Anne Reed-Brown* (see Box 7.1) provides an example of this process. The case depicts several events that occurred in the fifth grade open-space classroom of this second-year teacher who worked with a culturally diverse group of 20 students in Northern Virginia.

BOX 7.1 Teaching Note for Videocase

Event One: Beginning the Day— (4 minutes, 30 seconds) Students enter the classroom on a Monday morning. Ms. Reed-Brown greets the children, shows a new student (Joshua) where to sit, assigns seatwork, takes attendance, determines who needs a hot lunch, and introduces Joshua to the class.

Edited Transcript. Ms. Reed Brown: "Good morning. Be careful of the things on the back table. Joshua, I'm going to have you sit right here today, okay? (Points to a desk.) Okay, let's come on in. Douglas, sit down right there. The Early Bird assignment is on the board, Let's get busy, please. I like the way Lucia and Joshua are working hard on their Early Bird. You guys need to come in and get busy right away. Okay. Christian are you buying lunch? . . . [Ms. Reed-Brown continues with the morning's introductory activities.]

Now, let me introduce you to Joshua, our new student. Be kind to him today. This is a new school for him, and we're glad to have him. Okay. Let me have Patricia's row push your chairs in and line up for gym. Slowly, please. [Class exits the room.]

Edited Comments (Reflections). Ms. Reed-Brown: Every morning we are scheduled to leave the classroom at 9:00. The first ten minutes of the day are taken up with getting the roll called, the lunch count done, and forms collected. The shorter I try to make that time, the longer it becomes. Students work on their Early Bird assignment, but they don't ever get to finish it. Early Bird is work that I have them do so that I can take care of management tasks. If you noticed, I also had a new student named Joshua. I was told on Friday evening as I was leaving the building that I was going to have a new student on Monday. At the time that Joshua arrived, I knew absolutely nothing about him. He came in with his entrance form, and he was introduced to me by the secretary.

Discussion Questions
1. What do you see happening in this event?
• What do the students do when they enter the classroom?
• Who is Joshua? What does Ms. Reed-Brown say to/about Joshua during this segment?
2. What are some relevant perspectives?
• How do you think Joshua feels?
• Why do you think Ms. Reed-Brown introduced Joshua as she did?
3. What do you know/what more might you want to know if you were in Mary Anne Reed-Brown's position?
• What makes some seatwork tasks more useful than others?
4. What might you do if you were in Ms. Reed-Brown's position?
• How might you introduce Joshua?
• Would you consider assigning Joshua a mentor? Why/why not?
5. What might be the consequences of your actions?
• What is the upside and downside of assigning Jason a mentor?

(Herbert & McNergney, 1995, pp. 2–4).

Critical Perspectives

Critical perspectives, a third component of videocases, were written from several experts' points of view to encourage students to assume different perspectives on videotaped episodes. When examined together, the analyses suggest there is no single best way to teach. Instead, there are many acceptable ways of thinking about teaching depending on the needs of pupils, the purpose of the lesson, the content of instruction, and the personal experiences and beliefs of the individual who is collecting and interpreting the data.

In one critical perspective, Patricia Pullen, a special education teacher with more than 20 years experience, notes the lack of control Ms. Reed-Brown has over her own day and the grace with which she handles potentially troubling events:

> *Ms. Reed-Brown does not appear resentful about these administrative decisions—just frustrated. She might wonder whether Joshua's transition would have been smoother if she had known his skill levels. Was he a behavior problem at the previous school? Does he have a medical problem she should be aware of, for example, asthma or diabetes? Is there family history she should be aware of, a recent divorce in the family or the death of a loved one? Why did the family move? Was a father transferred, a mother running from an abusive husband? Were they evicted from the last home because they couldn't pay rent? And how often has Joshua moved? (1995, p. 47).*

In another critical perspective Walter Doyle, a teacher educator at the University of Arizona who teaches courses on classroom processes and instruction, curriculum theory, teacher and student cognition, and research on teaching, draws attention to the importance of morning routines:

> *This event illustrates two centrally important aspects of classroom management. First, openings are enormously important in creating an orderly classroom environment. Second, situations such as this are a clear example that order in classrooms rests not on direct control exercised by the teacher or on how the teacher stops misbehavior after it starts, but rather on activities that create involvement (Doyle, 1986). Without Ms. Reed-Brown's decision to use Early Bird, she would likely be required to spend most of this 10 minutes admonishing students to behave rather than completing essential administrative responsibilities (1995, p. 64).*

Shari Saunders, who has several years' experience as a special education teacher in Brooklyn, New York Public Schools, and as a teacher educator at the University of Michigan, notes the importance of Mary Anne's interaction with Joshua. She does so by considering the situation from his point of view:

> *Joshua, the new student, has to figure out the routines in this new setting with or without assistance. As a new student, he probably wants to blend in and be as inconspicuous as possible. The degree to which he can do so depends on how quickly he learns how this classroom works (1995, p. 21).*

In further videocase work (Herbert & McNergney, 1996a; Herbert & McNergney, 1996b), we changed the design of our videotapes. Instead of always placing teachers' reflections at the end of each event, we sometimes used voiceovers during the event to convey the teacher's perspective as she or he was working with students. In one videocase (Herbert & McNergney, 1996b), we also included scenes from classrooms in several schools in the community, rather than focusing on a single school.

Evaluation of Videocases

I have used these videocases with second-year, fourth-year, graduate education students, and in-service teachers. A colleague has tested the cases with groups of parents, students, and administrators (Ford, 1995). Both of us have learned that a careful structuring of case discussions results in thoughtful analyses. The teaching notes, which I did not have when teaching the case of Marcia, have been a valuable tool in this regard.

I do not possess hard evidence that students' abilities to analyze cases transfer to their work in elementary and secondary schools, but my own observations and self-report data from teachers suggest that those who think incisively in case sessions demonstrate problem-solving skills deemed important in interactions with children. In one of the courses I taught, (EDIS 925: Readings and Research in Education), videocases were a core component of the curriculum. Seven students (three preservice and four in-service teachers) were enrolled in the seminar. Course feedback from a formal evaluation suggests that class discussions about cases were useful to students. One student commented, for example, that "course content was very meaningful because all of the cases were 'real' and could very well be my own classroom!" Another stated that the course was "one of the most helpful courses I have taken because we covered a broad range of issues that are often left unaddressed." Variations on a third student's comment that "the cases which were used tied together all of the information we learned in the course and allowed for analysis and application" were voiced by several others.

The last comment matched my own observations of students' inter-actions during class; that is, I noticed students were using information from assigned readings to help them think critically about problems and issues raised in the videocases. Critical perspectives also elicited thought-ful discussions from students who were intrigued by the several ways a single event might be interpreted by different individuals.

TEACHING WITH CASES ON THE INTERNET

Project Cape Town

A number of factors conspired to encourage me to begin exploring with colleagues the problems and possibilities of case-based teaching and learning on the Internet. With support from The Hitachi Foundation, a team of faculty and students at the University of Virginia developed *Project Cape Town*. This Internet-based case draws its material from three Cape Town, South Africa, schools that were making a transition from apartheid to racially integrated student populations in the fall of 1993. The case combines text, still images, sound, and full-motion video, recorded by Bob McNergney during visits to these Cape Town schools. The video depicts four events: (1) a music class at Camps Bay High School where there is remarkable human potential for learning and teaching and subtle tension between white and black South African cul-tures and students; (2) an Afrikaans language teacher at Camps Bay High School who provides insights into relationships among students varying in cultural background and interpretation of their behaviors; (3) a black senior student who speaks to her peers at a morning convo-cation, reflecting on the realities of her educational experiences at West-erford High; and (4) a white English teacher at Pinelands High School who organizes students in cooperative work groups to facilitate a dis-cussion of how people perceive one another. As with other cases we have developed, *Project Cape Town* includes critical perspectives to stretch participants to consider other ways of thinking about recorded events. (Elsewhere in this volume, Todd Kent discusses the technical side of the development of *Project Cape Town* and subsequent multime-dia cases.)

CaseNET

By January 1998, our case development team had produced 12 more multimedia cases. The cases were based on classroom experiences with interdisciplinary teaching and learning and on interviews with teachers in interdisciplinary situations. They included a variety of ancillaries, such as lesson plans and test scores, that could be used to inform students' analyses.

Cases form the core of CaseNET, a set of three Internet-based courses: *Teaching across the Content Areas, Standards of Learning and Assessment,* and *Using Technology to Solve Problems in Schools.* All the course materials and cases reside on our server at the University of Virginia at **<http://casenet.edschool.virginia.edu>** Faculty from institutions of higher education, and teachers and administrators from K–12 public and private schools, access this Web site through Netscape to offer the courses at their own sites.

An earlier version of CaseNET was offered for the first time in the spring of 1996. This initial offering included faculty from six colleges and universities in the United States and one in Canada. Several faculty had worked with us earlier as sponsors of teams of students from their respective institutions in live and virtual competitions sponsored by the University of Virginia between 1992 and 1995 (Kent, Herbert, & McNergney, 1995; McNergney, Herbert, & Ford 1993, 1994). Other faculty used cases in their courses and were eager to involve their students in an Internet-based course focusing on issues of interdisciplinary teaching and learning. By January 1998, we had 10 instructors from higher education and 20 public schools teaching sections of CaseNET.

To familiarize instructors with the Internet and with course materials, we offered a two-day training session at the University of Virginia. Sessions provided hands-on experiences with case materials, accessing the Internet, and CU-SeeMe, a technology that allows users to send and receive video and audio across sites. Sessions allowed participants to develop working relationships with one another and with members of the case development team. We have found that the enthusiasm and collegiality demonstrated during our time together at Virginia continues throughout offerings of the Internet courses.

CaseNET courses focus on issues teachers face when they try to work together to offer interdisciplinary experiences for their students. Courses are organized around a set of multimedia cases at elementary, middle, and secondary levels and are designed to be used with both preservice and in-service teachers. Because the cases are based on real classroom dilemmas, they also include issues of classroom management, grouping for instruction, dealing with administrators and parents, and diversity issues.

Some institutions have offered CaseNET as an elective, and others have made it a required course. For example, at the University of Virginia, students in the first offering of the course were in their final year of the five-year teacher education program; they took the Internet course in lieu of a field research project. At the University of

Dayton, the course was taught to experienced teachers enrolled in a graduate program on teaching with technology. At Dayton, the course fulfilled methods and research requirements. The content of the course is sufficiently complex and integrated that it can be applied to various programs.

Students who enroll in the course learn how to analyze cases of interdisciplinary teaching and learning using a five-step reflection process. As they do so, they work collaboratively in teams with their peers and colleagues. Each team competes against a set of external standards in a case competition on the Web, demonstrating abilities to analyze a specific case as well as their collective writing and research skills. As a final assignment, students are to complete an individual project. One option is to write a case of teaching and learning based on their own experiences in schools and "publish" the case on the Web. Another option is to create a teaching unit for young people that incorporates ideas learned in CaseNET. In addition, course participants must develop and demonstrate skills necessary for navigating the Internet and the World Wide Web.

During the first several sessions of the course, instructors focus on technology and case analysis skills. Two videocases, both filmed in elementary, middle, and high schools in Columbus and Deming, New Mexico, are used to introduce students to the process of case analysis and reflection (Herbert & McNergney, 1996a; Herbert & McNergney, 1996b). Instructors at each site demonstrate how to analyze cases. The course is taught largely as inquiry, with the instructor guiding students with examples and questions that stimulate critical thinking.

By the third week of the course, instructors begin to organize teams of students and to encourage their collaboration. Each team is composed of four or five people who work together to craft group analyses of cases. Teamwork is not merely desirable, it is essential for success in the course.

The last half of the course is concerned with cooperation in case analysis within sites and team competition across sites, and the creation of individual projects. All students and instructors are connected to one another by the Internet and, in turn, are also linked to my colleagues and me at the University of Virginia. We all also connect with each other at least once during the course with CU-SeeMe, a communications technology that allows users to see and hear one another via a tiny eyeball camera and microphone over the Internet. The course is generally taught once a week for three hours over a 14-week semester.

As I teach with cases, I try to make explicit to students the criteria for evaluation. I also provide students with the list of questions that I ask myself as I read a student's analysis to determine whether he or she has addressed specific issues, perspectives, knowledge, actions, and consequences. For example, if a student suggests forming cooperative groups to help resolve a problem, I look for evidence that suggests the student is aware of research supporting the use of cooperative learning. In other words, there are some explicit criteria by which I and others can assess students' abilities to engage in case analysis. As I discuss below, other criteria, not always so obvious, can figure prominently in judging the success of our teaching with cases.

ADVICE FOR THE CASELORN

Our work to develop and use multimedia cases on the World Wide Web has forced some important changes in my own thinking. For example, I have learned from working with instructors at different sites that cases are mechanisms for bringing together faculty around a common set of concerns. At one level, the case itself has a set of issues that serve to focus people's attention. These are common discussion points across sites and among faculty. On another level, however, cases provide opportunities for K–12 teachers and administrators and college and university faculty to talk with one another about teaching teachers. Although I have been a university-based teacher educator for more than seven years, until I began working with cases I could count the number of professional discussions about pedagogy that I had with other teacher educators on one hand. Most of my discussions with colleagues revolve around scheduling, requirements, electives, field placements, and so forth, but not about specific acts of teaching teachers or about assessing their abilities to apply what they know in real situations.

If cases present opportunities for college and university faculty to discuss the realities of their work, then cases do no less and probably more for teachers themselves. Whether working in small teams or as a whole class, preservice and in-service teachers have opportunities to share personal and professional knowledge while addressing common problems. Interestingly, our Internet-based course is one of the few times when general and special education teachers interact with another in preservice programs. The cases with implications for special services, mainstreaming, inclusion, and other issues that touch teachers' lives across settings often spark lively debate.

I do wonder, however, whether the cases I have developed and used are going to work with equal facility in all situations. Are issues in the cases important to all teachers, regardless of geographical location? When reflecting on the multimedia cases used in the Internet course, two students from Canada commented that most cases presented issues and problems that transcend cultural boundaries. But in one case, in which there was evidence of racial tension in a high school setting, the two Canadians indicated that they had difficulty identifying with the situation:

Canada is often referred to as a multicultural society. We recognize that racial issues and divisions exist in Canada. However, black–white conflict, with the exception of a few regions, is nonexistent. A more relevant issue for Canadian teachers might involve [conflict between] English and French–Canadians.

For those interested in developing multimedia cases, teamwork will be key to the success of your efforts. Members of the team must include people with sophisticated technological skills and individuals who have had a variety of experiences in the schools and in the larger community. Look for the unexpected. Many of the effects of case-based teaching on your students will be unanticipated: their willingness to participate in teams, their subtle resistance to teamwork; hunger for "the right answer" and concomitant unwillingness to defer snap judgments, as well as careful, thoughtful analysis that leads to reasoned and reasonable but unspectacular actions. All of these behaviors are not always obvious and rarely measured in systematic ways. All are also important to those of us who work with teachers, and who want to help them develop thoughtful professional approaches to teaching and learning.

REFERENCES

Calderhead, J. (1981). Stimulated recall: A method for research on teaching. *British Journal of Educational Psychology, 51,* 211–217.

Clark, C., & Peterson, P. (1981). Stimulated recall. In B. R. Joyce, C. C. Brown, & L. Peck (Eds.), *Flexibility in teaching: An excursion into the nature of teaching and training* (pp. 256–261). New York: Longman.

Doyle, W. (1986). Classroom organization and management. In M. Wittrock (Ed.), *Handbook of research on teaching* (pp. 392–431). New York: Macmillan.

Ford, R. E. (1995). *Perspectives on a videocase of education in a multicultural setting.* Unpublished doctoral dissertation. Charlottesville, VA: University of Virginia.

Gallagher, D. G., Tankersley, M., & Herbert, J. M. (in press). In R. F. McNergney & C. Keller (Eds.), *Images of integration: Educating students with disabilities.* New York: Garland Press.

Herbert, J. M., & Keller, C. (in press). A case study of an effective teacher in an inner-city mainstreamed classroom. In R. F. McNergney & C. Keller (Eds.), *Images of integration: Educating students with disabilities.* New York: Garland Press.

Herbert, J. M., & McNergney, R. F. (1995). *Guide to foundations in action videocases: Teaching and learning in multicultural settings.* Boston: Allyn & Bacon.

Herbert, J. M., & McNergney, R. F. (Producers) (1996a). *The case of Columbus, New Mexico: Educational life on the border.* [Videotape] Washington, DC: American Association of Colleges for Teacher Education.

Herbert, J. M., & McNergney, R. F. (Producers) (1996b). *The case of Deming, New Mexico: International public education.* [Videotape] Washington, DC: American Association of Colleges for Teacher Education.

Kent, T. W., Herbert, J. M., & McNergney, R. F. (1995). Telecommunications in teacher education: Reflections on the first Virtual Team Case Competition. *Journal for Information Technology for Teacher Education, 4*(2), 137–148.

McNergney, R. F., Herbert, J. M., & Ford, R. E. (1993, April). *Anatomy of a team case competition.* Paper presented at the annual meeting of the American Educational Research Association, Atlanta, Georgia.

McNergney, R. F., Herbert, J. M., & Ford, R. E. (1994). Cooperation and competition in case-based teacher education. *Journal of Teacher Education, 45*(5), 339–345.

Pullen, P. (1995). Critical perspective of the case of Mary Anne Reed-Brown. In J. M. Herbert and R. F. McNergney (Eds.), *Guide to foundations in action videocases: Teaching and learning in multicultural settings.* Boston: Allyn & Bacon.

Saunders, S. (1995). Critical perspective of the case of Mary Anne Reed-Brown. In J. M. Herbert and R. F. McNergney (Eds.), *Guide to foundations in action videocases: Teaching and learning in multicultural settings.* Boston: Allyn & Bacon.

TODD W. KENT

Todd Kent is a program administrator for the Teacher Preparation Program at Princeton University where he works closely with student teachers and is coinstructor of a course on teaching theory and methodology. Kent graduated from the University of Virginia in 1997 with a doctorate in educational evaluation. His specialty is the use of technology in teacher education and classroom instruction. He has taught courses on the use of computers and other media to preservice teachers and has been involved in several projects combining case-based instruction with telecommunication technology.

Before coming to Virginia, Kent worked at an independent school in Potomac, Maryland, where he enjoyed a variety of responsibilities that included teaching middle and high school science, heading the science department, and directing the upper school division. He has a bachelor's degree in economics from Princeton University and a master's degree in the social foundations of education from the University of Virginia. Todd met his wife, Mary Jane, while at Princeton. His main hobby is chasing after his four wonderful children (Colleen, Maggie, Sean, and Katie), although the occasional fly-fishing outing provides an additional distraction.

8

TECHNOLOGY AND TEACHING CASES

TODD W. KENT
PRINCETON UNIVERSITY

I held a camera in my hand that looked like a large eyeball, and I had just turned it toward Eric Wee. On the computer screen next to me were four video conference windows, each with small black-and-white images of instructors and students from four different universities. Eric, a newspaper reporter from *The Washington Post,* was talking into a speakerphone in response to a question posed by the students from the University of Dayton. The students from these four universities were all participating in the same case-based course. Roughly half their class meetings involved materials that were made available through the Internet via the World Wide Web. The Dayton students were asking a question about one of the teaching cases involving a partnership between a school and a local newspaper. Through the technical wonder of the Web, each university was able to access this multimedia case consisting of a text narrative supported by graphics (pictures of faculty, students, and samples of student work), sound bites from interactions between characters in the case, and a 25-second movie depicting a meeting between students working on the school paper. The Dayton students had raised an issue from the case concerning possible tensions that might develop between teachers with differing perspectives regarding the creation of a new school paper. "I think it's really essential to have a strong personality in the position of editor," Wee told this virtual audience.

In a sense, this vignette was the culmination of my 14 years in education: the melding of nine years of classroom and administrative experience with four years of graduate work in education and technology. That evening was powerful for me, and the most lasting impression was how technology could be used to bring together different facets of this world we live in. On a personal level, this virtual course united several different aspects of my professional background. I had to call on classroom and administrative experiences, instructional knowledge, and technical expertise in developing one of the cases used in the course. On a broader level, I watched how this evening brought together a myriad of different people to share in this common experience. Eric Wee and Rudy Ford, an assistant principal in a school just outside Richmond, Virginia, served as experts, and answered questions raised by students in reaction to the teaching case. Eric was not the only journalist involved in this evening: two of the remote schools had reporters present in a different capacity: They were covering the teleconference as a news event.

At one point, I looked at the screen and saw the tiny image of a man adjusting his camera as he took pictures of the conference from one of the remote sites. These four universities were participating in the first of two conferences we were hosting that night. Altogether, seven universities were participating in the course. Of the four universities on the computer screen, three were predominantly white, and one was predominantly African-American. Two of the universities were state schools, and two were private. Three were from the United States, and one was from Canada. How often, I wondered, would students from such different backgrounds and experiences have this kind of opportunity to share their perspectives and questions on a common experience? How often would they have access to individuals with the knowledge and expertise possessed by Wee and Ford? I felt that the true power of today's technology lay in the ability to facilitate connections between people.

As I looked around the room, I saw some of the individuals responsible for putting this all together: a bevy of graduate students with backgrounds including manufacturing, Hollywood animation, and classroom teaching; professors with expertise in evaluation, curriculum and instruction, and instructional design. In addition to these primary players was a host of characters who contributed to the content and media captured in the cases. I remembered the hours of hard work, the endless string of scheduled meetings, the occasional clashes of values and perspectives, but most of all the feeling that we were all contributing to something new, exciting, and important. As I watched the tiny heads on the computer screen, I realized that each of the classes at the remote universities had a similar drama and cast of players that brought them together from very different paths to participate in the conference that night.

I have been involved in a number of projects that integrated the realms of technology and case-based teaching. As the technology improved, so did the sophistication of the projects. As I look back just a few short years ago at the first project, the Virtual Case Competition, I am awed by how far we have come in such a short time. I suspect that, years from now, I'll look back and marvel at the crudity of the tools we are currently using. I am a bit fearful of the speed of technological development, and I sense from the students and teachers around me an undercurrent of anxiety about the omnipresent need to keep up. Technology takes time to learn, and most people do not have the luxury of abundant free time. I am reassured, however, by the realization that technology is simply one of many instructional tools, and the simplest tools can be used very powerfully. One does not need to know about every bell and whistle on the latest model computer or newest Web browser in order to provide good technology-assisted instruction. The good news is that, as the technology becomes more sophisticated, the tools are also becoming more accessible and easier to use. The Web, with its graphical point-and-click format, is much easier to use than the text-based system of gofers and newsgroups that dominated the Internet until just a short time ago. This morning, in fact, I downloaded a product, for free, from the Internet that allows you to create a Web page in much the same way you would word process any document. Very soon, perhaps by the time you read this passage, people who could not tell you a thing about HTML coding (Hyper Text Markup Language, the coding used to build a Web page) will be merrily developing and posting their own Web pages using such software applications.

In the pages that follow I will discuss a number of projects I have been involved with that integrated case-based teaching and computer technologies. This will not be a technical discussion, but an account of how some very good ideas were made accessible to others through the use of technical tools. Any technical terms will be explained as they are used. But first, I will begin with a brief explanation of how I became involved in the areas of case-based teaching and technology.

A LESSON IN SYNERGY: CASES AND TECHNOLOGY

I vividly remember sitting across from Greta Morine-Dershimer, the head of our teacher education program at the University of Virginia (UVA), and nodding politely as she explained why having a minor in instructional technology would be valuable to me. Being a first-year doctoral student, I was open to suggestions, but was also pretty certain that computers held no place in my future. After all, I could word process and had even taught a high school keyboarding class in my previous life as a school teacher, so what more was there to know?

The following year, at Greta's urging, I took a computer course from Glen Bull, one of the instructional technology faculty at UVA, and my life changed dramatically. Glen taught us about Hypercard, newsgroups, e-mail, PowerPoint, and several other applications I've since forgotten. Most of these programs allowed teachers to create their own instructional modules and presentations on the computer. At that time, four years ago (a span of time that qualifies as an era in the technology world), the World Wide Web was a barely known quantity and not a major topic of class discussion. In Glen's class I saw possibilities, and I also saw immediate applications. I enjoyed working on projects involving the instructional use of newsgroups in the Electronic Academical Village, a part of Virginia's Public Education Network. Newsgroups are public areas on the Internet that allow individuals to post public messages that can be read by anyone. Teachers were using these simple tools in incredibly creative ways. I saw kids getting excited about reading and writing as they "conversed" with elementary book characters through the Language Arts Pavilion of the Electronic Academical Village. Their messages remained indefinitely on the newsgroup for other children and adults across the state to read, and designated experts would respond "in character" to their messages. I wondered how I would have felt as a third grader if I had been able to correspond electronically with Winnie the Pooh. I marveled as classrooms across the state, via the Rockhound Project, investigated a series of clues in a contest to identify several rocks and minerals indigenous to Virginia. Other newsgroups were being used to provide a forum for teachers to exchange ideas and information. I would have loved having such a resource available to me in my classroom teaching days. This electronic world was an exciting frontier, and I could feel the energy and enthusiasm of the people working in it. What amazed me most, however, was that I had absolutely no idea this world even existed until I took that class.

That same year, I also took a course on teacher evaluation taught by my advisor, Bob McNergney. In that class, I became acquainted with videocases, depictions of real teaching presented in a videotape format designed to encourage analysis and discussion. This unique format was developed by Bob and another professor at Virginia, Joanne Herbert. In those videocases I saw a real teacher interacting with real students. The information on the tape was incredibly rich, and the issues were too numerous to be addressed in the context of any single course. I also remember engaging in a fairly heated debate regarding some of the issues raised by the tape, and such rigorous debate was a disturbingly absent feature in most of my graduate classes. I have always learned so much from my fellow students, and teaching cases provided wonderfully complex examples of real classroom life for stimulating the exchange of ideas and professional knowledge. That glimpse into an actual classroom opened a window that breathed fresh air into a graduate student's world of educational research and statistics.

Teaching cases seemed a nearly ideal way to bridge the gap between the academic world of university education classes and the real world of teaching. Like technology, the notion of teaching cases sparked an excitement inside me that other education courses failed to reach. I came to the field of education through a circuitous route and found myself all too often questioning the relevance or application of what I was learning. At times, I felt frustration at being so far removed from working with children in actual classrooms. The cases developed by Bob and Joanne provided a vehicle for allowing education students to test ideas and theories in a shared context. Although no substitute for actual experience, teaching cases provided a safe environment for taking risks, exchanging ideas, and validating lines of reasoning. For me, teaching cases provided a vital link between educational research and classroom experiences.

I had fallen into a teaching career quite by accident. I majored in economics as an undergraduate at Princeton and was headed at one time toward a life on Wall Street. During the spring of my senior year, I decided to stay close to home because my mother was terminally ill. That summer, I ran into an old friend who mentioned a teaching job that opened up in an independent school I was familiar with. I thought that teaching for a year was an ideal way to earn a paycheck while providing enough free time for me to take care of my mother. Well, I was wrong about the free time. I applied for and was offered a job teaching seventh and eighth grade science and coaching two sports. I worked extremely hard, had little time or energy left at the end of the day, but felt like I was doing something worthwhile. I began to doubt whether I could ever find such fulfillment in the financial world.

That first year of teaching eventually turned into nine, and I enjoyed a range of responsibilities that culminated in my unexpectedly becoming the principal of the high school division for two years during a difficult leadership transition for the school. After nine years, I realized that, if education was to become my life's work, I wanted to learn as much about the field as I could. Having not followed the conventional teacher certification path, I decided to broaden my experience and come to the University of Virginia to earn a doctorate. I had earned a master's degree in social foundations from the University of Virginia at night while I was teaching, and my original intention was to earn a doctorate in curriculum and instruction. Having been primarily self-taught, I envisioned myself on an academic quest to uncover the secrets of great teaching.

The chance meeting of technology and case-based teaching in my academic program opened a world of possibilities that I found incredibly exciting. For me, this combination offered a medium for allowing educational research to be learned in a realistic and interactive context. I sensed power behind these notions, and I was certain that if this combination worked so well for me, it would work for others as well.

THE VIRTUAL CASE COMPETITION

The central question regarding the use of technology in education is simple: Why use the technology at all? Richard E. Clark argues that the media chosen for instructional delivery are "mere vehicles that deliver instruction but do not influence student achievement any more than the truck that delivers our groceries causes changes in our nutrition" (Clark, 1983, p. 445). The choice of media is therefore primarily an economic decision: Technology can save time or money. In terms of instructional impact, however, the instruction model, not the medium, determines the effectiveness of instruction. Clark implies that these two decisions—instructional model and instructional medium—are mutually exclusive. In the case of the first Virtual Case Competition, the decision to hold the event on the Internet was driven primarily by economic factors.

The Commonwealth Center for the Education of Teachers was a state-funded institution housed at the University of Virginia's Curry School of Education. The center hosted a unique event in the form of an international and invitational case competition (see McNergney, Herbert, and Ford, 1994; Sudzina, 1995). The state funding for the Commonwealth Center expired in 1994, and the last "live" case competition was held in March of that year. Prior to the competition, Glen Bull proposed the idea of hosting a virtual case competition to help continue the tradition and enthusiasm generated by the live competitions. Bob McNergney met with the teams at the end of the competition, and the participants showed enthusiasm for the idea. April 15 was set as the date to begin a pilot competition over the Internet. This date only allowed a month development time. Because of the short notice and looming end-of-term demands, only two of the five "live" competition teams decided to participate. Three other teams were quickly found, and a truly international competition was arranged between the University of Calgary (Canada), the University of Dayton (United States), the University of Exeter (United Kingdom), the University of Pittsburgh (United States), and the University of Virginia (United States).

The Virtual Case competition used a mailing list and e-mail as the medium of exchange. The mailing list was set up with its own e-mail address at the University of Virginia using Majordomo software. Individuals were added to the mailing list through "subscribe" and "unsubscribe" commands that were sent to the Majordomo software as e-mail messages. This was a "closed" mailing list, which meant that any new subscriber had to be approved by the person who was administrating the list. Any message sent to the list's e-mail address was automatically copied and sent to everyone subscribed to the list. Creating a mailing list facilitated communication among a fairly large group of people via the Internet. Unlike newsgroups, mailing list messages are not public; they are simply received as e-mail messages in the person's account. Thus, part of the subscription process entails sending each person's e-mail address to the mailing list. To run the competition, we set up two lists: one for everyone connected to the competition and a second list for use by the judges of the competition. Most of the interactions in the competition took place through the general list, and we followed the same format as the live competitions. Messages sent to the list included, in roughly chronological order, the competition rules and schedule, team introductions, the teaching case, and provocateur questions (see Table 8.1 for the competition schedule). Each team received the same case, and the participants were instructed to frame their analysis by following the conceptual framework used in the live competition. This model required students to identify the relevant issues, account for different perspectives in the case, apply appropriate professional and personal knowledge, develop suitable plans of action, and predict the consequences of actions (McNergney, Herbert, and Ford, 1994).

In addition to the mailing lists, we also used ordinary e-mail. The most important use of e-mail was for receiving the analysis from each team; we avoided the mailing list for this purpose to prevent any team from benefiting from the work of another team. We also used e-mail to send the provocateur questions to individual teams and for receiving the question responses. These follow-up questions were used to help push each team's thinking beyond their original analysis.

The teams' analyses and question responses were sent to the judges through their mailing list. The judges included an education dean, a school principal, and an exemplary teacher. To facilitate the evaluation of these materials, we created a scale based on the same five criteria from the conceptual model used in the live competition (see Box 8.1 for the rating scale). The judges simply filled out a scale for each team and forwarded the message back to us through e-mail. We converted the judges' scoring to a numerical format and used these figures to determine the winner (in this case there was a tie between the University of Dayton and the University of Virginia) of the event. An announcement of the winners was sent out over the general mailing list. As with the "live" competition, this

TABLE 8.1   Case Competition Schedule of Events

March 28 to April 15	Assembly of CaseStudy@Virginia.edu mailing list
	Introductions made by participants to mailing list
	Development of case
	Instructions for analysis given to participants via mailing list
April 19	Case posted via mailing list
April 19 to May 2	Participating teams develop written analyses and e-mail them to:
	twk7y@virginia.edu
	Note: Correspondence concerning analyses by individual teams will be handled by e-mail and NOT through the mailing list.
May 2 to May 9	Provocateurs post to the mailing list general questions to be answered by all teams
	Individual questions and specific comments will be e-mailed to individual teams as appropriate
May 17	Last day for teams to send responses to questions via e-mail to:
	twk7y@virginia.edu
	Note: Question responses are sent by e-mail and NOT through the mailing list
May 17 to May 24	Judges review all analyses, questions, and responses
	Judges deliberate
May 24	Winner of competition posted via mailing list

announcement was followed by a spontaneous flurry of congratulatory messages and comments that were exchanged between teams.

The first Virtual Case competition was a great success, and we used that experience as a foundation for building other projects. There were several notable features of this pilot. The competition was put together in a relatively short period of time and at minimal cost. Having had the live competitions as a pedagogical model greatly facilitated the development of the competition's virtual counterpart. The participants were satisfied with the experience, and the Internet proved a satisfactory forum for the now defunct live competitions. Another interesting feature of the competition was the formation of a cadre of "lurkers." These were individuals who did not participate in the competition but were added to the general mailing list because they were interested in observing the proceedings of the event.

One drawback to the virtual competition was the lack of human interactions among the participants. In the live competition, the participating teams felt that having the ability to socialize with peers from other education schools was an important facet of the experience. We tried to humanize the virtual competition by having each team post an introduction of its members to the general mailing list, but there was

---

BOX 8.1   The Case Competition Judges' Rating Scale

Below is a rating scale for your use. One entire scale is supplied for each team in the competition, and the name of the team for each scale is given on the top left of the scale. To use this, reply to me, include this message in your reply, and edit the message. Type an "X" on the line that indicates your answer. Don't worry if your "X" shifts the characters on the line a bit. Fill out one scale for each team and return to me.

Rating Scale for Team Competition

	Strongly Disagree	Disagree	Agree	Strongly Agree
The overall quality of the team's performance was superior.	SD	D	A	SA
The team demonstrated an excellent ability to define relevant perspectives (e.g., student, parent, administrator).	SD	D	A	SA
The team effectively used professional knowledge in its analysis.	SD	D	A	SA
The team's projected actions were reasonable and appropriate.	SD	D	A	SA
The team effectively anticipated the consequences of action.	SD	D	A	SA

Comments:

little actual interaction between individual team members. The issue of creating a more "human" environment became an important theme in the development of future projects.

THE VIRTUAL COMPETITION REVISITED

Because the first virtual competition was such a success, Bob McNergney organized a second event for the following spring. We ran the competition with five university teams and again followed the model established by the live competitions. During the intervening months, I took a course with Mable Kinzie that explored the use of various digital media and the development of resources on the World Wide Web. In just a few short years, the World Wide Web has revolutionized how people are using the Internet, and it changed the way we developed virtual case resources. Unlike the text-only environment of e-mail and mailing lists, the Web provides a virtual world filled with text, graphics, sounds, and even short movies! The Web uses the same cables and computers as the rest of the Internet, but to access the text, graphics, and other media on the Web, the user needs to have a software application called a Web Browser. The browser takes digital information from the Internet and presents it on your computer screen in an interactive and graphical format. By clicking links (usually in the form of colored and underlined text), you can jump from one site to another or access sound and video media. Some of the more popular Web browsers are Netscape (the most popular), Mosaic, and Microsoft's Internet Explorer. On-line service companies, such as America OnLine, may use one of these browsers or one developed specifically for their service.

The metaphor for the organization of information on the Web is the "page." Web pages contain text, graphics, and other media in a format that looks somewhat like a page in a magazine or illustrated book. The text and graphics are contained in computer files, similar to files that contain word-processed documents, and these files are kept in a public directory on a computer (or server) hooked up to the Internet. The text files contain HTML tags that tell the Web browsers how to format the page or where to insert graphics and other media. For example, a pair of center tags (<center> and </center>—the first tag begins centering and the second stops it) will center any text or graphic located between the tags. These tagged text files form the backbone of the pages you see on the Web.

Because Web pages are kept in public directories, anyone can access them, unless they are specifically protected by a password or some other device. All you need is the address of the page you want to view. Thus

Web pages are public, much like newsgroups. Unlike newsgroups, however, the owner of the Web page controls what is put on the page. Users generally can only look at pages, not contribute to their content (although this is changing as new softwares allow the creation of Web areas that allow users to post comments in a newsgroup-like format). The use of the Web for the second competition allowed us to do a number of things not possible with e-mail and mailing lists. For the second virtual case competition, we took advantage of the graphics capability of the Web in presenting a case that included pictures along with text. Also, each participating team sent us team pictures and individual biographies. If you have access to a computer on the Internet with a Web browser installed, you can visit the competition site by directing your browser to the following address (Web addresses or locations are also known as URLs, short for Uniform Resource Locators):

http://curry.edschool.virginia.edu/~casecomp/

The first Web page of this site is also shown in Figure 8.1. Using the Web for the competition allowed teams to *see* who else was participating, and we felt that this small step contributed greatly to humanizing the Internet exchanges between teams. We also posted pictures and biographies of the three judges and two provocateurs. Most teams mailed us their team pictures, and we used a scanner to digitize the photographs in order to place them on a Web page. The University of Calgary, however, used FTP (File Transfer Protocol, a fancy name for sending and getting digital information from one computer to another over the Internet) to send their pictures. I remember clearly an e-mail exchange I had with Bill Hunter, the Calgary team's faculty advisor. We both marveled at the ability to send such information across the continent in mere seconds.

Using the Web also allowed us to organize the competition materials in a meaningful way. HTML tags can be used to create links that allow the user to jump from one Web page to another with the click of a mouse. Usually these links appear as blue underlined text on a page, or the links may take the form of a graphic or portion of a graphic. When the mouse cursor is placed over a link and the mouse button is pushed, the current Web page disappears and is replaced with a new one. Unlike the pages in a book, Web pages need not be sequential. In fact, one Web page may have links to many other pages, each accessed by clicking on a different part of the page. These links can take you to a different page in the same location (directory), or to a page located on the other side of the planet. This ability to skip from one page to another in a nonlinear path is how the Web gets its name. By using this linking feature of

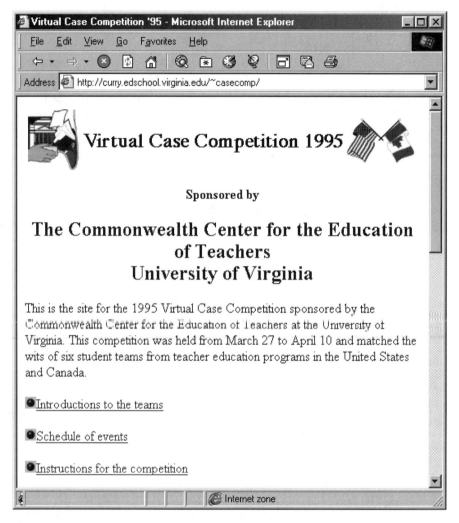

FIGURE 8.1   Web Page of the 1995 Virtual Case Competition

the Web, we were able to create a resource that allowed the user to access any part of the competition materials (such as accessing the text of the case or the biography of someone from one of the other universities) at any time and in any sequence, and all the resources stayed conveniently together in one location.

The Web format has several distinct advantages over mailing lists or e-mail. With mailing lists, each parcel of information is packaged in its own e-mail message. These messages, if not deleted, accumulate in a person's e-mail account along with every other message that the individual receives. It can be very difficult to attain any type of cohesion between messages that may be physically separated by other unrelated messages. In addition, if a message is deleted, that information is lost. On the Web, however, the information stays in one place and can be arranged in a way that facilitates its use. For example, we created one Web page that contained a schedule of events for the competition. That schedule remained in place throughout the competition and could be accessed by any of the participants at any time. Additionally, most Web browsers have a print button that allows the user to print out a Web page simply by pushing that button, so hard copies can easily be made of any Web page.

The forms feature is another useful tool that we incorporated into the competition Web pages. A form allows the user to send information to the owner of the Web page, via an e-mail message (see Figure 8.2 for an example of a form we used in the competition). Forms get a bit tricky to create because they not only require HTML scripting, but they also require a different type of file (called CGI-BIN) on the server that handles the mechanics of taking the information and converting it into an e-mail message. The text of the message is typed (or you can paste an already composed message into the box from a word processor) directly into the form box that is incorporated into the Web page structure. This feature facilitates receiving information from someone using a Web page, and the person need not have an e-mail account to send the information. We supplied forms for the participants to use in sending us their case analyses and responses to the provocateur questions.

An important aspect of the live competition was the audience. When teams defended their analyses they did so in public. In the first virtual competition we also had an audience, albeit a small one, in the lurkers that observed the exchanges taking place on the general mailing list. A nice attribute of the Web is that Web pages are public. In designing the Web site for the second virtual competition, we chose to construct the materials in such a way that they would make sense to any Internet pedestrian who stumbled on the resource. In fact, members of the Future Teachers Club at the University of Wisconsin–Eau Claire were cyberspace bystanders that went so far as to send us their own analysis of the teaching case. When the competition was over, we posted the winning analysis, from Winston-Salem University, and the unsolicited analysis from Wisconsin–Eau Claire (with their permission). After the competition we reconfigured the site slightly and have left it in place as a public resource.

Bob McNergney and Mary Sudzina, a professor at the University of Dayton, organized a third virtual competition that was held in the fall of 1995, and most of the Web development was done by Bruce Bourget,

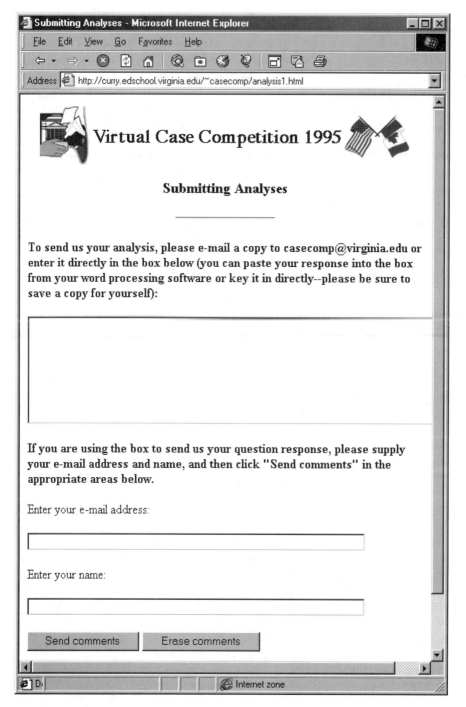

FIGURE 8.2   An Example of the Forms Feature

a graduate student in educational leadership at the University of Virginia. Like the second competition, the materials supporting the event were located on the Web. This competition differed from previous competitions in two important ways. First, the competition was dual, taking place only between the University of Virginia and the University of Dayton. The competition was run in conjunction with an introduction to teaching course for second-year students taught by Bob and a sophomore level educational psychology course taught by Mary. Although only two universities participated, each fielded several teams. The second important distinction of this competition was the scoring format used in evaluating the quality of team analyses. Unlike previous competitions, which judged team submissions on a normative scale, this competition used a criterion format that applied a rating (superior, excellent, good, etc.) to each analysis. Even though student analyses were subject to blind review and scoring was based on the conceptual model described above, there were no "winners" or "losers" in the dual competition. To view the site and results of this competition, direct your Web browser to:

http://curry.edschool.virginia.edu/~casecomp/dual

The virtual medium of the Internet demonstrated a versatility that accommodated a variety of purposes and applications of the case competition concept. In this instance, the competition was used to incorporate collaboration, technology, problem solving, and research into the required work of existing courses.

PROJECT CAPE TOWN

During the spring of 1995, I took a class on interactive media from Mable Kinzie. For that class, I proposed a project to develop a stand-alone teaching case resource on the World Wide Web. Two other graduate students, Frank Becker and Valerie Larsen, found the idea intriguing and joined me to form a development team. The raw material for the case came from videotape from several schools in Cape Town, South Africa. The footage was taken by Bob McNergney on an around-the-world sojourn during which he filmed classrooms in five countries. Bob was accompanied on that trip by Joanne Herbert, Jeff Harper (a graduate student at Virginia), and video cameraman, Ernest Skinner. The team visited South Africa in November of 1993, just a week before ratification of the constitution that set up the 1994 elections that put Nelson Mandela into power. Bob and company visited and videotaped several Model C schools that were among the first schools in South Africa to integrate their classrooms.

Our first task was to select several events from the South African videotapes to form the core of the teaching case. We watched hours of video and selected four sequences that we felt were particularly power-ful. The first sequence depicted a music class. The teacher was white, and all of the students were black. The students had formed a chorus to sing some of the tribal songs they had learned growing up. There was a ten-sion in the class because the teacher was trained in the Western tradition of prescored music. The students sang the tribal songs spontaneously, and each singing had its own character and interpretation that differed from previous versions. The tribal songs were free-flowing and jazzlike in their flexibility of form. The music teacher was visibly uncomfortable at times with the lack of formal structure, yet she encouraged the students to sing the songs that were important to their culture.

The second video sequence was an interview of a language teacher who discussed cultural differences between the black and white students. The teacher described how black students often traveled an hour or more to get to the school, and that they were often late to school because of strikes and other disruptions in the public transportation system. She de-scribed the dilemma teachers faced in having to address these realities while responding to the students' tardiness in a way that was perceived as fair and consistent by the white students. She also described some of the misconceptions that occur over cultural differences in the way stu-dents interact in the classroom.

The third sequence involves a black girl who gave an address at a stu-dent assembly in her school. She spoke to the issue of persistent divisions between races despite institutional integration. The last sequence recorded an English class in which a teacher donned a variety of hats as he taught a lesson on how people form perceptions of others.

After we selected the four video sequences, we needed to transform the material to a format that fit the Web. In doing this, we faced several design and technical problems, and Mable's expertise was invaluable in guiding us through major decisions. Because our primary audience con-sisted of educators in the United States, we wanted to include various media that would help convey the culture depicted in the tapes. A short-coming of the Web environment is the time it takes for Web browsers to load files containing graphics, sound, or movies. These files tend to be very large and can take several minutes to transfer from the server (the computer playing host to the files making up the Web page) to the client (the computer whose Web browser is trying to view the page). For ex-ample, a short, twenty-second videoclip can take nearly 30 minutes to load if someone was viewing the page from home over a modem.

Although movies and sound files can contribute greatly to the por-trayal of an event, Web browsers in use at the time we developed *Project Cape Town* needed software called Helper Applications to view and hear these files. These Helper Applications were available for free over the Internet, and they carried such catchy names as Popcorn, Soundmachine, and Sparkle. More current Web browsers more readily handle multimedia but may require applications called Plug-ins to access some types of media files. Unfortunately, the developer of a Web resource cannot assume that each user will have a Web browser configured with the appropriate Helper Applications or Plug-ins to handle sound and movie files. In fact, many computer labs in schools and universities do not support these files in an effort to help control the noise level in these public spaces. Our development team accepted these realities, but we nevertheless felt the inclusion of these media was important in giving an accurate portrayal of the individuals on the videotapes. We needed to strike a balance between the efficient delivery of information and the richness offered by such media as video. In the Web environment, people get very impatient if they have to wait for information or for files to load. Concurrently, one must resist the temptation to truncate substance in order to gain speed.

We decided that the four case events would be built on a foundation of text supplemented with graphics. To add depth to our depiction, we also included several movies and sound files, but we integrated transcripts of these files into the Web pages for those who could, or would, not load the files. We digitized the video using Macintosh AV machines. The AV nomenclature indicates that the computer is configured to record video and sound and has ports in the back that allow you to plug in jacks from a videotape player. We used a software called Fusion-Recorder to capture (or digitize) the video, and we used a second application called Adobe Premier to do our video editing. Once the video was digitized, we were able to use Premier to capture still images and to create files that contained sound only. In doing this kind of work, storage space becomes a pressing issue as these files can quickly become enormous. To cope with the management of these files, we employed external hard drives (a second, self-contained hard drive that hooks up to a port on the back of the computer) and MO drives and disks (MO is short for "magneto optical"; this storage format uses small optical discs, like an audio CD, that allow you to write and rewrite on them like magnetic tape).

Once we framed the four events of the case, we decided to supply professional practice questions and professional perspectives to accompany each event. This format followed the model that Bob McNergney and Joanne Herbert established with videocases: Each case was accompanied by a teaching note that supplied relevant questions for class discussion and several perspectives of the case from experts in the field. Bob helped us form a matrix to generate questions across the four events that covered the same five areas of professional thinking used to assess the analyses of the case competitions. We then incorporated the four questions into each of the four event Web pages. We also created a Web form for each event that allowed the user to send us their response to the questions as e-mail.

In order to expose users of the case to different perspectives on the issues raised by the events, we developed two professional perspectives for each set of event questions. One perspective was supplied by Joanne Herbert and another was given by Enrico Pedro, a graduate student from South Africa. Enrico had very little exposure to the Web prior to this experience, but he was so engrossed by the project that he has since created his own Web site providing information on educational issues in South Africa. Each week Enrico receives substantial e-mail about his site from around the world. We have linked his site as a resource to *Project Cape Town.*

After framing out the four events and supporting perspectives, we decided to provide some background information to help users understand the cultural and political context of the case. We received permission to use articles from *Newsweek, Time,* and *The Washington Post.* All three of these publications have since made their materials available through services on the Internet, but we were lucky enough to gain copyright permissions for the articles we needed prior to these publications going on-line. In addition to news articles, we supplied a number of links to other resources on the Internet related to South Africa or case-based teaching. We also added a technology support section that listed the necessary Helper Applications for viewing the media in *Project Cape Town* and provided links for downloading the applications. As a final feature for the resource, we created a number of Web pages for posting the responses we received to the professional practice questions to allow users to read what others thought of the issues.

After we developed *Project Cape Town,* we contacted a number of search engines and Web site catalogues to announce the creation of the project. Search engines are perhaps one of the most important features of the Web. These Web-based resources locate and record the content of millions of Web pages, and they allow users to perform key word searches (using a form on a Web page) to find Web sites related to particular topics. Some of the more popular Web search engines are Yahoo, Alta Vista, InfoSeek, and Lycos. In addition to announcing the project to various entities on the Internet, *Project Cape Town* received mention in several journal articles and was also shown in a brochure produced by Apple computers. To date, we have had more than 10,000 visitors to *Project Cape Town.* You can access this resource by turning your Web browser to:

http://curry.edschool.virginia.edu/go/capetown

CONTEMPORARY ISSUES

In the fall of 1995, Joanne Herbert, Bob McNergney, and Mable Kinzie launched the idea of a case-based course using material disseminated through the World Wide Web. (Joanne has written about the instructional issues associated with the course in her chapter in this text.) I will discuss some of the technical and design issues associated with the course.

Like *Project Cape Town,* the course cases (twelve in all) contained an array of movies, sound files, and graphics. Unlike *Cape Town,* the movies were captured with a SpigotPower AV system (consisting primarily of a smaller circuit board that plugs into the main board of the computer) on the Macintosh, which improved the quality of the videos noticeably (of course, this upgrade had a substantial price attached!). The cases for the course contained much more text than the events in Project Cape Town, so each case was divided into several scenes, and a table of contents with links to every scene was placed at the beginning of each case to allow the user to jump directly to a particular portion of the case. Because the course was full-credit and tuition was charged to each of the six participating universities, and because the venture was supported with a grant from the Hitachi foundation, which owned the rights to the case materials, it was necessary to implement a level of security for the course materials. We used a CGI-BIN script (the same kind of scripting used for the forms feature on the Web) to ask the users for a password before allowing them to connect to portions of the course materials. In order to give casual Internet surfers a taste of what was contained in the course, we selected a portion of one of the cases for public display. This "trailer" was accompanied by a form that allowed the user to e-mail the course instructors for more information. To see these course materials, direct your Web browser to:

http://casenet.edschool.virginia.edu

The course also had several features in common with the virtual case competitions. We solicited pictures and biographies and posted them on a Web page so students and faculty could see who else was involved with the course. As the students analyzed the course cases, we departed from previous practices by posting all of the analyses so that individuals could benefit from each other's thinking. Like the first virtual competition, a Majordomo mailing list was established to facilitate communication between the course organizers and the remote instructors, and this list was essential for making announcements regarding curriculum and answering questions or resolving technology and instructional issues. The course had a case competition as part of the curriculum, and the judging of the analyses followed a criterion format similar to the dual case competition.

The course had several notable features that were new for us. One design feature that helped students with their research on the issues raised by the cases was the Virtual Librarian. This resource provided links to library data bases (for example, ERIC) and also provided an "Ask the Virtual Librarian" option that allowed students to e-mail questions to Kay Cutler, our resident library technology expert at the Curry School. There were also links to other resources on the Internet that might prove valuable as students searched for information. The course also provided tutorials on navigating the Web and links to sites for downloading useful tools and Helper Applications for accessing the course materials.

Perhaps the most remarkable feature of the course was the video conference described in the opening pages of this chapter. We have been continually searching for means to promote a human feel to the interactions on the Internet, and we decided to use the CU-SeeMe software developed at Cornell University to hold a video conference among the remote sites. In keeping with the instructional model of providing a variety of perspectives to promote student thinking, Eric Wee and Rudy Ford were solicited as experts to discuss one of the course cases. The video conference provided a common forum for the students to ask questions.

Using CU-SeeMe software was exciting and challenging. This course provided us with the first true test of the software, and the remote sites were incredibly patient as we worked through the inevitable technical glitches. Our first task was to set up a reflector that allowed us to connect up to eight locations at the same time. The reflector software simply provides a common address that everyone connects to in a virtual version of a party line. We then needed to provide schools with a means to transmit video images, so we purchased a number of QuickCams, a tennis-ball shaped camera that plugs into the back of a Macintosh computer.

Before the course started, the remote instructors were flown into Charlottesville for a training weekend that addressed both curricular and technical issues. At this session, we gave each instructor a QuickCam and ran through a trial of the CU-SeeMe software. We realized very quickly that the performance of CU-SeeMe was inconsistent, and the problems that emerged were tied primarily to the level of traffic on the Internet. Most problematic was the quality of sound. Inconsistent quality of the video images, characterized by partial or frozen images, was tolerable, but poor audio quality was devastating to the instructional mission of the video conferences. We also found that the software worked better on some Macintosh models and less well on others.

After the instructors returned home (some were delayed by unusually large snowfalls in the Charlottesville area), we ran several trial video conferences with only the instructors and technical support personnel. We decided that the audio was not dependable and moved to using CU-SeeMe for the video and a conference call using conventional telephones lines and speakerphones for the audio. Although somewhat jury-rigged, the evening was very successful, and there was the thrill of having broken new ground. We held a second conference on a new reflector in Washington, D.C., that improved the audio so substantially that we did not need to use telephones. This new reflector improved the audio quality simply because it was located closer to one of the major Internet hubs than was our first reflector in Charlottesville. As I write, there are advances being made in the live transmission of audio on the Internet, and a computer technician told me this very morning that within a year we should have several new software alternatives that would improve the audio transmission for future projects.

CONCLUSION

More than ever, I hear Clark's arguments echo in the back of my mind as I work with new technologies: The choice of medium is primarily a question of efficiency, whereas the effectiveness of the instruction is tied to the instructional process used. Good technology simply cannot make up for poor instruction. The projects described here met with very satisfactory levels of success because their underlying instructional model was built on a firm foundation and the instructors were superb. All of the professors involved in these projects were experienced teachers, and many had previously participated in case-based teaching and/or case competitions. They understood their content, their students, and their instructional context. Using the technology to enhance the educational experience was a new and exciting challenge for everyone involved. The ideas and techniques contained in these projects worked well in the classroom long before they were tested on the Internet. Access to *people* was the primary advantage gained by using the Internet. We could have flown individuals to Charlottesville to speak with Eric Wee, but only at enormous cost. However, I believe that there are benefits to using technologies that are missed in a traditional cost–benefit analysis. Technology, I believe, has an inherent power to motivate. I believe this motivation comes from two levels. First, as human beings, we are curious creatures who derive pleasure from new experiences. We may experience fear and uncertainty in the face of the unknown, but I believe most of us interpret these feelings as excitement and anticipation. I believe technology can allow us to put a fresh face on many good ideas. I see this phenomenon whenever I work with children and computers. What may seem like a tedious task to a student using a pen and paper may suddenly become "fun" when transferred creatively to a computer. Curiously, this delight and motivation was also observed in seasoned instructors as they posted their own photos and biographies to the Web pages of these projects. Of course, like any instructional model or educational resource, computers can be used poorly in instruction, and the use of technology is certainly no guarantee to enhanced motivation. But, like classroom teachers everywhere, we need to be awake to and aware of the classroom potential in the resources that are available to us.

Second, and perhaps most importantly, this age of telecommunications is giving us access to a variety of people in ways that were never possible before. Suddenly, a student in Duluth, Minnesota, becomes "published" as students from around the country (and world!) read what she has to say about issues in a teaching case. This student is no longer writing just for her professor, but for a larger Internet community that includes unimaginable diversity, and this reality cannot help but change the way students think about their writing. Perhaps some day soon these tools will all be taken for granted, like so many other technical wonders in our planet's history. Education has seen many technologies (the stereoscope, film, radio, and television to name only a few) that have made many unrealized claims for revolutionizing instruction. The obvious question is whether the computer will someday rest in the closet next to the filmstrip projector. I think the computer is different from other technologies because it affords individuals access not just to information, but also to people. The computer allows us to make connections across the globe in ways that were unimaginable just a short time ago. These new possibilities present us with a teachable moment: Students are readily intrigued with the possibility of touching lives across the planet as they explore and expand their own understanding. If we are clever enough and careful enough in not using technology simply for technology's sake, we can use new tools and sound instructional methods in a way that helps us generate new excitement and joy in learning. The combination of teaching cases and technology can be a potent combination in helping minds extend beyond the walls of the conventional classroom and toward our ultimate goal: to provide the best possible teaching and learning for all children.

REFERENCES

Clark, R. E. (1983). Media will never influence learning. *Educational Technology Research and Development, 42*(2), 21–29.

Clark, R. E. (1994). Reconsidering research on learning from media. *Review of Educational Research, 53*(4), 445–459.

McNergney, R. F., Herbert, J. M., & Ford, R. E. (1994). Cooperation and competition in case-based teacher education. *Journal of Teacher Education, 45,* 339–345.

Sudzina, M. (1995, April). *Case competition as a catalyst to restructure the teaching and learning of educational psychology.* Paper presented at the annual meeting of the American Educational Research Association, San Fransisco (ERIC Document Reproduction Service No. ED 382 683).

THOMAS D. PEACOCK

Thomas D. Peacock, an enrolled member of the Fond du Lac Band of Lake Superior Chippewa (Anishinabe), is an associate professor of education at the University of Minnesota–Duluth. Peacock received his master's and doctorate degrees in educational administration from Harvard University. Peacock has served as a teacher, counselor, director of Indian education for the Duluth Public Schools, secondary school principal, and superintendent of education for the Fond du Lac Reservation.

His research and publication interests focus on American Indian education and policy issues. He coauthored *Collected Wisdom* in 1998 with Linda Miller Cleary on teachers' perceptions of American Indian students. Peacock is also conducting an impact study of casino gaming in reservation communities, a qualitative study of American Indian student's perceptions of teachers and schools, and writing case studies to enhance the knowledge base of non-Indian preservice teachers about American Indian culture, history, teaching strategies, and methods.

9

USING CASES IN MULTICULTURAL STUDIES

THOMAS D. PEACOCK
UNIVERSITY OF MINNESOTA–DULUTH

My initial exposure to the case study method came from three distinct and seemingly unrelated sources, with each contributing in different ways to my interest in using cases. The first and foremost influence has been my Anishinabe heritage, which is rich in both oral and written stories. Second, graduate school exposed me to lengthy, complicated case studies that forced me to apply theory to case situations. Finally, as a faculty member at the University of Minnesota–Duluth, I attended a seminar on using case studies that gave me insight into combining my knowledge of Anishinabe storytelling with educational theory and the contemporary case method, thereby using *cases as stories* to teach about American Indians to primarily non-Indian undergraduate students.

Much of my interest in the case study method comes from the research and study of my Anishinabe heritage, in which stories have been used in teaching for tens of thousands of years. My Anishinabe ancestors were primarily an oral people, although they did record their history, culture, ceremonies, songs, stories, and sacred teachings on bark scrolls and "teaching rocks," writings on large rock outcroppings that line many of our northern lakes. To Euro-Americans, these seemingly cryptic writings appeared to be simple drawings of spirits, animals, people, or events and places in the natural world. To the Anishinabe, however, each symbol was a highly compressed representation of an entire story, or series of stories. For example, the entire history of the Lenni Lenapi (the

Delaware people who are considered by some historians as the traditional ancestors of the Anishinabe and other linguistically similar tribes) consists of a mere 687 richly descriptive word symbols. Anishinabe oral stories were also similar to their written language, simple yet profoundly complex at the same time. Anishinabe children's stories were rich in deeper meanings, subtlety, metaphor, and indirect teachings. Stories were the primary means by which these teachings and lessons of life were passed down through the generations. Their purpose was to engage children in a lifelong quest for wisdom and the truth.

The coming of the Europeans to North America changed this way of being forever and much of the ancient knowledge was lost. The sacred teachings in the stories, songs, prose, and parables that had guided the direction of the people's lives for many thousands of years were denigrated and called primitive myths or paganism. Today, a highly descriptive native language (which contains over 6000 verb forms) is spoken by less than 500 people in the United States.

If anything, the people called "Indians" by the colonizers, are survivors. Despite everything we have lost, we retain a rich storytelling tradition, even though many of the people today are primarily English speakers. Stories (both oral and written) are still the primary means by which the history and legends are passed down from elders to the young. Stories are still used to teach the lessons and deeper meaning of life. Seemingly simple stories, written or told orally, are complex at the same time, rich in subtlety, metaphor, and multiple layers of meaning. This storytelling tradition is strong in me because I was raised in a home rich in stories. The important lessons of life I teach to my own children are passed on in stories, to engage them in their lifelong search for wisdom and the truth. Because they have been raised in this way, the manner in which they describe their own lives is often done in story form. We are a story people, and what I refer to as the case study method is just an extension of a very ancient way of teaching.

Another significant source of exposure to the case study method came while I was in graduate school at Harvard University. Until that time, neither my undergraduate or graduate study in Minnesota universities had given me any exposure to cases. The graduate school of education (HGSE) at Harvard didn't have many education-based cases, but relied on those developed at the Harvard Business or Law Schools, each of which had an established tradition of using the case method. These cases dealt with significant leadership issues in business, law, finance, and ethics. Typically, the cases accompanied theoretical/knowledge-based readings, and teams of students analyzed lengthy (often over 100 pages in length) and complicated cases according to the constructs provided in the literature. Each team prepared a written paper in which they applied theory to the case. HGSE called it the Harvard Inquiry Method, something we today refer to as cooperative learning.

In the fall of 1993, I attended a case method writing and teaching workshop conducted by Mark Mostert of Moorhead State University, Minnesota. Mark was using cases in special education courses at Moorhead State, and the workshop focused on the how's, when's, and why's of using cases, as well as offering writing tips for developing our own cases. At the workshop I reflected on the myriad issues confronting American Indian students in our schools, with inadequate teacher preparation being one of those major issues, and began to wonder if using cases might be an avenue for better teacher preparation. A fellow native educator had reminded me that many non-Indian teachers knew little about native teachers, saying, "They just don't get it."

I remember responding, "What is the 'it' they don't get?" She replied they don't understand US. They don't know us because they haven't walked in our world. They don't perceive things the way we do. They have never experienced things the way we have.

Suddenly the workshop on using and writing cases in teacher education courses melded with my knowledge of Anishinabe storytelling: *Cases* could be used to help non-Indians understand us, walk and perceive in our world in a literal sense, and experience things the way we do, albeit in stories. In combination with theory/knowledge-based readings, cases could temporarily transport preservice teachers into the Anishinabe world. Thus began a journey into searching out, writing, and using cases.

A PROCESS FOR DEVELOPING CASES

A search for cases on American Indian education led me down a series of lonely roads. There just wasn't much out there because not many native educators were developing case studies. So I sat down and developed a complex matrix of issues facing American Indian students and possible scenarios, situations, and characters that might be used to address them. There were certainly enough issues to keep me writing forever: racism; oppression; dysfunctional institutions, communities, and families; native language loss; literacy; discontinuity; living in both worlds; learning styles; teaching methods and strategies; and interpersonal styles. Moreover, there was a whole spectrum of culture, history, and value differences that most non-Indians know little about.

I looked at the matrix again. It was too complicated. Too linear. Where would I begin? In frustration I set it aside and drew a large circle (see Figure 9.1), which in my culture symbolically represents the way and seasons of all things.

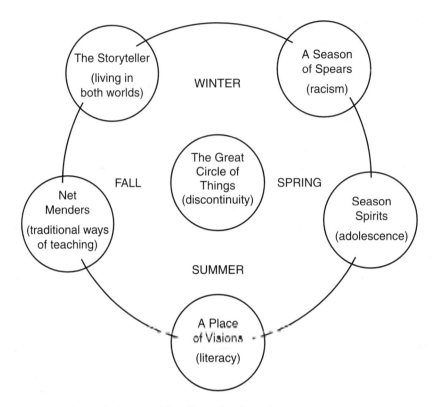

FIGURE 9.1   A Process for Developing Cases

Using this more holistic approach, the ideas began to flow. In the spring of the circle I would develop a case around a season of spears, the time of spring spearfishing. It would address issues of racism in schools, revolving around the Indian treaty rights issues that have torn many native and white communities apart. In late spring/early summer I would write a case on season spirits, the eternal battle between the spirits of winter and summer, and also focus it on issues of good and evil, decision making, and growing up. Season spirits would be a coming-of-age case, of the internal conflicts inherent to adolescence, and of growing and moving on. It would be set in a summer math and science program for native students. In late summer I would write a case about visions, and the continuity many Anishinabe people see between the past, present, and future. It would focus on issues of literacy in oral cultures, about a student faced with trying to decontextualize, or describe his vision, in writing. In fall I would develop a case that outwardly centered on mending fishnets, and it would deal with the traditional reasons and ways of teaching, as a way of enlightening prospective teachers about the need for cooperative group learning, active learning, and integrating traditional knowledge across the curriculum. So with a circle of potential cases before me, I began to lay out story lines, characters, settings, and ways I might weave the complexity of the native world into seemingly simple cases.

It seemed to me my first case should address issues of discontinuity, the differences in values, thinking, and ways of being between the schools and the communities American Indian children live in. There just seemed to be a tremendous gulf in the way the two saw the world. That is how the case, *The Great Circle of These Things,* was born.

In designing the case, I first listed the major and minor issues I wanted to address. It seemed important to describe the differences between the ways of school and the ways of community, as a way of helping non-Indians understand the gulf in world views. Moreover, it was important to demonstrate the need for multicultural education in schools, most of which are Eurocentric to the core, showing how most schools completely ignore the diversity of cultures in their communities. It would demonstrate the traditional ways of teaching, of using stories and direct application, and of teaching the whole of things (the layers of meaning in all things) rather than the obvious, superficial meaning. It would demonstrate how a parable that has been passed down from generation to generation is still used by elders in teaching the young about life. Moreover, the case would be structured in such a way as to appeal to both superficial and deep thinkers.

Like traditional Anishinabe stories, it would be both simple and complex, with layers of meaning. Superficial thinkers would be able to see the obvious issues of discontinuity. Deep thinkers would see the parable of an uncle telling his nephew the traditional creation story about Turtle Island, of a spirit woman having a vision of the new earth, and of her creating it with the help of a muskrat from the back of a giant turtle. Deep thinkers would recognize the uncle was not only passing down the Anishinabe creation story to the next generation, but he was telling a parable to the young person about the need to have vision and direction in life, and that the purpose of vision is to fulfill it. Depending on the reader, issues would be obvious, subtle, indirect, or hidden in metaphor.

The case is about Ron, an Anishinabe secondary student, who attended a primarily non-Indian school just off the reservation. It revolves around him missing several days of school to go netfishing with his uncle, acknowledging the traditional roles of paternal uncles as teachers in Anishinabe culture. It is written in a circle, beginning with Ron getting up in the morning and readying himself for school, and ending with him doing the same. He goes to school, a place that seems oblivious to his culture. He comes home. He goes netfishing around the sacred islands of the Apostles in Lake Superior, and returns home. During the trip, his uncle tells him stories and those stories reflect the circle of things. The case reflects the wholistic, messy reality of schools and the students who attend them.

PREPARING TO USE CASES

Students in my *Secondary Apprenticeship* (a required prestudent teaching field placement seminar) and an elective, *Teaching the American Indian Pupil,* served as guinea pigs for the first case drafts. The American Indian pupil course has primarily enrolled graduate students and those with a sincere interest in native issues, and is an in-depth study of all the issues and strategies of teaching native students. The class revolves around *case as story.* In the apprenticeship course, undergraduate students were required to respond to the cases in groups, as well as in an individually written analytic paper, which would connect theory/knowledge-based readings, the case, the reality of the classrooms of their field placement, and their own reflections. In addition to teaching about native education issues, a stated purpose of using cases was to challenge students to become critical thinkers, see connections, and be able to integrate knowledge from multiple sources.

Initial discussion and papers in the apprenticeship course indicated that although students gained a much better understanding of native students, most of them had a difficult time integrating their newfound knowledge and applying theory to the actual practice of teaching. The exception to this has been students with strong liberal arts backgrounds in the humanities, particularly English or composition majors, who have prior experience in being challenged to engage in the critical analysis of literature and the arts. The majority of the other students, however, soon "get it" (see the relationship between theory and teaching) after the first several cases and both their discussions of the case and accompanying readings, as well as their analytic papers, reflect this. My sense is the superficial thinkers continue to analyze the obvious issues in cases, while the deep thinkers notice the subtlety, nuances, metaphor, parable, and indirect meanings. I simply tell them all that cases, like life, are complicated, and that there are many views of the forest of reality.

In the three years I have been both developing and using cases, the only thing that has changed from my initial experiences has been my expectations of undergraduate preservice teachers. Initially, many have a difficult time with the complexity of case analysis, of finding the relationship between cases and theory/knowledge-based readings, as reflected in both their initial discussions and written analyses. Many undergraduate students have not been challenged to engage in the critical analysis of issues, and cases are a conduit for doing it. So the road to wisdom begins with simple steps.

There is some advice I would offer to someone contemplating using cases about multicultural issues in their content areas. Euro-Americans should have their prospective cases reviewed by a person of color before using them. This will help ensure they actually "get it" themselves, and don't offend anyone in the process. Euro-Americans should write the case from the perspective of a Euro-American (something they are experts at) with a multicultural situation. For those who contemplate writing and using their own cases, be prepared for ego deflation when some cases receive low evaluations from students or peers. In a sense, it is similar to sharing any writing with colleagues or students. The author must feel comfortable and expect to get suggestions, advice, and sometimes demands to edit their work.

CASE APPLICATIONS

This section explains the case-based multicultural course I teach, *Teaching the American Indian Pupil,* and describes how cases are an integral part of my instructional methodology. I discuss finding existing cases for use in the course, linking author-written cases to Anishinabe tradition, modeling traditional Anishinabe ways of teaching, teaching the class as story, additional teaching methods and strategies, course evaluations, and references for using cases in American Indian education.

Teaching the American Indian Pupil (Education 5381) has been an undergraduate and graduate elective course offered at the University of Minnesota–Duluth (UMD). That changed in 1995, when the Education Department at UMD made it a required four-credit quarter course beginning with the 1997 school term for all education (early childhood through secondary level) majors. Traditionally, the course has had a mix of both undergraduate and graduate students, primarily non-Indian (although there has usually been one or more native students), who have completed a minimum of 10 quarter credits in education courses. With an average class of under 20 students, all have been in the course at their own choosing, so there has been internal motivation (singing to the choir so to speak) on the part of most of them to know more about native education. Once the course is entirely composed of students who need the course to meet departmental requirements, the tone, demeanor, and methodology of the course may change. Class sizes will swell to 30 and higher. The change may be a reflection of the reality of

living in northern Minnesota, where non-Indians and Anishinabe people live near each other in an uneasy peace, where racism is both covert
and overt in communities and schools, where even institutions of higher
learning, like UMD, which purportedly are bastions of open and enlightened thinkers, nevertheless reflect the predominant Euro-American
society. Simply put, there will still be choir members in the class, but
there will also be skeptics, bigots, racists, the misinformed, and the un-
enlightened awaiting to be enlightened.

The course has been case-based, focusing on introducing students
to: (a) the socio-political and historical background of American Indians; (b) the issues, methods, and strategies for working with native students in a variety of contexts; and, (c) *American Indian Learner Outcomes,*
a curriculum framework developed by native educators for the Minnesota Department of Children, Families, and Learning. The course
seeks the integration of theory and content (using a collection of readings, journal articles, research findings, and book chapters), issues
(found in the cases), and reflection (students' own experiences and reflections based on the cases and theory/knowledge-based readings). Beginning with a brief history of American Indian education and bringing
students up to the present is important for establishing context for the
issues faced by native students today. Moreover, students are familiar-
ized with an understanding of oppression theory, of the effects of oppression on both the oppressor and the oppressed, and how that is
played out in schools. Table 9.1 shows the major topics covered in the
course.

Once the socio-political and historical backgrounds are laid, the class
is introduced to a curriculum frameworks document, *American Indian
Learner Outcomes* (1995), developed by native educators as a guide for
teachers to integrate Anishinabe and Dakota history and culture across
the curriculum. The book contains 17 curriculum frameworks, including
learner outcomes, their relationship to Minnesota's graduation standards, teacher contexts, sample lesson plans for elementary, middle, and
secondary classrooms, and resource lists. This outcome document is used
as a resource guide for the course.

A fruitless search for cases to use in the course forced me to expand
the notion of what constitutes a case. Mark Mostert's faculty development
seminar had taught me that most cases present a dilemma, and at the
end, there are questions or issues that the reader must explore further to
arrive at their own conclusions and solutions. My search couldn't find
anything that met those requirements, thus I looked to short stories with
American Indian characters that were set in schools. Most short stories
have definitive conclusions, but many stories written by native authors
are still influenced by the authors' oral traditions and are strong in

TABLE 9.1   Teaching the American Indian Pupil: Course Topics

- History of American Indian education: traditional forms of education; the boarding and mission school era; the age of self-determination

- Issues of oppression: overt and institutional racism; internalized oppression with all its characteristics, including alcoholism, drug abuse, anger, passive–aggressive behavior, a sense of helplessness and purposelessness, the absence of an educational legacy, mistrust of schools, and all the other attributes of individuals and communities suffering from dysfunction

- Native language issues

- Literacy issues

- Discontinuity: the differences in values, worldview, and cultural beliefs between predominantly Eurocentric schools and the homes of many native students

- Living in both worlds

- Learning styles

- Research-based teaching methods and strategies that have worked with native students

- Interpersonal skills that have proven effectiveness in working with native students

metaphor, subtlety, and indirect teachings. Conclusions in many of these native written stories leave the reader with more questions than answers. One such story I use is Stephen Barse's *Grandson,* which is about a native student experiencing cultural, personal, and academic problems in a university setting. The case is usually the first case assigned in *Teaching the American Indian Pupil* because it is a good introduction to the complex cultural and oppression-driven issues facing many native students.

The cases that I have written parallel the Anishinabe tradition. In traditional times, education was done in three phases. Children spent their early years with grandmothers and aunties. Skills in observation and listening were enhanced by setting babies outside to see and hear all of the natural world around them, where they learned the language of plants and animals, grasses, clouds, and wind. Adults sang to them and told them stories to enable them to dream because it was believed that dreams are a child's first visions. As they grew older the children went with men or women to learn the skills of living, how to hunt, plant, gather, and the making of things. When they entered adolescence, boys were sent on their vision fast, because a vision would give them purpose and direction in life. For girls, the vision fast was not required, because they were born with the miracle of childbirth in them. The final phase, which went on the rest of their lives, was spent in the search for wisdom and the truth, things that can only be found by searching for the deeper meaning of life's events, its nuances, subtlety, simplicities, and complexities. Wisdom is the whole of these things.

The course begins with describing this traditional form of education and offers to students a parallel with the goals of the course. The purpose of the course, I explain, is to begin them on their search for wisdom and the truth. They already know many of the *how's* of living, and some of them know the *why's*. The course is intended as an intellectual, philosophical, and fundamentally internal journey as well as a forum for offering concrete methods and strategies for working with American Indian students.

Twelve cases are used in the course, nine of which I wrote (see Table 9.2). Six of my cases have the same main character, Ron (a native secondary student), and are set in the community of Red Cliff, Wisconsin, a reservation community located on the south shore of Lake Superior. The other three cases are set in Big Lake Schools, a fictional school district in northern Wisconsin. Two of those cases revolve around Molly and Beverly, a rebellious pair of junior high girls. The other case is about Lenny, an attention deficit, hyperactive kindergartner. Because many of the cases are related, (six Ron cases, three Big Lake cases), the class is taught as story.

The teaching methods and strategies used with *The Storyteller* and the other cases is similar. The class is assigned a case and supplemental readings several days before class and asked to identify the issues, perspectives of the main actors, and proposed solutions to the case. The readings provide background material to facilitate discussion and to broaden their

TABLE 9.2   Author-Written Cases

Case Title	Subject Matter
A Place of Visions	Cultural continuity; literacy
A Season of Spears	Racism
Another View of the Forest of Reality: A Squirrel's Perspective	Classroom management
Lenny	Hyperactivity; classroom management
Net Menders	Traditional ways of teaching
Season Spirits	Coming of age
The Great Circle of Things	Discontinuity
The Storyteller	Living in both worlds; racism
They're Acting Really Squirrelly	Classroom management

knowledge about potential case issues. Other readings generally come from the *American Indian Learner Outcome* document. With the introduction each week of another case, the class comes to know the characters, especially Ron. To facilitate discussion, the class is divided into cooperative groups of four, and students are given up to half an hour to discuss the case in its entirety. A whole class discussion of the case then takes place, with each group giving an oral report of their discussions. [I follow this with either a 10-minute lecturette, or a cooperative group problem, based on the key application concepts raised during the discussions.] For example, a lecturette following a case on classroom discipline (*They're Acting Really Squirrelly*) is focused on cultural and community discipline issues in American Indian communities.

Students often remark in discussions about other readings or issues, "What do you think Ron would think about that? How might doing such and such affect Ron's education?" There is an interrelatedness and connectedness of cases and case issues. Each new case builds on the others, while focusing on specific issues. All the cases have multilayered issues and meanings that involve interweaving story, parable, subtlety, indirect lessons, and practical application.

An example of this complexity is found in the case, *The Storyteller*. To prepare for the case, students read a chapter on oral tradition from the *American Indian Learner Outcomes*. This theory/knowledge-based reading gives students necessary background about Anishinabe oral tradition and the importance of including it in the curriculum. It also offers teachers practical advice on how to ask an elder into the classroom by offering storytellers some tobacco, which is used in prayers. Students then read the case in which Ron has asked his Uncle Eddie to come into the school to tell stories. In one scene, Uncle Eddie tells a story to Ron's American literature class:

> *Uncle Eddie stepped forward. From his front shirt pocket he pulled out the pouch of tobacco his nephew had given him. He looked at the tobacco the whole time, never once looking directly at the class. He explained how his nephew had approached him to come into the school and tell stories, and how he had offered the tobacco and how important that was. He went on to explain that after he had told the stories and left the school he would offer some of the tobacco to the animals and spirits that live in the stories. The class was pin-drop quiet when he said that.*
>
> *"Now I am going to tell you about the plant-beings," he said, and the story began:*
>
> *"Plants were here on this earth before our elder brothers, the animals, and before humans. They can exist without either animals or*

humans. *All the plants, like all the animals and humans, have their own unique soul-spirits. It gives them their form. It allows them to grow. When they get ill or injured, it allows them to heal. One of the most wonderful things about plants is that they can join with other plants and animals to form a larger spirit. When we say a place has spirit, that is what we mean. When we say a place is sacred, that is what we mean. It is the spirit of a place. Each one of the Apostle Islands out there on Gitchi Gummi, what you call Lake Superior, possesses a spirit which reflects the state of being of that place. If the soul-spirit is peaceful, the island is peaceful. It* **feels** *peaceful. If it is angry, the mood of the place is angry."*

Uncle Eddie was fingering the tobacco. Never once did he look directly at the class.

"I can prove this to you. If you destroy a part of a sacred place, a special place, the mood and spirit of that place will not be the same as it was before. If you cut down the trees or pick all the flowers, the mood and spirit of the place will change forever. All of us, you know, we have special places where we go when we want to think and to be with Gitchi Manito, God. They are sacred places. Even you white people have these places, even though you might not think about it the same as we Indians do. I think about that. That is why the plants are so important to the Anishinabe people."

The case continues to describe an incident that follows Uncle Eddie's storytelling in which a white student, Matt, mocks Ron's uncle to his friends by saying, "Why did we have to listen to that old Indian dude anyway?" Later in the case, Ron, who in all the other cases has been portrayed as a caring, functional adolescent, gets even with Matt by beating him up. When Uncle Eddie finds out, he is disappointed, and teaches his nephew a lesson in the indirect way so common among traditional American Indian people. Before he departs from a visit to Ron's house, he leaves Ron with a life lesson.

"I have something for you to read," Uncle Eddie said, digging in his jacket pocket. He took out a book.

"I've been reading this Momaday book and I think you might like it, Ron. It's filled with all kinds of Indian stuff."

Eddie laughed softly. His eyes were serious. Ron took the book and thanked his uncle for letting him borrow it. After Eddie left, he took it into his room and set it on the lamp table.

His first intention was to go immediately to bed because it was getting late but he decided to page through the book to see if it might interest him. It wasn't all that unusual for Uncle Eddie to offer books to people to read after he was done with them. It was unusual for him to offer one to his nephew.

As Ron was paging through the book, he noticed one of the pages was folded over. It was the only page in the book where an ear had been folded over as a marker. Page 14. And he opened it and saw a sketch of an Indian man, and written above it Momaday told of "The Fear of Bo-talee":

Bo-talee rode easily among his enemies, once, twice, three—and four times. And all who saw him were amazed, for he was utterly without fear; so it seemed. But afterwards he said, "Certainly I was afraid. I was afraid of the fear in the eyes of my enemies."

So what outwardly seems like a case about the hows and whys of storytelling, and a boy's reaction to racial intolerance, is actually much more than that. The case provides lessons on eye contact, the roles of paternal uncles as teachers in Anishinabe culture, the indirect way of teaching used in many Anishinabe homes, and fundamental information about the Anishinabe worldview.

The course is graded in a traditional A–F manner and the requirements consist of three papers. The grading system and scale used for each paper is as follows: mechanics (grammar and sentence structure), 30 percent; content (synthesis of ideas, use of research, relevancy of topic), 30 percent; and, overall strength of argument, original thinking and clarity, 40 percent.

The first paper describes an issue about teaching American Indian students. It consists of five to ten pages written in American Psychological Association format with a minimum of five references. The paper begins by introducing the issue, followed by a discussion of the issue based on the literature, and closes with a summary. The second paper, using a similar format, proposes solutions to the issues presented in the first paper. The final paper is a written case (five to ten pages) that poses as one of its issues something from the other two papers. Students present their case to the entire class in the final class session, reading it aloud as well as furnishing written copies to the instructor. Racism in schools is an example of the types of subjects selected by students for their papers. One student prepared her first two papers on issues of racism in public schools educating American Indians, and presented a true life case about racism involving one of her Indian friends.

The course is formally evaluated at the final class session using a university seminar evaluation form. The form is a rating scale from one to six (very strongly disagree, disagree, agree, strongly agree, very strongly agree, and not applicable), assessing 24 areas: challenging/stimulating material, enthusiasm in teaching, inspired interest in subject, motivated me to do best work, used examples and illustrations effectively, explained what was expected from students, prepared adequate course outline/syllabus, clarified material, was an effective speaker, referred to recent applications or developments in the area of study, maintained an atmosphere that encouraged learning, related to students in a way to promote mutual respect, was available outside the classroom for help/advice, maintained consistent evaluation procedures, was clear on how student work would be evaluated, had reasonable pacing of assignments, gave helpful feedback of student performance, broadened student knowledge of the information in the readings, developed my ability to conduct research, included student presentations, got students to participate in class discussions/activities, was open to viewpoints that differed from his/her own, facilitated discussions effectively, and course on a whole was good.

I use the summary of these course evaluations to help me improve my teaching methods, to assist in determining what worked or didn't, and as a planning tool to better meet the learning needs of the next group of students. Students have consistently rated the course positively (between strongly agree to very strongly agree). Students also have an opportunity to discuss the course on an informal basis after their case presentations, over goodies (soda, candy, and healthy snacks) provided by the instructor. They have generally mentioned reflection (linking case scenarios to their own personal experiences) and writing their own cases as high points of the course.

SUMMARY AND CONCLUSIONS

Teaching using cases has invigorated me as a teacher in several important ways. Case-based teaching has helped me understand the importance of challenging students to think critically and to apply what they read (theory) with what they see and do (practice) and what they believe (reflection). Using cases has challenged me to model teaching practices I advocate to students to use as teachers: active learning, cooperative groups, experiential learning, and inquiry. Finally, case-based teaching has reminded me of the importance of fun in the teaching–learning process, as well as the reciprocal nature of teaching and learning.

REFERENCES

American Indian Learner Outcome Team. (1995). *American Indian learner outcomes*. St. Paul, MN: Department of Children, Families, and Learning.

Barse, Stephen. *Grandson.* Unpublished manuscript.

Deer River Public Schools. (1992). *Everyday heroes.* [Film]. Available from Deer River Schools, Deer River, MN.

Miller Cleary, L., & Peacock, T. (1998). *Collected wisdom: American Indian education.* Boston, MA: Allyn & Bacon.

MARK P. MOSTERT

Mark P Mostert is an associate professor of special education and coordinator for programs in learning disabilities at Moorhead State University in Moorhead, Minnesota. He graduated with distinction and a higher education diploma in elementary teaching and special education from the Johannesburg College of Education in Johannesburg, South Africa. His master's degree is from the University of South Alabama where he was also the 1985 outstanding graduate in special education. He received his doctorate in special education and teacher education from the University of Virginia.

Mostert was the recipient of the 1996 Jason Millman Promising Scholar Award from Cornell University and was Moorhead State's Dille Distinguished Lecturer for 1997. He served as visiting professor of special education at the University of Cologne, Germany, in 1998. His research interests include case-based pedagogy, teacher cognition and practical knowledge, and research synthesis.

10

A CASE OF THE PERSONAL IN THE PEDAGOGICAL: SPECIAL EDUCATION CASE-BASED INSTRUCTION AS SHARED EXPERIENCE

MARK P. MOSTERT
MOORHEAD STATE UNIVERSITY

I became a teacher as a matter of survival. In the context of the early 1970s, white South African males were offered two options after finishing high school: automatic drafting into the military with an excellent chance of gaining combat experience (or worse), or having the draft deferred by entering an approved university. I chose the latter course, hoping that my four years in college would be time enough for the draft to end. My decision immediately led to another hurdle: I did not qualify for university entrance.

In the heavily tracked and segregated South African schools, I had not done well enough. For years I was baffled by my dismal high school performance. I had left elementary school with a string of academic awards dating back to the first grade, but by the end of the 8th grade, my first high school year, I had gone from a straight "A" student to "Bs", "Cs", and the lowest quartile in math and Latin. I remember being despondent because I didn't understand what had gone wrong, even though I worked as hard as I knew how. I was raised with many dictums,

157

among which was that if you work hard enough at anything, you will conquer it. Attempting, in vain, to apply this dictum to math and Latin led to the first notion I can recall that was later to influence my teaching: *Working hard does, fortunately, create a willingness to apply oneself diligently to any task.* Unfortunately, if applied indiscriminately and unrealistically to every task one attempts or feels one should attempt, the result can be quite debilitating. One is also, in this latter condition, likely to blame oneself almost entirely, which I often did.

In retrospect, and now that I am a teacher myself, I am convinced that my problems in math and Latin, and, to a lesser extent, in my other high school subjects, were not a result of my laziness or even lack of application. What happened to me was bad teaching. In the past several years I have studied my old high school report cards carefully. The fall from grace in math clearly shows that I entered high school well prepared, close to the top of my graduating 7th grade elementary class, in the "A stream", of course.

Within the first two quarters of the 8th grade, I began to fail math. In remembering my 8th grade math teacher, I now understand what happened: She was a first year teacher with a university degree in math and only a course or two in *how to teach math.* I clearly recall badgering her with questions and requests for help as I fell further and further behind, and always leaving her desk more confused than when I arrived. Soon, my embarrassment became quite acute and I stopped asking questions. In a class of 40 students, no one noticed. I think Miss Strauss was relieved that I was no longer asking questions she was having difficulty answering.

Things were a little different in Latin. Mrs. Bell was a highly experienced, well-liked teacher. Her class was heavy on drill, pop quizzes, unpredictable demands in class to come up with *exactly* the correct verb form, and so on. Aside from my dismal performance, what I remember most was the sense of panic that enveloped me each day as I went to her class. Invariably, when I was asked a question, I needed a little more time to find the answer than what she was prepared to give me, and besides, there were others eager to answer and who made more sense of things than I.

However, I remembered the dictum about hard work and knew how well it had served me in elementary school. I redoubled my efforts in math and Latin but I had lost too much ground in that 8th-grade year. In the ensuing years I barely passed math and by my senior year there was a good chance that I would fail the final national math "A stream" examination. My performance in math was in stark contrast to some other subjects, where, in retrospect, the teaching was different. I excelled in geography, which was taught by my rugby coach, Mr. Verster. I had started, that freshman year, to play rugby and, working as hard as I could, soon began to excel. Going to Mr. Verster's geography class was a pleasant extension of hard work on the rugby field. He was enthusiastic about his subject, had a sense of humor, and I always understood what he was teaching us. It was a clear, unmistakable contrast to Latin and math.

I continued working as hard as I knew how in math, but to no avail. My parents paid for extra lessons, and I spent many afternoons along with several other dullards trying to understand a retired math teacher who didn't seem particularly interested in whether we learned anything or not. I recall that by that time, however, I was acutely ashamed about my lack of progress, and studiously pretended that I knew what I was doing. In contrast to my lack of success in math, my application of the "hard work dictum" worked extraordinarily well on the rugby field (as it would years later when I turned my attention to ultramarathon running). I made the first rugby team as a junior and remained through the rest of my high school playing days.

Academically, I eventually graduated high school from the "B stream," a major stumbling block to defer military service. Only "A stream" pupils went to universities, institutions that graduated most of the public schools' secondary teachers. My single option was to enroll in the Johannesburg College of Education (JCE), a teacher training institution that accepted "B stream" students and was responsible for graduating the vast majority of the public schools' elementary teachers. Everybody knew that if you went to JCE, chances were that you hadn't made the university cut. By this time I had learned another bit of information that would help when I taught preservice teachers: *Doing your best was the surest way of succeeding.* However, this was not the only factor influencing success. The trick was to know when you had done all you could so as not to blame yourself unfairly for failing, or, in understanding when you had not done your best, to keep trying. Determination and persistence, when finally rewarded, are wonderful encouragements.

THE CONTEXT OF THE PERSONAL: THE STRUGGLE FOR COMPETENCE AND CREDIBILITY

Very quickly, as a college freshman, things began to change. I worked as hard at college as I had at school, and suddenly I flourished. Coursework was exciting and my practicum experiences revealed an unexpected, but unmistakable, talent for teaching. Four years later, I graduated very near the top of my college class. To this day the memory of begging to be admitted to a first year bachelor's program smarts. I taught for several years and gained as much experience as I could by teaching in both elementary school and secondary schools, and in general and special education.

My early struggles and subsequent positive initial educational experiences as a preservice and novice teacher began to lay a pedagogical foundation of the personal in the pedagogical that would, many years later, support my own teaching of special educators, particularly in relation to interprofessional consultation and collaboration. I soon discovered that in spite of my "B stream" teaching qualification, maintaining high levels of motivation, hard work, persistence, and a willingness to do the most with the skills I possessed vitally shaped my emerging skills. I did the best I could to take advantage of every learning opportunity and constantly sought more experienced colleagues for advice and help. Several veteran teachers were very encouraging of my work and assured me that I was adjusting well. Very soon, I began to notice marked improvements in my teaching skills and relationships with my students and their families. It was the first inkling I had that, contrary to my belief that "teachers were born," that effective teaching, technical skill, and working effectively with others could be learned. In my college teaching today I stress that students can learn to be teachers, if they are willing to apply themselves.

Even as my success in those first years grew, the specter of my "B stream" schooling bothered me. Surely if I had not done well in grade school, should I be doing this well at teaching? These thoughts persisted until I realized what highly experienced teachers know about their pupils, and that, as a teacher, I had to relearn for myself: *Underachievement in one educational area or experience does not necessarily preclude satisfactory or superior achievement in others.* It also became clear early on that I was doing more, and doing more effectively, than two colleagues who had begun their careers with me. One seemed less motivated and more preoccupied with other things in his life outside of work. He seemed to be largely ignored by the school faculty. Simultaneously, I noticed that I was being relied on by more senior faculty and the principal. This helped me deduce that, at least in my case, there was a correlation between my effort and the extent to which I learned and applied practical skills, including interprofessional collaboration, in the classroom. I was motivated to work harder and learn more.

I also seemed to be moving ahead of my other novice colleague whom I had always considered "superior" because she had completed her elementary degree at university (an "A stream" high school pass, no doubt). In this case I understood my advantage more clearly: At JCE I had been exposed to student teaching experiences and methods courses from my freshman year with much less focus on academic liberal arts coursework. My female colleague, however, had spent three years in purely academic courses and a hurried fourth year cramming in all her required teaching experience and methods courses. My advantage in terms of working with children and being resourceful in my lesson planning and execution was significant. Understandably, I struggled with how it could be that my (self-) perceived "inferior" preparation actually stood me in better stead than had I been able to attend a university preparation course. I came to realize that, in essence, my broader educational experience appeared generally more effective and adaptable in learning about teaching, in relating to children, and in interprofessional collaboration, than the narrower professional preparation provided to my colleague.

THE PERSONAL IN THE PEDAGOGICAL: EARLY CAREER LESSONS—THE POLITICS OF COLLABORATION

In those years I learned many of the things most novice teachers do about their jobs, but I also began to notice that what I term the *technical* (the melding of the *theoretical* and the *pedagogical*) aspects of teaching were only half the story. I began to encounter another dimension for which I had received no training; a dimension in which all my enthusiasm, curiosity, hard work, and willingness to learn were not necessarily assets. I slowly perceived that the realm of the *personal,* consisting of the *political* (the complex partisan milieu of teaching in which personal and professional agendas, implicit or obvious, exert considerable influence on professional decisions) and the *relational* (the intricate connectedness or disconnectedness generated by both personal and professional social interactions) were equally pivotal in effective teaching.

Both the technical and the personal appeared to be moderated by the *contemplative* (the ability to consider past actions, situations, and perspectives as an agent for future improvement). For example, I soon discovered that, for some of my colleagues, personal friendships could be more professionally influential than honesty, or that professional recognition could depend on past reciprocal favors rather than legitimate achievement. I also knew that such personal skill was, at that point, quite undeveloped in my teaching.

As I reflected on this new, unexpected dimension of teaching, several things became quite clear. Most rudimentarily, as I observed this new world swirling around me, I came to believe that the political realm, especially aspects related to power, could be as important, or even more important, than the technical skill of teaching. Indeed, it became quite clear that the contemplative was a means of uncovering, understanding, and acting more reasonably to become a better teacher. This realization was reinforced by the uneasy understanding that my teacher preparation program explicitly addressed the technical. Addressing the contemplative, which I was finding increasingly important in improving my ability to teach and collaborate interprofessionally, was never mentioned.

Predictably, lacking contemplative and reflective skills, I soon became involved in several scrapes, most of a minor nature to be sure, but significant enough for me to understand that this lack held potential for professional disaster. To steer an ethical, considered, and responsible course through such waters required knowledge, maturity, and, above all, astute, consistent reflection.

In my final two years of teaching before leaving South Africa, now at a high school, I resolved to learn more about these aspects of teaching. It immediately became disturbingly clear that attempting to uncover the personal as a means of increasing interprofessional collaborative skill without prior sensitization and practice was time- and energy-consuming, to say nothing of dangerously mired in trial-and-error learning. One example will suffice.

Because of my special education background, along with my regular teaching duties, I fulfilled a quasi-counselor role at the high school. I was often asked to conduct formal and informal academic testing, to work with problem students and their families, and to meet with related county and state service providers. In one instance, a pupil alluded to some rather unusual goings on at home to the point that, after consulting with the principal, we decided to interview the father, the sole custodian. In my customary zeal I commandeered the meeting and pressed hard for details that might help us serve the child better. The principal, having more sense than I, did not attempt to chastise my obvious fire openly (in retrospect, I was quite inappropriately overwrought), but was supportive and calm when I allowed him to be. I didn't achieve much in that meeting. I did, however, reflect that my lack of communicative skill, overbearing presumptions that I was to run the meeting, and the crestfallen look on the principal's face as we concluded the meeting, to say nothing of the furious parent, meant that in terms of the personal, I had a long way to go.

By the time I immigrated to the United States in 1983, I felt that I had met most of my teaching goals in the classroom. Subsequently, I completed a master's degree in special education and taught at a private school for students with learning disabilities. Teaching in a private school considerably honed my notions of the personal, given that my work environment was largely ruled by an elite board of parents who clearly dictated the course of the school and many of the routine minutiae of my teaching day. The school advertised itself as a private school exclusively for children with learning disabilities. Almost every student enrolled had passed through a detailed (and expensive) assessment conducted by one of two board members, one a nurse with an interest in special education, the other a clinical psychologist. The evaluations of children, irrespective of the chronological age or their specific strengths and weaknesses, were remarkably similar. They also all ended with the same recommendation: enrollment in the school. Clearly, not everyone was learning disabled. Several students were mildly retarded, others were obviously emotionally disturbed, and several seemed to have been enrolled simply because they demonstrated some rather common behavior problems. Diagnosis increased enrollment, elevated enrollment inflated revenue, more revenue meant a bigger school and more prominence in the community, which in many ways seemed the ultimate goal of the board. They achieved their wish several years later when the school was amalgamated into the most prestigious private school in the city as a special education department. I learned more explicitly that in many contextual ways, the personal can dictate the pedagogical.

More convinced than ever that the personal agendas often directly influenced the teaching that was done, I looked for clues that might alert me to, and help make more explicit, people's hidden agendas and motives. I quickly learned that the political and the relational are often hidden and difficult to define for effective professional performance, especially in terms of interprofessional collaboration. As I became a careful observer of the implicit and explicit dances that shaped school policy and my teaching, the powerful results of the personal often generated strong feelings of frustration and helplessness: Very little was as it first appeared, and the dangers of misperception and misinterpretation were infinite.

Thus, I learned that teaching, especially in collaborative relationships, can become problematic if the political and relational are either ignored or taken at face value. Central to my growing experience was the realization that whatever my level of political and relational collaborative skill, there always seemed to be others who were more powerful or politically astute. I managed to avoid serious blunders, but increasingly found myself uncomfortably compressed, with much of my energy being diverted to the personal and away from the technical aspects of teaching.

Soon, an intriguing opportunity came my way. I became the director of education, and subsequently the program director, for a 30-bed adolescent inpatient psychiatric unit of a for-profit psychiatric hospital. The work was challenging, exciting, and very different from teaching. Even with my growing sense of the political and relational intangibles of interprofessional work, I was, in retrospect, still hopelessly naive. Primarily, I trusted everyone I worked with to maintain high standards of integrity; I expected my codirector (a psychiatrist and the medical director), and subordinates, (nurses, mental health technicians, social workers, counselors, teachers) to work as hard as I did; I assumed that everyone wanted what was best for the patients. Most disappointing of all, I thought I could earn my colleagues' loyalty by being their advocate to the higher levels of the administration. However, my efforts were hardly appreciated by upper management, and my budding career was cut short.

Subsequently, I reflected deeply on what went wrong. My integrity was never in question. My commitment to hard work and being willing to learn were beyond reproach. Everyone agreed that my repeated, voluntary advocacy for my subordinates to upper levels of the administration was greatly admired. I also remembered that all these attributes made me enemies among those who were more politically and relationally powerful. This distressing experience, though, focused several new layers of understanding. It taught me that, when engaging in interprofessional collaboration, being a sincere advocate without exceptional political or relational skill or a commanding knowledge of sources of power can exact an exorbitant professional price. However, I also understood that not all of my experience had been negative.

It was quite clear from my hospital experience that those who were more successful politically and relationally than I, and, irrespective of their power status, generally fared better in interprofessional collaboration than the politically naive. I took a special interest in a colleague who had managed to weather numerous corporate purges and staffing upheavals and whose ability to survive in this charged setting was commonly acknowledged as masterful. His understanding of the delicate layers of power, hidden and explicit worlds, and an acute sense of timing allowed him an extraordinary level of professional freedom, to say nothing of survival. It taught me that understanding issues of power within the political and relational are imperative for effective, uninterrupted professional performance with both pupils and colleagues. Over time, my reflections and observations also taught me that it takes considerable time and effort to develop discriminatory intercollaborative skills that take into account, and use to positive pedagogical advantage, issues within the political and relational.

I returned to teaching with a deeper understanding of what I did not need. I did not need more technical teaching expertise. I was clearly able to perform even outside of the field for which I was trained. I could outwork almost all of my peers and colleagues. But it wasn't enough, and the understanding of what I needed was yet to come.

In returning to education, I assumed the principalship of a private elementary school with a renewed sense of commitment to children and the teachers I supervised. Once again, the attributes that had historically stood me in such good stead were evident. It was in this job, though, that I finally realized that I did not have the level of the personal that would assure my survival and enable me to do professionally what I wanted to do. The very same currents I had so painfully discovered in my previous private school and the hospital setting were here, in a vastly different context, and even more pronounced.

As I strove to improve the image of the school and implement what I believed to be policies beneficial to the pupils and teachers, I soon learned that some of the teachers who had long alliances with certain members of the board did not see the need to abide by my policies and directives. It was clear in this case that interprofessional collaboration could be delineated by those who had more power, although not necessarily more status, by virtue of their deeper understanding of the political and the relational to further their own goals. As these battles became more frequent and protracted, I soon learned again what most experienced teachers might say was the obvious: *That the forces at play in teaching and schools sometimes overlook, deliberately or inadvertently, the pupils' educational needs in favor of intrigue, authority, or a collective will based in the personal desires, whims, or needs of a few.* Not only was the focus not the pupils and their educational needs, it was also apparent that educational needs of the pupils were sometimes used as a mask for furthering political and relational aims.

I was consistently astonished at others' willingness to coopt and contaminate legitimate educational issues for largely personal, noneducational ends. Putting aside competing interests to better serve children and their families was almost always framed in terms of the victorious and the vanquished. It became obvious that aspects of power through the political and the relational could be used for many things aside from effective service delivery and professional problem solving to further teaching and learning. I continue to be fascinated with this hidden, yet significant component of educational practice.

My personal experiences in education, quite predictably, have shaped and prepared me as a teacher educator with a distinct point of view. It was these experiences, and what I have found in the juxtaposition of the technical and personal in the pedagogical, that has became the bedrock of my approach to case-based instruction. Irrespective of efforts in teacher education to do otherwise, I believe that student teachers are technically largely trained in two important, yet restricted, areas containing aspects of (1) the theoretical, and (2) the pedagogical. Within this largely traditional emphasis, almost all students find the accumulation of teaching skills, most often through their teaching practica, to be the more valuable of the two. We have only recently begun to make explicit a third area for more effective teacher training, that is, issues in personal and practical knowledge.

First, this line of research acknowledges, as in my story above, a hidden but integral part of teachers' lives that profoundly influences teachers' thinking and everyday work. Second, and, in my view, even more importantly, it acknowledges the intimate intertwining of the personal in the professional. Equally, if we accept the premise of practical knowledge to be personal, idiosyncratic, and a principal mediator of teacher thinking, decision making, and pedagogical action, we must increase efforts to uncover the personal, especially, in this case, as to what this means for interprofessional collaboration. There is little evidence, however, that teacher training programs explicitly address, as a matter of teacher preparation, the personal as found in the political and the relational, concentrating, instead, on the technical aspects of learning to teach. Teaching with cases can help make personal agendas more explicit for both the teacher educator and student.

CASE-BASED TEACHING: SHARING THE TECHNICAL AND PERSONAL ASPECTS OF INSTRUCTION IN SPECIAL EDUCATION

In reflecting on my work as a teacher educator, I have asked myself these questions: What was the purpose of all my past experience? How could I use these experiences for my professional growth and the growth of my students? How could I use what I had learned to better prepare my students for life in their classrooms and schools?

Prior to designing my own case-based courses, I had extensive experience in teaching with cases as a doctoral student both to large groups of students in a behavior management course, and in a more intimate setting with a dozen graduate students in a similar summer class. Very early on, as I taught using cases, I found my rich professional experience pouring into the case discussions. While my contributions to case discussions sometimes attended to the traditional explication of the educational dilemmas presented in the cases, that is, the technical, I found that I increasingly emphasized the personal in terms of contemplating the political and relational. It seemed that for almost every case the technical and educational dilemmas were rather obvious.

My students were intrigued by the educational dilemmas of the cases, and true to their training in the technical, diligently worked to understand the problem, relate it to some theoretical framework, and then attempted to operationalize their solutions in practice (Mostert & Kauffman, 1993). I was even more fascinated, however, that almost all the cases I shared with my students had some form of personal dimension, a dimension that, in the educational case literature and in practice, was largely ignored. I was not surprised that the political and relational remained largely hidden to my students, or, that when these issues were made explicit, they learned a great deal about the unseen and unsaid, which learning, it seems to me, is key to surviving as an educator in the classroom, school, and community.

Given these emphases, since becoming a teacher educator, I have shaped a senior undergraduate course to reflect my belief that the technical must be coupled with the personal if we are to send novice teachers into classrooms well-rounded and well-prepared. The semester course, *Consultation and Collaboration in Special Education and Human Services,* is a required, case-based, capstone course for all special education majors in their final semester, concurrent with student teaching. The course text is a standard reference on professional consultation and collaboration (Thomas, Correa, & Morsink, 1995), and linked to cases (see Table 10.1) that are drawn from a variety of sources (Greenwood & Parkay, 1989; Kauffman, Mostert, Nuttycombe, Trent, & Hallahan, 1993; Silverman, Welty, & Lyon, 1992; Wassermann, 1993). The current text for the course will be replaced shortly by my own (Mostert, 1998).

All of the cases I use contain common educational dilemmas in practical areas such as classroom management, instruction, and interprofessional collaboration. To a greater or lesser extent, all of the cases also reflect, albeit more implicitly, problematic issues in the personal. For example, *Amanda Jackson* (Silverman, Welty, & Lyon, 1992), details an ethical issue between a new teacher and a principal. Another case, *Grandma's Boy* (Kauffman, Mostert, Nuttycombe, Trent, & Hallahan, 1993), reveals a teacher attempting to deal with hostile parents, and so on. Additionally, students are required to complete an initial reflective essay about their teaching goals, read, analyze and critique assigned journal articles, and finally, complete a final 10-page reflective essay about their teaching goals, evaluative strategies for increased interprofessional collaboration, and their emotional reactions to becoming a teacher.

Students are required to prepare the cases prior to class by: (a) becoming completely familiar with the facts of the case, (b) reflecting on, and identifying, obvious or potential problems, (c) attempting to match the course content on consultation and collaboration to each obvious or potential problem, and (d) reflecting on what they have uncovered to identify alternative solutions or plans of action. Students are also required to respond and support their answers for each case to three questions (see Box 10.1).

The assigned case is discussed in class, usually in a large group format. In the initial cases, students focus on the obvious educational problems. As they become more familiar with the format, I begin to add a distinct emphasis on the political and relational. In later cases, once students have developed some awareness of both the explicit (obvious educational problem requiring interprofessional collaboration) and the implicit (the political and relational which appear as mediators to interprofessional collaboration), they are required to consider both aspects in their decision making for professional action in the cases. Subsequent to the discussions, the students construct in-

TABLE 10.1   Course Sequence

Week	Topic	Assignments
1	Introduction, Overview, Course, Requirements, etc. Historical Context	
2	Framework & Rationale for Interactive Teaming	Morsink ch. 1
3	Historical & Legal Foundations	Morsink ch. 2
4	Definitions Case: *Helen Franklin*	Morsink ch. 2 Case
5	Roles & Responsibilities Case: *The Power Struggle*	Morsink ch. 3 Case
6	Professional Roles Case: *The Ghost of School Years Past*	Morsink ch.4 Case
7	Communication Skills Case: *Alison Cohen*	Morsink ch. 5 Case
8	Families of Children with Disabilities Case: *Grandma's Boy,* Part A	Morsink chs. 6 & 10; Case
9	Teamwork with Professionals and Families Case: *Grandma's Boy,* Part B	Morsink ch. 7 Case
10	Siblings of Children with Disabilities Case: *They Failed Derrick*	Case
11	Journal Article Critiques	Critiques
12	Case: *I'll Come Back When You're Teaching*	Case
13	Interprofessional Leadership Skills Case: *Values in the Workplace*	Morsink chs. 7 & 9; Case
14	Ethical Issues in Professional Practice	APA Ethical Guidelines
15	Ethical Issues Case: *Amanda Jackson*	APA Ethical Guidelines Case
16	Putting It All Together: Case: *Mostert* (1998)	Case

BOX 10.1   Case Questions

1. In this case, what do you think the teacher (or central character) saw as important for his or her teaching?
2. Do you think the teacher in this case was doing the job to the best of his or her ability?
3. What was your emotional reaction to the issues raised in this case?

---

dividual written analyses for each case based on their preparation and class discussion.

In all of these efforts, however, it is not yet clear how students learn from cases (e.g., see Barnett, Harrington, Levin, Lundeberg, Morine-Dershimer, Mostert, & Sykes, 1995; Kauffman, Mostert, Trent, & Hallahan, 1998; Mostert, 1994, 1996a, 1996b, 1996c; Mostert, Keller, Peacock, & Rallis, 1996; Mostert & Sudzina, 1996; Sudzina & Mostert 1997; White & Mostert, 1995), or how to codify the purposes for which case facilitators use cases. I remain certain, however, that it is insufficient, at least for inexperienced undergraduate students or novice teachers, to simply present a menu of alternatives to case dilemmas and insist that students choose the option of individual best fit. This is especially crucial in the political and relational, for experienced teachers understand, as my own experience has shown me, there are sophisticated implicit rules and modes of political and relational interactions that can dictate professional competence and teaching effectiveness.

SUMMARY AND CONCLUSIONS

Not only is the notion of the technical linked to the personal crucial in educating teachers, especially when teaching with cases, but such a perspective is closely tied to the pedagogical decisions instructors must make if they choose to use cases in teacher education. It is insufficient, therefore, to present cases as stories with several possible solutions or answers, or to allow case discussions to ramble on in some directionless morass in the hopes that students will "get it." It is also insufficient to marvel at the "magic process" of cases in the naive and feeble hope that a simple discussion will somehow teach what needs to be taught. Indeed, it is primarily insufficient, in my view, to glibly ignore the pedagogical rationale and decisions made by case instructors before, during, and after case discussions.

Case facilitators must grapple with the understanding that a combination of the technical and the personal, situated in the contemplative, presents the best possible potential for effective case teaching and learning from cases. Such a dual emphasis requires that case facilitators take careful stock of their own and their students' technical and personal framework to better use cases as a catalyst for learning in teacher education. A beginning point, in my view, is for teacher educators to consider how their own perceptions and knowledge are made explicit, especially in terms of their pedagogical decisions about how to teach with cases. The case literature reflects very little attention to the pedagogical role of the instructor, although there have been some tantalizing beginnings (Wineburg, 1991).

Case-based pedagogy has a relatively long, exciting, yet unfulfilled history. Teaching with cases can be challenging, stimulating, and, happily, worthwhile. However, the intuitive appeal of cases and their potential for transforming teacher education must move beyond enthusiasm, fascination, and unchallenged doctrine. There is much about using cases that we do not know. As our expertise and knowledge about case-based teaching grows, so too, will our ability to positively affect teacher preparation through illuminating the personal in the pedagogical.

REFERENCES

Barnett, C., Harrington, H., Levin, B. B., Lundeberg, M. A., Morine-Dershimer, G., Mostert, M. P., & Sykes, G. (1995, April). *In search of methodologies in studying teachers' thinking about cases: A critical look at current practices.* Symposium presented at the annual meeting of the American Educational Research Association, San Francisco, CA.

Greenwood, G. E., & Parkay, F. W. (1989). *Case studies for teaching decision making.* New York: Random House

Kauffman, J. M., Mostert, M. P., Nuttycombe, D. G., Trent, S. C., & Hallahan, D. (1993). *Managing classroom behavior: A reflective case-based approach.* Boston: Allyn & Bacon.

Kauffman, J. M., Mostert, M. P., Trent, S. C., & Hallahan, D. P. (1998). *Managing classroom behavior: A reflective case-based approach* (2nd ed.). Boston: Allyn & Bacon.

Mostert, M. P. (1994, October). *Cases for teaching: An analysis of their levels of difficulty.* Paper presented at the annual meeting of the Mid-Western Educational Research Association, Chicago, IL.

Mostert, M. P. (1996a). Special education teaching cases: The case is not enough [Review of case studies for teaching special needs and at-risk students]. *Teacher Education and Special Education, 18*(3), pp. 3–4.

Mostert, M. P. (1996b, April). *Cognitive aspects of case-based teaching.* Paper presented at the annual meeting of the American Educational Research Association, New York, NY.

Mostert, M. P. (1996c, October). *Students' cognitive representations of practical knowledge in case-based teaching.* Paper presented at the annual meeting of the Midwestern Educational Research Association, Chicago, IL.

Mostert, M. P. (1998). *Interprofessional collaboration in schools.* Boston: Allyn & Bacon.

Mostert, M. P., & Kauffman, J. M. (1993). Preparing teachers for special and general education through case-based instruction: An analysis of their perceptions, learning, and written cases. *Australasian Journal of Special Education, 16*(2), 40–47.

Mostert, M. P., Keller, C., Peacock, T., & Rallis, H. (1996, February). *Using cases to connect theory, knowledge, and practice in reflective, perservice educators.* Paper presented at the annual meeting of the Association of Teacher Educators, St. Louis, MO.

Mostert, M. P., & Sudzina, M. R. (1996, February). *Undergraduate case method teaching: Pedagogical assumptions vs. the real world.* Paper presented at the annual meeting of the Association of Teacher Educators, St. Louis, MO.

Silverman, R., Welty, W. M., & Lyon, S. (1992). *Case studies for teacher problem solving.* New York: McGraw-Hill.

Sudzina, M. R., & Mostert, M. P. (1997, February). *Teaching with cases: Strategies for success.* Paper presented at the annual meeting of the Association of Teacher Educators, Washington, DC.

Thomas, C. C., Correa, V. I., & Morsink, C. V. (1995). *Interactive teaming: Consulting and collaboration in special programs* (2nd ed.). Boston, MA: Allyn & Bacon.

Wassermann, S. (1993). *Getting down to cases: Learning to teach with case studies.* New York: Teachers College Press.

White, B. C., & Mostert, M. P. (1995, April). *Using case-based instruction to improve preservice teachers' practical arguments.* Paper presented at the annual meeting of the American Educational Research Association, San Francisco.

Wineburg, S. S. (1991). A case of pedagogical failure—my own. *Journal of Teacher Education, 42,* 273–280.

WILLIAM F. LOSITO

William F. Losito is professor of educational philosophy in the Department of Teacher Education at the University of Dayton. He earned his doctorate in philosophy of education from Indiana University–Bloomington.

Losito has presented and published papers nationally and internationally on a variety of topics related to the philosophy of education. A major responsibility of his is doctoral teaching and inquiry pertinent to the ethical dimension of educational leadership. Of particular scholarly interest to him is the role of religion in democratic education and he has served on the education committee of the United States Catholic Conference. Prior to his appointment at the University of Dayton, Losito was Heritage Professor of Education at the College of William and Mary.

11

USING CASES IN TEACHING PROFESSIONAL ETHICS

WILLIAM F. LOSITO
UNIVERSITY OF DAYTON

W hen I attended graduate school in the early 1970s, I was
trained in analytic philosophy of education. Analytic philosophy was the predominant mode, at the time, in both general
philosophy as well as educational philosophy. A central tenet of the analytic approach is that philosophy does not aspire to say anything about
the external world. (This, of course, students have known for several centuries.) Rather, the function of philosophy is to analytically clarify the
meaning of terms in other disciplines used to describe the world.

The analytic premise excludes philosophy from saying anything pertinent about practical experience. Instead, the educational philosopher
ponders the meaning of terms like *teaching, learning,* and *education* themselves. I recall endless discussions, for example, about whether the correct
use of *teaching* implied that learning took place. I sometimes questioned
the extent of my own learning achieved by participating so intensely in
these academic discussions. The hope of the analytic approach was that
the careful clarification of key terms would result in a more adequate educational science. And, indeed, there is some merit in this approach, although I have since come to believe that it is a very limited perspective
on the function of philosophy.

Nonetheless, when I began teaching my own educational philosophy courses at the College of William and Mary in the mid-1970s, my
approach was a continuation of the analytic project. I tried to engage the

students in discussions to clarify the meaning of educationally relevant terms, such as *freedom, authority, competency,* and the like. Not surprisingly, while some students participated with intellectual zeal in the task, many were frustrated by our (my) failure to apply the clarified concepts to practical decisions in concrete situations. The students, understandably, wanted to know how much authority and freedom they should have and not what is meant by the terms.

In moments of candor, I was also feeling disappointed by the seeming impotence of analytic philosophy to effect practical recommendations. My concern, like that of my students, was for reflection and inquiry that would result in practical recommendations. It was my interest in ethical issues that provided the catalyst for helping me break through the intellectual glass ceiling inherent in the analytic approach.

Lawrence Kohlberg's early work in moral development and education stimulated my interest in a more practical approach to the activity of philosophizing about ethical issues. An essential ingredient of Kohlberg's model for moral education was to engage the students in discussions about concrete moral dilemmas. Kohlberg's paradigmatic example was the Heinz Dilemma in which the students debated whether it was ethically justified for Heinz to steal a very expensive drug to save his wife from a life-threatening illness. Kohlberg's contention was that there is a hierarchy of reasons that undergird decisions about moral dilemmas such as that of Heinz. For example, at one end of the hierarchy, reasons of fear and self-interest inform moral decisions, while at the other end of the hierarchy, reasons for stealing or not stealing the drug would be expressed in terms of ethical principles, such as justice and fairness. What struck me most about Kohlberg's moral education approach was that it was an example of practical philosophizing. The students were not simply engaged in discussing the meaning of *fairness* and *justice* but rather the bearing of those principles on practical conduct.

A second intellectual movement encouraged me to ponder further the practical relevance of ethical reflection about specific cases. In various areas of public life, such as business, politics, and medicine, a field of inquiry emerged referred to as "applied" or "practical ethics." Public concern about professional misconduct in these areas, as well as the increased complexity of contemporary social life, had stimulated a closer scrutiny of professional decision making from the perspective of applied moral philosophy. The goal of this inquiry was to develop ethical principles and guidance for practical ethical issues involving professional integrity, such as confidentiality, conflict of interest, respect for client autonomy, and the like.

INITIAL CASE USE

Taking the lead from Kohlberg's theory of moral development and the emergence of applied and practical ethics in other professions, I began to reconceptualize my teaching of educational philosophy. I started developing a course in ethics and education that would engage the students in applying theories, such as utilitarian and contractarian perspectives, to concrete case dilemmas. By the late 1970s, I was teaching ethics and education as part of the master's requirement for special education, educational administration, school and agency counseling, and elementary and secondary education. After teaching the course a few times, I felt the need to discuss this approach with other colleagues. Not only pedagogical problems, but also theoretical questions, were starting to emerge for me.

Shortly thereafter, I attended a workshop on applied ethics at Princeton University, sponsored by the Hastings Center. I approached one of the Center's Fellows, Art Caplan, about the possibility of planning a conference on the pertinence of applied ethics in the formation of professional educators. A few weeks later, Caplan called to inform me that the Carnegie Corporation had awarded the Hastings Center a grant to foster the development of applied ethics in several professional fields. Caplan requested that I help plan a small conference to explore the development of applied ethics in schools of education. In the fall of 1981, a small group of educational philosophers met over a weekend with several Fellows at the Center at Hastings-on-Hudson, New York. At great length, we discussed the desirability of developing applied ethics inquiry in the field of education. The consensus of the group was that an applied or practical ethics approach was a much needed emphasis in educational philosophy.

The conference confirmed for me the importance and academic credibility of developing a case-driven approach in teaching ethics and education. As a result of the conference, two of the participants, Kenneth Strike and Jonas Soltis, developed a highly regarded text, *Ethics and Teaching* (1985). Subsequently, they organized and edited the *Professional Ethics in Education* series published by Teachers College Press.

EMPHASIS ON APPLIED ETHICS

Developing an applied ethics and education course in the late 1970s raised many pedagogical challenges. First, I needed to orient theoretical discussions to practical cases. The cases I initially used followed the simple Heinz formula: a few simple facts that shaped a dilemma context for a moral agent. In the cases I found in texts or created, the facts were minimal and the choices typically were bimodal: keep or break a professional confidence, evaluate student performance under one scheme or the other, accept or deny a parent petition for an educational classification for his/her child, and so on.

While using these simple dilemmas stimulated student interest in practical applications of ethical inquiry, I quickly became uneasy with an exclusive regimen of these formula dilemmas. While my objectives for the course included the emphasis on practical applications, several other ideas were also very important to me. First, I hoped that the course experience would help the students become deeply engaged with, and personally committed to, ethical conduct in their profession as educators. Simple dilemmas stimulated interest, and sometimes passionate discussion, but I was skeptical about discussions of these simplistic cases opening up the deeper moral recesses of character. Because the cases were simple and remote, one could discuss these cases in a rather detached way without changing fundamental moral dispositions.

Secondly, I intended students to recognize and reflect thoughtfully on the complexity of moral issues confronting them as professional educators. The simplistic nature of the Heinz formula dilemmas was not fully sensitive to the multidisciplinary context of human decision making and the textured dimensions of diverse cultural, religious, and gendered voices.

Thirdly, an intended course objective was for the students to develop a model for ethical decision making, whereby they could defend the rational acceptability of moral judgments about particular case situations and the theoretically principled grounds on which the judgments were based. My initial efforts to relate ethical theories to practical cases yielded modest results with respect to developing a model for ethical decision making. My continuing efforts over the past several years have been to enhance the quality of case examples and develop a model for ethical decision making. These prior efforts yielded modest suggestions for rationally acceptable judgments, at best.

LITERATURE FOR CRITICAL ENGAGEMENT

Over several years, I have made efforts to enhance the case approach to practical educational ethics to meet my broader educational goals. The following is an account of what I presently do to (1) enhance the soulful engagement of my students in ethical decision making, (2) develop students' sensitivity to the varied texture of moral issues, and (3) promote the development of skills in rational moral discourse. My present approach is an ongoing effort to integrate literary narratives, detailed student-developed cases, and a heuristic model for practical decision making. Well-written literary narratives stimulate the reader's involvement with the moral situation as well as introduce the multiple considerations in the decision-making process.

In an ethics course designed for graduate students, I frequently introduce a short novel such as Tolstoy's *The Death of Ivan Ilych*. This novel, as with most literary works, is used as a concrete case with multiple foci for analysis, rather than as a moral dilemma for reaching the appropriate ethical decision. In this Tolstoy classic, Ivan is the central character. As a young man, Ivan devoted his energy to acting "comme il faut," doing as one must do for professional and social advancement in 19th-century Russia. In his chosen field of law, Ivan selected and treated his clients according to how he perceived their potential for enhancing his career rather than the merits of their case or legal need. Later, as a judge, he rendered his decisions according to the same criterion.

While still in the prime of his career, Ivan was confronted with the realization that a disease was slowly claiming his life. Ironically and tragically, others treated him as he treated them, and he was "without a single person to understand and pity him" (p. 83). His wife and daughter viewed his illness as an inconvenience to their attendance at the theatre. The doctors were interested in Ivan as a challenging case but did not display empathy for him as a person. Even Ivan's legal colleagues responded to his illness, and later to his death, according to "what effect it would have on their own transfers and promotions or those of their acquaintances" (p. 36). Ironically, it was Gerasim, the servant from peasant stock, who "showed that he alone understood what was happening" and did not lie to Ivan (p. 104). Only the simple servant, Gerasim, and Ivan's son, Vanya, displayed genuine empathy for Ivan's plight. In typical Tolstoy convention, Ivan's spiritual and physical suffering occasioned a deep illumination experience:

> *His official duties, his manner of life, his family, the values adhered to by people in society and in his profession—all these might not have been the real thing. He tried to come up with a defense of these things and suddenly became aware of the insubstantiality of them all. And there was nothing left to defend (p. 127).*

The death sequence, while ambiguous, suggests a religious conversion and moral transformation of Ivan to an ethic of caring and forgiveness.

I initiate the discussion of the novel by asking the students to analyze the moral character of various individuals and groups of individuals: the lawyers, doctors, Gerasim, Vanya, Ivan's wife and daughter, and

Ivan himself. The discussion, which commences with a critique of Russian aristocratic morality of the time, quickly turns to an engaged conversation concerning contemporary professional moral attitudes. Invariably, the students begin to unmask motivations contrary to moral leadership in education, such as dispositions to use professional roles as a means to prestige, power, and material advantage. Eventually, the students personalize the discussion and share reflections about their own individual histories as professionals. My own contribution to the discussion is to emphasize that the moral point of view is more than exercising a rational, detached competency in deciding the right thing to do. Developing the moral dimension of one's professional conduct involves a commitment in the deeper recesses of one's moral and spiritual personhood.

There are other novels and plays that work equally well to provoke the students to a deeper level of moral critique and personal reflection. On occasion, I have used *The Fall* by Camus. The main character in the novel is Jean-Baptiste Clamence, who, again, was a lawyer. From the perspective of an external observer, Jean-Baptiste led an exemplary moral life both as a professional and in his private life. He helped the poor, offered solace to widows, rendered compassionate advice, attended wakes, and so on. He commented, "I never accepted bribes, it goes without saying" (p. 19). Like Ilych, Jean-Baptiste "progressed on the surface of life, in the realm of words, as it were, never in reality" (p. 50). But his flaw was that he performed good moral works only when there were other people as witnesses to commend him at least implicitly. When the opportunity presented itself to save the life of an individual jumping off of a bridge, Jean-Baptiste was frozen, "inaction in time of real need" (p. 70). There was no one present to witness his intervention. This episode and Jean-Baptiste's torment throughout the rest of the novel raise pertinent questions for the students about ethical behavior, motivation, and the social context of professional expectations.

There is a second reason why I am trying in a concerted way to integrate selected literary narratives into my educational ethics course. Over the past several years, two approaches to professional moral education have gradually developed: virtue theory and moral reasoning theory. The latter emphasizes the development of impersonal moral reasoning skills, while virtue theory stresses the importance of developing habits of moral character. While my course continues to accentuate the application of a moral reasoning model to case dilemmas, I include several literary narratives to enhance an aesthetic and ethical critique of habits of virtuous conduct. Discussing the Tolstoy or Camus novel opens up the terrain, but neither presents an extended portrait of the purported virtuous hero or saint.

I have frequently used several of Plato's dialogues as literary–philosophical texts for the students to test their aesthetic and ethical affiliation with the moral character of Socrates. One particularly useful edition, *The Trial and Death of Socrates,* includes "The Euthyphro," "Apology," "Crito," and the death scene from "The Phaedo." In "The Euthyphro," Socrates was engaged in an intense discussion about the nature of piety. Euthyphro attempted to justify his action at court as an act of piety. Socrates ostensibly hoped to attain a clearer understanding of the nature of piety, because he himself was accused of impious acts. Meletus claimed that Socrates was "a pestilential fellow who corrupts the young" (p. 27). Through intense and incessant questioning, Socrates demonstrated to Euthyphro that his understanding of piety was foolish. Ironically, what we witness in the "Euthyphro" narrative is exactly the kind of conduct that gets Socrates into trouble. He unremittingly questioned what appears to be wisdom and unmasked it as foolishness. Discussing the professional conduct of Socrates from the moral point of view opens up rich lines of analysis for the students. Instead of focusing on a specific decision, the discussion ranges over the entire pattern of moral character traits suitable for a professional.

In "The Apology," Socrates tried to defend himself before the court against the claims that his teaching was weakening belief in the gods and tainting the minds of the young. Socrates did not attempt to inculcate a specific set of beliefs, but his masterful inquiry destabilized unquestioned beliefs and simplistic ideas. He claimed that since youth his "whole concern was not to do anything unjust or impious" (p. 35). Socrates realized that his death was in the balance, yet he claimed before the court that "wherever a man has taken a position he believes to be best there he must I think remain and face danger, without a thought for death or anything else, rather than disgrace" (p. 31). The jury found Socrates guilty. Even though Socrates had several opportunities to escape the death penalty by modifying his views, he claimed that the honorable thing to do was to stand by his views and take the poison hemlock.

Discussion of these dialogues with educators raises questions about the correctness of Socrates' decision and certain aspects of his personality. Many students think that the Socrates of "The Euthyphro" was pretty arrogant. Nonetheless, the character of Socrates looms large as a preeminent educator who was willing to put his life on the line rather than compromise his beliefs about the nature of the examined life and education.

As a bookend to the discussion of Socrates, I have sometimes used Robert Bolt's *A Man for All Seasons* later in the semester. The dramatic rendition of Thomas More's refusal to take the oath prescribed by Henry VIII involves the students in similar questions of character. Also, I use literature as dilemma cases on occasion. May Sarton's *A Small Room* provides a good example. In this novel, Lucy Winter was confronted with the situation of what to do when she came across a plagiarized essay submitted by an outstanding student. This narrative adds the personal emotional dimension to the case dilemma. Also, it enables one to introduce diverse experiences in an authentic way. In this case, it is the introduction of the feminist perspective. One could also use Chaim Potok's *The Chosen,* for example, to illustrate a multicultural religious perspective. Should Danny, from the moral point of view, be justified in breaking away from Reb Saunder's vocational goals for him? The character development in good novels is particularly helpful for adding a realistic dimension to the cases.

At the same time, paramount among my course objectives is the development of a rational approach for deciding problematic issues. So, much of my course over the years has been devoted to improving the constructed cases and a heuristic model for clarifying moral views and their application. The latter provides a theoretical support for the professionals making rationally acceptable decisions from the moral point of view. To achieve this objective, both the content and the process of reasoning about decisions must be realistic.

There are a few ways of making cases more realistic. Cases can be made more elaborate and complex. Another way of making the cases more realistic is to have the students write the cases themselves. When the students, especially those experienced as teachers and administrators, write the cases from their own experiences, the cases are much richer and the students become more engaged in the discussion.

FORMULATING A MORAL VIEW

As important as engaging students in moral discussions through case studies is, it is not enough. My instructional hope is that students develop rationally acceptable ethical theories and a process for applying them to specific cases. A fundamental problem in applied ethics is establishing criteria for determining the rational acceptability of an ethical theory. In our contemporary intellectual climate, ethical theories are susceptible to rejection as simply being expressions of subjective opinion or emotion.

Ethical theories and their applications can be rationally justified, at least to a reasonable degree, by standards widely accepted by respected individuals in our society. For the purposes of my course, I use a two-part heuristic model for articulating and assessing ethical theories. This approach includes the assumption that there are identifiable rationales as bases for our practical ethical decisions and that these rationales can be assessed as to their rational acceptability or unacceptability. The first part of the heuristic model I refer to as "Moral View Components." A *moral view* is the interpreted and justified moral belief. It is the equivalent of what is commonly referred to as an *ethical theory.* A moral view includes the following components:

- *Formulation of Ethical Norm:* Statement of general or intermediate ethical norm as prescriptive ideal standard.
- *Interpretation of Ethical Norm:* Explanation of the meaning of the ethical norm as a whole and/or individual phrases or terms.
- *Justification:* Reasons in support of public acceptability of the ethical norm (and its interpretation) as an ideal guide for moral conduct.

The notion here is that with respect to a given ethical decision-making case, the application of one or more moral views is telling, at least implicitly, with respect to the decision we make. In particular, it is the ethical norm, under a given interpretation, that we apply to a particular case situation. The moral view does not preclude other influences, such as habit and sentiment, as explanatory of practical moral decisions. Likewise, moral views may be more general or more applied, e.g., a general moral view focusing on the norm "do no harm" in contrast to an applied moral view about counselors not exceeding their competency in psychotherapy.

APPLYING A MORAL VIEW

To illustrate the relationship between a plausible moral view and practical decision making, consider the hypothetical case in Box 11.1.

To judge the ethical appropriateness of such a policy, the following moral view is offered to students for discussion:

Formulation of Ethical Norm

- Educators should encourage intrinsic rewards whenever possible in the teaching–learning process.

Interpretation of Ethical Norm

- "Intrinsic rewards" refers to those feelings of satisfaction and personal accomplishment that are derived from successful completion of worthwhile learning tasks.
- Educators should not use direct or indirect monetary rewards as a means of modifying students' attendance.

BOX 11.1   An Ethical Reward System

A large, urban public school system has developed a chronic problem of high student absenteeism. As a result of the high rate of student absence, instructional programs are severely disrupted and the dropout rate is alarming. The school board is considering an experimental program for the high schools to increase the rate of attendance. If the new policy is enacted, each high school student would receive a coupon for each day that he/she arrived at school punctually and remained in attendance at each period during the day. The coupons would be redeemable (at a value of 25 cents) for a variety of school related items, such as pencils, payment of library fines, extra cafeteria food, and so on. For six weeks of consecutive attendance, students could select from a display of small recreational goods, such as tennis balls and athletic socks. For a year of perfect attendance, there would be more expensive items from which the students could select rewards. The school board realizes that the reward system might be relatively costly, but since the state provides funding based on student attendance, the program's cost would be more than covered by the state's increased funding. Also, the school board considers the attendance problem so severe as to consider a reward system for attendance. Critics strongly oppose the program on the grounds that paying students to attend school is a grossly misdirected idea. Is such a policy ethically justifiable?

- Educators should make curricular activities as interesting, appropriate, and worthwhile as possible, so as to provide motivation for school attendance.
- One might legitimately use direct or indirect monetary rewards, however, when the educators have exhausted all other legitimate alternatives for providing attendance or learning incentives.
- Educators can use, however, verbal praise and other certificates of recognition as means to stimulate pride and satisfaction in academic accomplishment.

Justification of Ethical Norm and Interpretation

- A major goal of general education is to help the learner become self-motivated, so that the student will be a lifelong learner. Reinforcing intrinsic rewards furthers that goal.
- Because learning presumes attendance and participation, using token economy modification systems (including indirect monetary rewards) can be justified as a last resort.

This moral view is abbreviated in that much more interpretation of the ethical norm is possible. In fact, a particular ethical norm can be interpreted without limit. What I try to point out to the students is that, if they hold the above moral view, it will make a difference in the practical judgment they make about the case. The students proceed to debate whether holding to the above moral view would justify the school board policy. On the one hand, the interpretation explicitly rules out the use of "direct or indirect monetary rewards," but another part legitimizes them when other alternatives have been exhausted. The function of class discussion and exercises is to help the students make explicit their implicit moral views, construct them when they are only partially thought out, and learn to apply them to concrete cases. I have the students construct and analyze moral views similar to the one presented. They articulate their moral views after discussing their responses to particular cases. Very quickly the discussion focuses on the adequacy of the moral views themselves in addition to their application to particular cases.

CRITERIA FOR OBJECTIVE REASONING

The fundamental thrust at that point of my work with the students becomes helping them develop objectively adequate moral views, i.e., those views acceptable to reasonable individuals. In this postmodern era, indeed, the challenge is trying to preserve a degree of rational objectivity and acceptability in ethical discourse. Because articulating and justifying definitive criteria for determining the rational acceptability of a moral view is not possible, I take a pragmatic approach similar to that of Soltis and Strike as developed in their *The Ethics of Teaching* (1985) and other places.

Their approach to ethical theorizing and judgments is to assume that moral views and their applications cannot be justified with certitude. Nonetheless, our justification of ethical theories can achieve what they call "provisional reflective equilibrium." The notion here is that there are a number of standards by which one can determine the objectivity of the ethical theory in question. These standards include congruence with public philosophy, intuitions, and consequentialist and nonconsequentialist reasoning. None of the standards, taken separately, is decisive in determining objective acceptability, but a theory is said to have achieved "provisional reflective equilibrium" if it satisfies to a reasonable degree the standards taken collectively.

Below is a list of the standards with a brief explanation of their meaning. These criteria are a slight modification of those proposed and used by Strike and Soltis (1992).

1. Public Philosophy
   Is the theory and its application consistent with the public moral philosophy as it might be expressed in professional codes, public policy/law, and/or the consensual opinions of respected people in our culture/community?

2. Intuitions
   Is the theory and its application consistent with our immediate, personal response?

3. Consequentialist Reasoning
   If one applies the theory to concrete cases, does it support desirable consequences? Those desirable consequences may be calculated in terms of benefit maximization, personal well-being, and so forth.

4. Nonconsequentialist Reasoning
   Is the theory a credible expression of a more fundamental, nonconsequentially derived and accepted philosophical ideal standard, such as respect for persons, doing one's duty, being benevolent, and the like.

5. Deciding Provisional Reflective Equilibrium
   The theory and its application are considered objectively acceptable, if it reasonably satisfies the conditions of consistency in the above areas. Of course, because the bases in these areas may themselves be open to criticism (e.g., the opinions of respected persons), the judgment of objectivity is provisional, hence "provisional reflective equilibrium."

SUMMARY AND CONCLUSIONS

Formulating a model for a moral view and using a model for provisional reflective equilibrium provides a common focus to my course. The theme of the course has become debating practical moral judgments in specific cases based on moral views that have demonstrated provisional reflective equilibrium. Thus, much of the debate in class is both theoretical and practical. In some sense, I have been striving after my own reflective equilibrium. On the one hand, a balance between the theoretical and practical is achieved by discussing both the adequacy of theoretical moral views as well as their practical application to specific cases. I strive for a balance between the cognitive and affective dimension of the moral life by integrating narrative materials as a source of the moral situation as well as a perspective for reflection on a given issue. Using narratives can be extremely useful in engaging students in moral discourse, critiquing the moral dimension of professional conduct, and offering models of inspiration.

One of the ongoing challenges in my course is trying to integrate diversity of thought with the effort to develop an objective basis for moral views and their applications. Trying to establish a provisional reflective equilibrium is always situated in a particular culture and community. To serve as a corrective to this inherent bias, I envision that the cases and moral views proposed for consideration will be drawn increasingly from a diversity of perspectives, including those of culture, religion, and gender.

As a result of these and similar efforts, the applied approach to educational ethics has become respected in the academic community. Rather than supplanting the analytic tradition, it has evolved into a complementary approach. The seemingly minor effort to incorporate cases in my ethics teaching several years ago has opened up a challenging intellectual and pedagogical project. It has forced me as an academician and teacher to confront directly the elusive relationship between theory and practice, and thought and action.

REFERENCES

Bolt, R. (1956). *A man for all seasons.* New York: Vintage Press

Camus, A. (1956). *The fall.* New York: Random House.

Plato. (1975). *The trial and death of Socrates: Euthyphro, Apology, Crito, death scene from Phaedo.* (G. M. A. Grube, Trans.) Indianapolis, IN: Hackett.

Potok, C. (1967). *The chosen.* New York: Ballantine.

Sarton, M. (1961). *A small room.* New York: W. W. Norton.

Strike, K., & Soltis, J., (1985). *The ethics of teaching.* New York: Teachers College Press.

Strike, K., & Soltis, J., (1992). *The ethics of teaching* (2nd ed.). New York: Teachers College Press.

Tolstoy, L. (1981). *The death of Ivan Ilyich.* (L. Solotaroff, Trans.) New York: Bantam.

WILLIAM J. HUNTER

They want me to tell you that I am William J Hunter and that I am an associate professor of teacher education and educational psychology at the University of Calgary in Alberta, Canada. However, I want you to know that:

- you can call me hunter@acs.ucalgary.ca
- or you can call me 136.159.135.35
- or you can call me http://acs.ucalgary.ca/~hunter
- but you doesn't have to call me William.

My research has been diverse in method and content (educational measurement, computer application, moral reasoning, school psychology). If you want to know more, you may want to read *Spirituality in Moral Education* (Hunter, 1993a) or, for fun, the special issue I edited of the *Journal of Educational Thought* entitled "A Bucket of Words," a collection of creative writing and poetry about teaching and learning that includes three poems and a short story by yours truly (Hunter, 1993b). Of course, I have written a couple of things since 1993, but none of that has aged sufficiently yet.

12

APPLYING CASES TO A COMPUTER APPLICATIONS COURSE

WILLIAM J. HUNTER
UNIVERSITY OF CALGARY

I suppose that my earliest exposure to the use of cases dates back to elementary school where the nuns liked to embed moral lessons in little stories. A whole class of such stories was *Butler's Lives of the Saints,* but I liked the more fanciful cases. I especially remember a story about Virtuous John, who, to the best of everyone's knowledge, had lived an exemplary life. This was a source of considerable consternation to Satan, of course, and he set out to rectify the matter. The meat of the story was a series of graded temptations (in brilliant detail) in which Satan attempted to get old Virtuous to commit murder, to do violence to someone, to steal, or to swear. Finally, to get Satan off his back, John agrees to a little overindulgence in alcohol. As he swaggers home after a night of drinking, a group of young boys begins to taunt him, and John swears at them. They persist and he steals a bottle of milk from someone's doorstep and throws it at them, but they continue. John then hits one of the boys, but the others keep pestering him until finally he picks one boy up and throws him against a wall breaking his skull and killing him instantly. I think the moral must have been "Sin early and often lest Satan take you on as a special case."

My first academic use of cases was in the arena of moral development research involving the moral dilemmas that Kohlberg used to assess moral reasoning. I imagine most readers will be familiar with the story of Heinz and his wife dying of cancer in a town where the local druggist has set an exorbitant price for a cure he personally developed. Heinz struggles with the dilemma of whether or not to steal the drug. About three decades of interesting research has emerged in an attempt to understand the ways people reason about such dilemmas, but I, steeped in quantitative methods in my doctoral program, sought to improve on Kohlberg by developing an "objective" measure of moral reasoning. My method was simple: forced choice items that required people to decide which of two statements most closely resembled their own thinking.

A. *If you steal somebody's stuff, they might steal from you.*
B. *Stealing is bad because they'll put you in jail.*

A. *Conventional laws do not apply in life and death situations because life is the most precious thing we have.*
B. *Property cannot have any value unless there is a higher value placed on human life.*

Yeah, I know. My research subjects didn't like it either. Talking about those little stories is much more interesting. I am still not convinced that the Kohlberg interviews measure any enduring characteristics of the research subjects, but I was and am convinced that people enjoy the challenge of solving problems set forth in hypothetical dilemmas.

None of this led me to think seriously about the role that the analysis of cases could play in teaching. In fact, I would probably have been pretty skeptical about that had any one cared to ask. I am sure that in my early career, the words "case studies in teaching" would have conjured up images from my undergrad days of waiting for my roommate in the halls of the business school. Everywhere I looked there were groups of students engaged in apparently serious discussions about such things as "Should they call the client on the phone or send a letter?" and "Well, what about sending a postcard?" or "So, how should the conversation start? 'This is Mr. Nemesis of Out 2 Get U Corp. and I need to talk to you about your past due account.' Would that work?" I would then ask my roommate: "What are those people taking—Common Sense 101?" This was the sixties: If it wasn't about Vietnam, it wasn't serious.

Since then I have been actively engaged in the preparation of teachers and other education professionals (counselors, school psychologists) and have occasionally worked with nurses, home economists, and other professionals. I don't think there is a year that goes by without my hearing several students singing the "I-get-my-diploma-in-the-morning and I-go-to-work-on-Tuesday, don't know what I'm doin' " blues. I now see that the analysis of cases may be the preventive medicine for that particular brand of the blues. Somewhere in professional education, people need to work out the details of how "Common Sense 101" plays out in the day-to-day practice of teaching or whatever profession they are learning. Perhaps I should have understood this because I read Donald Schon (1983), but that didn't do the trick. For me, the lesson had to be up close and personal.

But I don't want you to think that I was some kind of hyper-resistant anticase stuffed shirt. I used cases from time to time to spice up my teaching, especially in quantitative areas like statistics or educational measurement. These areas lend themselves to a very particular use of cases, I'd say a genre of sorts. The cases are short mystery stories with irrelevant information as the red herrings, the current crop of formulas as the suspects, and an ironclad logical path to the correct solution. What? Am I boring you again? Would it help to know that I also spiced up such courses with "statistical poetry"?

> I
> am
> going
> to illustrate
> that concept here
> using visual
> poetry
> in
> a
> Normal Curve

CASE COMPETITION

I didn't really understand that cases had more to offer than variety in teaching methods until I encountered "The Commonwealth Center Invitational Team Case Competition" at the University of Virginia. As with so many good things, that was an accident. I saw a call for proposals somewhere and, because I was a department head, I sent for it. I knew two people in the department made extensive use of cases in their teaching. I was sure one of them would welcome the opportunity to put together a team and get a free trip to Charlottesville. The materials arrived at a bad time of year for my colleagues, so I asked the executive of the students' association if anyone was willing to work with me on the proposal in exchange for a place on the team. One go-getter jumped at the chance and we quickly put together a proposal that was long on promises but short on actual experience. We were a little surprised and very pleased when we were invited to participate. I immediately approached my two potential coaches with the good news, but it turned out that each of them had firm commitments for the dates of the competition. I asked one other colleague with a tangential interest, but he felt already overburdened. So, now it was mid-January in the Northern Rockies and I had a student leader with a guaranteed trip to sunny Virginia in the springtime and no coach and no team.

My two colleagues were most helpful in providing me with readings (sorry, these were source-not-identified photocopies of stuff from the days of yore—perhaps I could cite that as Anonymous, YORE) and advice and samples of cases they had written themselves. Each of them did some training with the team and one helped with selection of team members. That was the one area where I felt I made a contribution early in the process. I organized a minicompetition with the help of the students' association and set up some criteria for observing and evaluating performance in the competition. (That hard-core quantitative stuff pays off from time to time.)

The application form that I developed requested information on academic background, availability for training sessions, willingness to work long weekend and evening hours, practicum experience, any personal characteristics, broadly defined, that would contribute to team diversity, special skills (e.g., computer skills), and permission to check academic record. I observed a 15-minute case discussion and took note of willingness to contribute, ability to draw on personal experience, interest in the contributions of others, and any idiosyncratic skills or weaknesses that caught my attention. Three professional educators listened to a case analysis presentation and made note of speaking skills, organization, preparedness, ability to respond to questions, and contributions to group cohesion. In every instance, we placed a high priority on indicators that the individual was more interested in the success of the group than in demonstrating personal prowess.

We had 32 competitors in six teams over a three-hour period—marathon case analysis. When a team had been selected, it was my duty to call each of the unsuccessful participants to say "Sorry, but thanks for coming out." As it turned out, that experience made me a case study enthusiast. To my amazement, every one of the "failed" competitors said something along the lines of "Oh, gee, thanks for calling. I had a really good time in the minicompetition. It was (one of) the best educational experiences I've had. We should be doing that sort of thing in classes more." Interesting. That was the whole point of the case study competition at the University of Virginia, to promote the uses of case-based teaching in education. We had only begun, but already I had learned my lesson.

As it turns out, the Faculty of Management at the University of Calgary has an outstanding record of achievement in case study competitions, at that point, 14 successive first- or second-place finishes in international competitions. I sought the advice of Dr. Bob Schulz who had coached all of these teams. Bob was generous and supportive in sharing the secrets of his success, but his style was much more top-down than I could carry off personally. I shared all of his ideas with my team, but I asked them to try them out, test them, and see what worked for them. They were an extraordinary bunch and they worked really hard. They learned to be frank and brutal in their criticism of one another's ideas while maintaining a very high level of mutual regard.

There would be a whole story in the trip to Charlottesville, the competition itself and the camaraderie surrounding the competition. One of the things we learned from Bob was that the winning attitude is not "We are going to win," but "We are going to do well." This is something Bob learned from athletic coaches: The objective is always to perform well, do the best you are capable of individually and collectively, and let the end result take care of itself. After writing their analysis of the competition case, the team was depressed. They felt that they had not worked as well together as they had on trial runs and that the written analysis left much to be desired. I advised them to take a couple of hours off, to relax over dinner and talk about other things, and then return to prepare for the oral presentation with a renewed sense of purpose. They did. Together they prepared the opening comments and chose a speaker (changing our original plan based on trials at home) that they felt could best present *this* case.

Their performance on the stage the next day was inspired and we all felt that now we could honestly say that we did well. We all told each other that winning wasn't important, that we had had a great time, learned a lot, seen historic sites, met some marvelous people, and heard Julian Bond. Mr. Bond delivered a dinner speech that was memorable for its erudition, passion, and compassion. For an old 1960s troglodyte, this was manna; for a team of Canadian students it was a lesson in history and politics. The trip had been an extraordinary success. We did, however, win and that certainly did add to the overall experience.

RETHINKING CASE APPLICATIONS

Needless to say, such an experience would cause one to be enthusiastic. I began to see that an in-service course I teach, *Teachers in Film,* is a form of case-based teaching in which the case is professionally written and acted. The cases I used in quantitative methodology courses became more elaborate and I began to incorporate some of what the competition taught me about methods of analysis and group dynamics. I started using cases in my computer applications course where I had not previously seen the need, and I revised my graduate course in teacher evaluation so that it was largely organized around the writing and analyzing of cases.

I also began to see that case-based methods could permit simultaneous treatment of multiple topics. In an in-service for the staff of a large local high school, I was initially asked to "do something on moral education," but the sponsor was also interested in focusing attention on problems in classroom testing. I wrote a case about a young Native Canadian teacher who faced a professional ethics problem as a result of observing the callous disregard her colleagues had for the administration of tests and reporting of results in a province-wide standardized testing program. Discussion questions focused some groups on the moral issues, others on the testing questions embedded in the case. Subsequent discussion with the whole group brought out ideas about both kinds of problems and about the interaction between them.

I guess that I teach in what people would call the "hard" side of education, statistics and technology. Many of my colleagues tend to be dismissive about any recommendation that does not have its basis in a statistically significant difference. The problem with this attitude, as it applies to decisions about one's own teaching, is that the "control" is always whatever I am doing now. That is, I will change only when something is shown to be significantly better than my current practice. I see this as a recipe for stagnation in teaching. Case-based methods may or may not be "better" than whatever you currently happen to be doing, but I can assure you that the processes of writing cases and involving students in analyzing them will bring you a fresh outlook on the material you teach. It may also help you to see your content in a different light as the detailed realities of case discussions ("Should she phone the mother or send a note home?") reveal the ways in which knowledge of your content (for the students) is embedded in much broader networks of knowledge and skill.

CASES AND COMPUTER APPLICATIONS

The course I teach is a second-year teacher education course called *Introduction to Computer Applications in Education*. It is required for all teacher candidates at the University of Calgary and focuses specifically on the educational uses of computers. Normal enrollments run from 80 to 120 students per section with students assigned to groups of 20 for lab experiences. The course outline and other contextual information is available at:

http://www.ucalgary.ca/~edtech/edts325/

A combination of lectures and lab activities is used. Students learn educational uses of telecommunications, of productivity software (word processors, data bases, spreadsheets, and paint/draw programs), and of computer-assisted instruction, especially hyper/multimedia. A major project involves students in a group production of a multimedia presentation or classroom activity. Students are encouraged to develop a personal understanding of how computers and other technological aids fit in their overall conception of teaching. A major goal of the course is to have students leave confident that they can continue to learn about educational technology on their own.

In the past in this course, I have written and used only short cases intended to get students to deal with some very practical issues. One such case presents students with an equipment purchase budget and price lists. The case requires the student to equip or update their school's technological facilities. The case is about a page in length, but what makes it interesting is that each case group is given a different school description on a variety of dimensions (rural/urban, small/medium/large, poor/middle-class/wealthy, well-equipped/poorly equipped). The consequence of these variations is that the case engages students in a discussion of what considerations *ought* to affect purchase decisions. Another example, about a half page in length, is a dialogue in which a teacher who has her students creating "multimedia books" is challenged by a colleague who wants to know "the point," how is this different from text with an accompanying audiotape? This case challenges students to look beyond the easy assumption that newer is better and to think more deeply about *whether* multimedia offers something new and if it does, *what* that something is.

I write such short cases tailored to the group (elementary or secondary teachers-to-be) and current issues in educational computing. One frequent guest speaker also presents a case, derived from his actual experience, involving the sudden uninvited appearance of a sexually explicit and violent poem in an English class that is using electronic mail to communicate with students elsewhere. It is presented as narrative with minimal student interaction, but the content and brevity of the case combine with the dynamic delivery of the speaker to make a lasting impression (revealed in references to the case in exams and papers).

With the case competition experience behind me, I knew that I wanted to make use of a longer and more complex case. I also wanted to change the way in which cases fit into this class. So I developed a case with no single, direct, identifiable, practical problem addressed in it. Rather, I tried to create a problem that was large and theoretical even though it arises in the context of a short parent–teacher conference. The problem might be simply stated as "the role of computers in instruction," but I will return to this later. First, let me introduce you to the case in Box 12.1.

BOX 12.1   May I Have a Couple of Words with You?

by Bill Hunter

"Where's Hannah?"

The question registered as a question, but the contents didn't come through. "What? What do you want to know?" I asked as I turned to face Mr. Blade who, as it turned out, had been hovering only centimeters behind me. "Sorry," I said, in the mi(d)st of a shower of coffee, I had no idea you were so close." But now I did have an idea what the content of the question had been, "Hannah's at the computer, next room over, working on transformational geometry."

"Right, thanks."

That man had a gift for brevity. People sometimes complain that you can't get two words out of him, but that's not true: you can nearly always get two words, the problem is getting more than that. But I won't complain. You can't change people overnight. It was enough that he was a father who took an active and continuing interest in his child's education. Other men were learning to be communicative. It would all work out in a few short centuries.

It was perhaps 10 minutes before I could leave the ecology work groups (three sets of five fourth graders each) and be confident that the name "work" group would hold true long enough for me to visit

Hannah and her loquacious dad. "So, how is Hannah doing?"

"Really well."

"Does she seem to have the idea?"

"Guess so."

"Right. Sometimes parents have trouble understanding this approach to mathematics, so I like to be sure that you know what we are trying to achieve with Hannah."

"Of course."

"Of course I want you to know what we are doing or of course you understand? Are you familiar with the concept of transformational geometry?"

"Plane geometry."

"Plain geometry? Well, I guess so, it's the only kind we teach. Oh, *plane* geometry! I can't say I know a lot about that. I'm afraid my interest in mathematics started in my education courses, so I know the new better than the old. Do you know a lot about plane geometry?"

"Grade 10."

"Right. Okay, so what do you think of this computer program?"

"I'm glad you asked. I've been meaning to talk to you about that. I have some concerns, but I don't want to take you away from your work."

Way more than two words. I used both hands to lift my jaw back

BOX 12.1 *continued*

into place. "No, that's OK. Talking to parents is part of the job. Just let me get the aide to monitor the discussion in the next room and I'll be able to spend about 20 minutes with you in the conference room. "See you there?"

"Sure thing."

Two minutes later, I was preparing myself for a marathon session of my favorite teaching game, get-the-reticent-parent-to-open-up. I won this one in short order; he was talking before I was sitting."

"Okay, here's the thing. I'm not sure about transformational geometry; I like the old stuff, but things change, I can cope with that. I just don't know if that computer program is teaching her anything at all."

"Well, yes, I understand. I was a little reluctant about it myself, but our own local results show the same thing as the research literature: Kids do better with this type of CAI than they do with worksheets and class presentations. And to be honest with you, the computer is better at math than I am."

"Better how?"

Back to two words. Oh, well. "I mean I understand the general concepts and I can do the problems, but . . . "

"No, I mean the kids do better how? On what?"

"Oh. Classroom quizzes, tests provided by the publisher, that sort of thing." "

"May I see them?"

"Sure. I have samples here in Hannah's portfolio."

He looked them over, but it didn't take him long.

"This is what I was afraid of. Miss Barker, I don't think that Hannah is learning anything *real* here."

"What do you mean? She has near perfect performance on all of this stuff."

"Yes, and she has near perfect performance at the computer screen too, but I think it is all memory work and no understanding."

What is this guy, an education professor? This is not the kind of turf I expect to cover in a parent conference. Maybe it should be. Okay, put on my graduate student hat. "That's a very interesting observation and a distinction too few parents make. But why do you think Hannah doesn't understand?"

"Look at the examples on the screen. They tell her 'this is a slide' then they show her two or three examples. Next it wants her to make a figure slide, but the only part of the screen that responds to the mouse is the figure they have chosen and the only thing it will do is slide. Same thing with rotations and all that other stuff. She mimics what she sees like some sort of trained monkey and she gets little rewards in the form of smiley faces and 'stickers' in the corner of the screen."

"But what about the test results?"

"By the time she gets to those, she knows that squares or triangles can slide or rotate. She knows the vocabulary and that's all she is really tested on. May I use this computer over here? Thanks. Look. Here's a triangle in a paint program. I am going to click on this vertex

BOX 12.1   *continued*

here and then I'll drag it over. See what happens? Only that point moves so that the shape of the triangle is now quite different. It's really acute now."

"Yes."

"Well, I did this at home with Hannah and she said I made the triangle slide. I don't know transformational geometry, but I know English; I made the point slide, not the triangle. Now that I've watched her on that program, I know that I am right. This is not what they mean by a slide, but Hannah thinks it is. She knows the answers, she doesn't understand the principles."

"I see your point. I have to get back to class now, Mr. Blade, but I promise I'll look into this. Could you come back next week and we'll talk again?"

"Sure thing."

"Very well. See you then."

"Good-bye."

Selected Readings for the Case

De Corte, E. (1990). Learning with new information technologies in schools: Perspectives from the psychology of learning and instruction. *Journal of Computer Assisted Learning, 6,* 69–87.

Kulik, J. A., Bangert-Downs, R. L., & Williams, G. W. (1983). Effects of computer based teaching on secondary school students. *Journal of Educational Psychology, 75*(1),19–26.

Lockard, J., Abrams, P. D., & Many, W. *Microcomputers for 21st century educators* (3rd ed.). Boston: Little, Brown (especially Chapter 9).

Papert, S. (1993). *The children's machine.* New York: Basic Books.

Pressey, S. L. (1932). A third and fourth contribution toward the coming "Industrial Revolution" in education. *School and Society, 36,* 934.

Skinner, B. F. (1986). Programmed instruction revisited. *Phi Delta Kappan,* October, 6–11.

Taylor, R. B. (1980). *The computer in the school: Tutor, tool, tutee.* New York: Teachers College Press.

I generally have the students discuss this case in class after they have done some relevant reading. If the reading has not already been assigned, the case is distributed with a note such as: "Miss Barker needs to do some homework for her meeting next week. In preparing for that meeting, she might benefit from reading some of the studies listed at the end of the case." To add dimension to the discussion, I sometimes have students read slightly different sets of readings with some getting a behaviorist article like the Skinner piece above and others getting something more provocative or future-oriented (see Hunter, 1996, in which I try to describe my thoughts on what may lie ahead). At other times, I ask students to find and read any one article about computer-assisted instruction on the Internet and to use it to inform their thinking about the case. In the near future, the case will likely reside on the class Webpage with links to appropriate on-line readings.

When the discussion begins, it is usually guided by discussion questions:

> *Imagine that you are Miss Barker and that you are preparing notes for your meeting with Mr. Blade.*

- *What do you see as the key problem to be dealt with in regards to Hannah's learning with the computer?*
- *Are there any contributing minor problems that also need to be dealt with?*
- *In any event, what do you see as the action that you must take in the future?*
- *Do you need to change the instruction? If so, how?*
- *Do you need to do a better job of informing parents? In what respect and how would you go about doing it?*
- *Is this case not really about computer-assisted learning but about some other problem altogether? If so, what is that problem and how did it get mixed up with computer-assisted learning?*

> *Or,*

> *The following questions are meant to help you consider some of the possibilities in this case. Do not let them restrict your thinking.*

- *From Mr. Blade's description, what can you infer about the program Hannah was using? Try to describe a typical interaction a student might have with this program.*
- *Is Miss Barker correct in her assertion about the research literature? Give some examples of research that supports her view.*
- *What part of the problem in this story is due to the computer and what part is due to the teaching?*
- *Mr. Blade seems to know math pretty well. At least, he sounds more confident than Miss Barker. Is this a problem? If not, why not? If yes, what could be done either to prevent it or correct it?*
- *Is there ever a place for the kind of program it seems Hannah was using? If so, what is that place?*

SUMMARY AND CONCLUSIONS

In general, I'd say that this case works well. It raises serious concerns about the use of computers in the manner Taylor labeled "tutor," for the delivery of instruction. More importantly, it raises questions about instruction versus construction if the students' prior readings prepared them to see this distinction. If not, then the case can be a useful point of departure from which to introduce such concepts. Exam responses (I have used the case as part of a final examination in a class in which it had been discussed early in the term) and case discussion show that the case leads students to be skeptical about computer-assisted instruction, particularly to be skeptical about unthinking uses that put too much faith in the claims of program developers or vendors. Students sometimes have novel ideas about how such a program could still be used to good effect in the hands of a creative teacher.

One of the surprises for me with this case is the extent to which the students are critical of Miss Barker. They are not as sympathetic about her discomfort with math as I thought they would be (because many are similarly uncomfortable) and are quite likely to accuse her of a lack of professionalism for failing to learn the mathematics better herself. They will say this even while acknowledging that they themselves do not know what transformational geometry is.

In general, work on cases has not been part of my course evaluation scheme. The case work is usually carried out during lecture time in lieu of some formal presentation, film, or other activity. Often, though, my examination questions have been structured in such a way that students must decipher a problem and present a solution (or choose one in a multiple-choice framework), so the benefits of working through in-class cases should be apparent. The use of the above case as part of an examination was an important element in the increasing shift in my thinking about the value of cases. As I make increasing use of cases in teaching, it seems essential that the testing format also reflect this emphasis so that students can demonstrate the skills they have acquired in a format that is well suited to the task.

Miss Barker and Mr. Blade do not face the kind of decisions that faced poor old Virtuous John. Nor do any of my other case characters. But each of them is embedded in a situation that may well occur in an actual classroom setting and each is designed to bring forth the students' knowledge and experience in a challenging group problem-solving situation.

Some students recently asked me what working with cases would give them when they became teachers. I think there are a lot of good answers to that question. It might even make a good case itself. But what I said focused on the group problem solving process. All too often, teachers seek to solve all of the problems they encounter by relying entirely on their own resources. I suspect that they learned to do that partly in response to the kinds of demands that teacher education put on them, demands that too often focus exclusively on individual performance, individual responsibility, and individual assessment. If case-based teaching can communicate to teachers that there is value in shared decision making, then we may see both more collegial schools and better solutions to the inevitable problems that arise in teaching.

An early draft of this paper presented Hannah's case as a sort of proposal. I was on sabbatical leave and I developed the case for use on my return. Sufficient time has passed that the case has now been used several times and the reader will understand from the preceding material that this usage is part of an ongoing change process. Interestingly enough, this change process is not simply a personal one. During my leave, a team of my colleagues was revising our entire teacher education program to become case-based. When I returned, I was asked to conduct workshops in case analysis for faculty and students. We have now completed a pilot year and are committed to a completely new program in which the major body of teacher education content and skills will be acquired through interaction with cases and increased practicum experiences. Just last week, a group of us submitted a proposal to fund the development of more dynamic cases and to create a case analysis support system on the Web. Another of my colleagues is proposing a complete shift in infrastructure that would replace many of our computer labs with much smaller case discussion rooms equipped with one or two computers for use by one or two case groups at a time. These rooms will be in close proximity to the Education Materials Center so that students have ready access to information sources.

We feel we are engaged in something important. We believe that we will be doing a more honest and a more comprehensive job of preparing teachers in this new program. But whether that proves to be true or not, a commitment to more serious and more comprehensive use of cases in teacher preparation has invigorated our faculty and encouraged us all to struggle with fundamental questions about teaching and teacher preparation. It's a kind of Virtuous John escalation in reverse; so I guess I should be looking for the angelic intervention that put the case competition advertisement on my desk nearly five years ago.

REFERENCES

Hunter, W. J. (1993a). Spirituality in the service of a larger moral tradition. *Religious Education, 88*(4), 595–605.

Hunter, W. J. (Ed.). (1993b). A bucket of words: Creative writing about teaching and learning. *Journal of Educational Thought, 27*(1).

Hunter, W. J. (1996). Wild speculations and sober thoughts. *Computers in New Zealand Schools, 8*(1), 47–57.

Schon, D. A. (1983). *The reflective practitioner: How professionals think in action.* New York: Basic Books.

THEODORE J. KOWALSKI

Theodore Kowalski is a professor of educational leadership at Ball State University. A former teacher, principal, and superintendent, he served as dean of the Teachers College at that institution from 1983 to 1993. His more than 150 professional publications include 12 books, the most recent of which are: *Keepers of the Flame: Contemporary Urban Superintendents* (1995), *Case Studies in Educational Administration* (2nd ed., 1995), *Public Relations in Age of Information and Reform* (1996), and *The School Superintendent: Theory, Practice, and Cases* (1998).

13

USING CASES IN A SCHOOL ADMINISTRATION DOCTORAL SEMINAR

THEODORE J. KOWALSKI
BALL STATE UNIVERSITY

The import of case studies in the preparation of school administrators is associated with changing conditions of practice. In today's reform context, educational administration entails a greater emphasis on leadership, which means that principals and superintendents are being encouraged to devote more of their time to three critical responsibilities: (a) creating climates for shared decision making, (b) facilitating decisions that focus on what schools should be doing, and (c) motivating individuals and groups in the school community to achieve the agreed-on goals. Because professionalism and democracy are core values in school renewal, administrators also are relying less on transactional strategies, largely political tactics involving an exchange between an administrator and subordinate for purposes of achieving one or more goals they deem important (Burns, 1978). And, rather than attempting to appeal to baser emotions (e.g., fear, greed and jealousy), real leaders seek to influence behavior by appealing to "higher ideals and moral values such as liberty, justice, equality, peace, and humanitarianism" (Yukl, 1989, p. 210). This reconceptualization of school administration is called *transformational leadership*.

Case studies are especially powerful tools for preparing administrators to perform functions that are core to school renewal (e.g., identifying and solving problems). For example, policy initiatives for school reform are moving toward a balance of centralization and decentralization; many states are giving local districts and individual schools substantial freedom to determine goals and processes. At the same time, however, local districts and schools are being made more accountable for results. This policy shift—a transition from an emphasis on inputs to an emphasis on outputs—produces the need for *directed autonomy,* a construct that focuses on leaders empowering others to achieve specified objectives (Waterman, 1987). Within schools, this means that administrators provide direction and facilitation to connect school decisions to more global goals (state or school district goals). Functions such as collaborative visioning and planning become foundational to operating schools (Kowalski, 1995b). Unlike the 1960s and 1970s, when the preparation of school administrators concentrated largely on political frames of decision making, professors of educational administration are now encouraged to view schools as moral institutions (Capper, 1993; Power, 1993) and to infuse moral and ethical aspects of practice into professional preparation (Sergiovanni, 1992)

UTILITY OF CASE STUDIES
IN EDUCATIONAL ADMINISTRATION

The changing landscape of administrative practice that I have briefly described is largely responsible for the emerging interest in the case method as a paradigm for preparing school administrators. Case studies can be used for a variety of purposes ranging from research to evaluation to teaching. As a teaching tool, however, I believe they serve one of two broad purposes:

- reinforcing new information, concepts, or theories, and
- permitting students to apply acquired knowledge and skills to specific situations.

In the former, the case study is used to exemplify key facets of the new information being provided to the student; in the latter, emphasis is placed on objectives such as reasoning, critical thinking, and problem solving (Kowalski, 1995a). When cases are used to apply knowledge, both the Socratic method (the dialectical process relying on questioning to set students to think logically), and situational knowledge (facts about individuals, schools, communities, and problems that place the case in a specific context) play an important role in teaching (Weaver, Kowalski, & Pfaller, 1995). These two elements nourish psychological and personal involvement on the part of the student, qualities that make the application of professional knowledge and the use of cases more meaningful (Christensen, 1987).

Although the popularity of cases escalated in the late 1980s and early 1990s, they have been used in the graduate study of school administration for some time. In the 1950s, for example, several case studies texts were published (e.g., Hamburg, 1955; Sargent & Belisle, 1955); in the early 1960s, several leaders in educational administration advocated the use of cases and simulations (e.g., Culbertson & Coffield, 1960; Griffiths, 1963). But until recently, there was little evidence that case studies had become an integral part of many preparation programs.

CASE TEXTS

Today, increased interest in using case studies is evidenced by the growing number of school administration texts based on this format. These books vary with regard to structure (complete versus open-ended cases), length (several pages to nearly 50 or 60 pages), and basis (real, disguised, or fictitious).

The following texts serve as examples:

- *School Leadership and Administration,* a text authored by Richard Gorton and Petra Snowden (1993), provides a mix of theoretical concepts and research on decision making with 58 cases. The length of a typical case in this book is only about two pages; each case is followed by a list of suggested learning activities that encourage the reader to analyze the case, examine larger issues, and solve the problem presented. The cases do not include the final actions of the administrators, and the reader is encouraged to assume the role of the problem solver.
- *Administrators Solving the Problems of Practice,* authored by Wayne Hoy and C. John Tarter (1995), is a book that attempts to teach both theoretical content and application of decision making. There is a common structure to the chapters: a decision-making model is explicated and analyzed; the model is demonstrated through a case; the reader is guided through the case as the model is applied; and, after the guided illustration, a new case is provided challenging the student to apply the model. The authors indicate that the cases were generated from the experiences of working administrators in various school environments.
- *Educational Leadership: Case Studies for Reflective Practice,* authored by Carl Ashbaugh and Katherine Kasten (1995), is a book that contains 62 relatively short case studies. The first two chapters are devoted to

a rationale for using cases and suggestions for analyzing them. The cases are presented in four chapters and grouped according to topics. Many of the cases are less than two pages in length. Questions related to the cases are provided in an instructor's manual rather than in the text. The cases are open-ended.

- My own case book, *Case Studies in Educational Administration* (Kowalski, 1995a), is designed to facilitate decision making and the application of acquired knowledge. An introductory section provides the reader with explanations about the case method, a rationale for using case studies, and suggestions regarding participation in case analysis and classroom discussions. The book contains 23 open-ended cases. Each case begins with a one- to two-page introduction that informs the reader of relevant theories and concepts and provides him or her with a list of key areas for reflection. The average case study in this book is approximately eight pages in length. Each case is followed by a primary challenge (that asks the reader to assume a specific role), a list of key issues and questions (approximately 12 after each case), and suggested readings. An accompanying instructor's manual provides suggested formats, additional learning activities, and additional readings.

In addition to these types of books, a growing number of traditional educational administration textbooks are including a short case study at the end of each chapter. The purpose is to engage the reader in reflection by placing the chapter content in the context of a problem.

Differences in case books often reflect continuing disagreements over definitions of case studies and their appropriate use in graduate study. Individuals espousing rigid structure often ignore the reality that case studies are used for different purposes. As such, success is not dependent on a specified type of case, but, rather, is determined by synchronizing instructional objectives with the types of cases used. In school administration, cases have been used predominately in the areas of decision making and problem solving. For this reason, open-ended cases (referred to as *Type B* cases) have been common. When cases are used in school administration for these purposes, they should not have a formalized, didactic structure leading the reader to infer a single correct answer (Prestine, 1993), because problems are multifaceted, and variables such as school environment, community standards, and past practices help determine the efficacy of decisions. For example, a decision about reprimanding a teacher may be influenced by past practice, school district policy, laws, and the culture and climate of the school. So rather than encouraging the notion of single, correct answers, students are encouraged to use a multidimensional approach that leads to contingencies that then can be analyzed and evaluated in the context of the problem.

USING CASES IN AN ADVANCED DOCTORAL SEMINAR

Doctoral students majoring in school administration at Ball State University are required to enroll in a yearlong advanced seminar that focuses on applications of professional knowledge and the political, moral, and ethical dimensions of decision making. Only doctoral students who are at advanced stages of their degree programs are permitted to enroll. Typically, the class size ranges from 8 to 13 students. Among the specific objectives for the seminar are the following: to expose students to the case method, to study and apply various decision-making models, to apply professional and craft knowledge in problem-using open-ended cases, to develop an appreciation for multiple perspectives and to use a multidimensional approach to problem solving, to develop reflective practice skills, and to provide an opportunity to teach with cases.

Case Implementation and Evaluation

The cases used in the seminar are contained in the second edition of my case book that has already been described. A minimum of 16 of the 23 cases in the book are used over the two semesters. During the first semester, at least five cases are presented by the instructor. I purposely select cases that focus on different administrative positions (school-based and central office positions) and different contexts of practice (rural, small town, suburban, urban). Additionally, I try to demonstrate several different teaching techniques. Among those used are the following:

1. Students are assigned to read a case a week in advance of the class period during which it is discussed. They are instructed to respond, in writing, to the challenge and other selected issues and questions at the end of the case. As the case is discussed in class, students share perceptions, using their written assignment as a guide. At the end of the class period, the written assignments are collected. In grading the assignments, I focus on three issues: (a) the quality of decisions exhibited by the students, (b) the responses in the written assignment in relation to the class discussion of the case, and (c) the degree to which students associate their decisions with their professional knowledge base or their previous experiences in schools.

2. Having already read the case in preparation for class, students divide into small discussion groups. The task is to reach consensus in each

group on a course of action. This method is an especially effective technique for fostering collaborative decision making. After the groups complete their assignment, there is a discussion of the proposed solutions; and the entire class evaluates the quality of each group's proposed course of action. Additionally, each group comments on the dynamics that occurred in trying to reach a consensus decision (e.g., notation of problems, how conflict was handled).

3. Role playing and simulations are used with some cases. Roles are assigned to students at least one week prior to the case presentation. Typically, this format is used when multiple actors are divided over a course of action. The time frame for role playing is set at some point following the end of the case in the text. For example, the setting may be a meeting of the key actors (e.g., principals, teachers, parents, board members) in the superintendent's office that has been called in an effort to resolve conflict described in the case (e.g., a dispute over the enforcement of a policy on plagiarism).

I do not direct students on how to play their roles. Because they are assuming a role that has already been described in the case study, they have the choice of either maintaining the described behavior pattern or assuming a different posture. For example, a student may be assuming the role of a principal who objects to a certain policy by challenging the authority of the superintendent. The student playing this role may decide to sustain the belligerent behavior or to become cooperative. Typically in role playing, one or two students who are not assigned roles have the responsibility of being evaluators. During the discussion that follows role playing, the following topics are addressed: (a) evaluator perceptions, (b) the degree to which students maintained or altered behavior patterns described in the case, (c) verbal and nonverbal behaviors that may have contributed to resolution or additional conflict, (d) outcomes, and (e) alternative approaches to solving the problem presented.

4. I present students with alternative solutions to the primary problems detailed in a case, and the students are directed to identify the strengths and weaknesses of each (typically as an out-of-class assignment). Discussion of the outcomes occurs in class. Students also are encouraged to suggest possible decisions beyond those that I provided.

5. Practicing school administrators or professors are invited to participate in class discussions of certain cases. For example, one case involves the use of corporal punishment by a middle school principal in an urban area. Several administrators from urban settings and an educational psychology professor read the case and share their opinions with students. Prior to this discussion, students are prompted to observe the basis for the positions taken by the visitors. For example, to what degree are the practitioners influenced by their personal experiences and working con-

ditions? To what extent is the educational psychology professor ignoring political issues commonly found in urban schools?

Prior to working with any of the cases, the students are given a multidimensional model for studying problems that has five components:

- legal considerations,
- ethical and moral expectations,
- political expediency,
- economic constraints, and
- professional dispositions (includes both managerial and education-driven considerations).

The purpose is to have students identify perspectives within each dimension prior to making a decision. Often these perspectives are in conflict. For instance, a decision may be politically advantageous but illegal. Or a decision may be sound from a management perspective, but clearly not in the best interests of student needs.

During the second semester, each student is required to teach a case. As the instructor, the student has license to make assignments and determine the format for teaching the case. Students are provided with a list of potential strategies in the course syllabus, but they are not restricted to these options. In completing their lesson plans, they are required to identify specific instructional objectives and to link these objectives to the proposed activities.

Feedback about the case studies is obtained through both program and performance evaluation. These evaluations include information about the value of the course, the effectiveness of the cases, my performance as an instructor, and personal and peer performance. First, students complete an anonymous course evaluation at the end of each semester. Because cases are an integral part of the seminar, some information about the case method is obtained through this process. Second, student performance is evaluated for purposes of determining a course grade. Students earn points for participating in each case. Students receive their participation points one week following the presentation of each case. Students also earn points for teaching a case (approximately one-third of the points for the course grade are associated with this activity). These are assigned by both the instructor and peers; the number of points earned from peers is a mean score. Third, students are asked to reflect on their experiences with cases at the end of the second semester in writing. Students are told at the beginning of the first semester that they will need to provide this information, and they are encouraged to keep a log or notes to assist them.

POTENTIAL PROBLEMS

Because case studies are so engaging, some instructors are tempted to rely on serendipity. This is a precarious practice, because students often can sense when the activities lack direction. In truth, effective use of cases requires a great deal of planning, especially with regard to dealing with contingencies and staying on task. Unlike the lecture method, in which students are passive learners, the case method provides greater opportunities for them to shape and direct classroom discussions. However, there are several problems that also may be encountered in using cases:

Graduate students in school administration often struggle with the concept of ideal practice. That is, they find it difficult to describe behaviorally an ideal principal or superintendent. When asked to do so, students often describe a role model, and not uncommonly their admiration is associated with a referent power relationship (i.e., the student idolizes the administrator because that person is seen as ideal). Ideal practice relates more directly to expectations embedded in the professional knowledge base. Without such a conceptualization, students are prone to assess their behavior in cases in the context of self-interests or political expediency. For this reason, discussions of ideal practice are recommended prior to working with cases. This is done by providing a behavioral description of a practitioner, emphasizing both relevant theoretical constructs and ethical and moral dimensions of practice.

Some students avoid problem solving, creating an obvious obstacle to the effective use of the case method. This behavior is often characterized by either quick, intuitive responses to problems or the excuse that the case study does not facilitate a proper decision (e.g., contentions that the case is too abstract or does not provide sufficient information). Interestingly, this same behavior has been observed by several colleagues at different universities working with both undergraduate and graduate students. For instance, those professors working at the undergraduate level in teacher education collectively estimated that one-third of their students exhibited this problem. Correspondingly, professors working at the graduate level in school administration collectively estimated that one-fifth of their students exhibited this problem. This behavior may reflect a disposition of fearing responsibility and decision making. Given the increasing demand for leadership in school administration, this topic certainly merits formal study.

Because of the interactive nature of the case method, the potential exists for a few students to dominate the discussions. This is one of the most probable problems associated with a lack of planning. You do not want to discourage students from being open and candid, yet you want everyone to have a meaningful part in case discussions. Unfortunately, some students have been socialized to the role of passive learner, and they are willing to let others dominate. I attempt to encourage passive students to become active by asking them to enter discussions (e.g., asking them if they agree with opinions stated by others).

As in all types of educational exchanges, some participants may not be properly prepared. Students who enter class without having read the case or doing their assignment may try to "fly by the seat of their pants." Allowing them to do so sends the wrong message. Tactfully students need to be told that intuition and "gut feelings" are insufficient to guide professional practice. I frequently ask students to identify research or literature that influenced their position. After a period of time, students know they may be asked this question, and they become less likely to be unprepared.

Getting sidetracked by unrelated topics is a problem in all college level courses, but it is especially true when using the case method. Again, this possibility is enhanced by the interactive nature of the teaching model. Often students will want to relate issues in the case to personal experiences, and this certainly should be encouraged. But there is often a fine line between relating this element of reflection and sacrificing instructional objectives. I try to set time parameters for peripheral discussions (usually about five minutes). As a student begins talking about a personal experience, I might say, "Because this is an important experience for you, let's take just a few minutes to have you share it with the class."

Teaching has often been described as an isolated activity. That is to say, teachers rarely engage in peer consultation when problem solving (an activity much more common in medicine or law). Because most school administration students are teachers, they are not accustomed to sharing their philosophies and judgments openly. This task involves human relations skills, and concerns that emerge often are related to insensitivity, overly aggressive behavior, and poor communication skills (especially listening skills).

Problems can also emerge when students do not clearly understand the reasons why they are working with cases. Those most conditioned to lecture-type teaching may initially see the case method as too disordered.

POSITIVE OUTCOMES

The case method produces many positive outcomes, some of which are truly by-products. Among the more cogent are the following:

- Experiences with cases teach students to relate decision making to the professional knowledge base. This is accomplished by emphasizing conceptualizations of ideal practice. Over time, students become less likely to rely solely on intuition or personal values and beliefs, because they begin to accept professional responsibility for their behavior. That is, they accept a moral responsibility at least to consider the professional knowledge they have acquired.

- Many students enter graduate study with erroneous and negative perceptions of research and theory. Rather than appropriately seeing theoretical constructs as depictions of reality, they are more inclined to believe that theory is a professor's dream or a bias about how things should be. Even more disconcertingly, they often see theory as having little relevance to success in administration. Their exposure to using research and theory is often abstract and not sufficiently relevant to change such perceptions. Immersing them in problem solving and requiring them to rely on a professional knowledge base often leads to attitude changes, because they know that others in class may challenge their decisions.

- Responding to a problem on the basis of opinion is quite different from responding on the basis of acquired knowledge and skills. In addressing problems, many administrators fail to look at issues from multiple perspectives, and either rely solely on personal opinion or restrict their analysis to the political aspects of the problem. By using a multidimensional framework for analyzing problems, they become more cautious and more reflective. This proclivity is exhibited by behavioral changes during the latter stages of the seminar. As their experiences with problem solving in the context of Type B cases increases, they are more likely to engage in peer consultation prior to rendering a decision.

- Although the process of reflection is discussed in many educational administration courses, it becomes more meaningful in the context of problem-solving activities. The vicarious experiences provided by the cases allow students to test their professional knowledge. This helps to dissipate disjunctions between theory and practice.

- The typical graduate student in school administration is a midcareer individual who has been teaching for approximately 10 to 15 years. As an adult learner, he or she seeks relevant experiences that link studies to everyday problems. Using cases based on real problems achieves this goal. Thus student reactions to cases are overwhelmingly positive.

- The interactive nature of the case method makes it an excellent vehicle for developing human relations skills. Activities such as professional consultation and consensus building are indicative of goals being pursued in school reform.

- A sense of closeness among students often emerges from working with cases; in many respects, the case method evolves into a form of cooperative learning. Students become better acquainted with each other; they can identify group strengths and weaknesses. Over time, they may produce a shared commitment to addressing problems.

- Knowledge about organizational behavior is reinforced through the cases. Students learn how individuals and groups, the community, and other situational variables shape problems.
- The most neglected element of practice involves ethical and moral leadership. Students often remark that the cases provided a clearer picture of their responsibilities to other people and to their profession.
- Exposure to cases provides critical lessons about accessing and using information. Students learn that information usually is fragmented and incomplete; they learn to sort and filter data provided in the cases; they learn to identify missing information that is vital to making a decision.

STUDENT COMMENTS

After completing the seminar, students submit a written statement detailing their opinions about their experiences with the case studies. They are also asked if their perspectives about school administration have changed. Approximately 80 percent of these students had not had previous experiences with the case method. Their comments demonstrate that they find the case method an exciting, interactive process; for many students, it is rewarding experience to be able to use their knowledge to address real problems of practice. The following is a sampling of comments collected in the past two years:

> *As a result of working with case studies, my perspective of administrative behavior has both broadened and deepened. These changes have been gradual and subtle. Before this class, I was less conscious of stepping back and thinking about a problem before giving a response. In fact, I often felt that administrators had to make quick and decisive moves. I am far more cautious about trusting first impressions; I make myself step back, rethink the facts, and delve more deeply into the problem. I've learned to walk around a problem. That is, I try to see it from different perspectives. I now see problems as sculptures and not as one-dimensional flat paintings. I also look beyond the smooth surface of the statue (problem) and into the depths of the thoughts, assumptions, values, and beliefs of all the diverse, multiple creators of the problem. I am now more conscious of my own biases, values, and attitudes. Also, I became aware of my tendency to filter information, to stress those facts that were in agreement with my philosophy and to*

ignore or downplay other information. The real challenge lies ahead. That is for me to continue to grow along the lines of an art critic, ever striving to understand the creator(s) and the work, the people, their paradigms, their perspectives, and their problems, then to use this intensely profound comprehension as a basis for wise action.

I have a deeper understanding of the necessity of situational leadership. It has become obvious to me that a great many variables impact an administrator's decisions, and many of these variables are beyond the control of the decision maker. Thus I have learned the importance of scanning both the internal and external environments. I also have a finer understanding of the linkage between theory and practice, and I believe I am more proficient at engaging in reflection. I find it easier, although not less complex, to evaluate administrative behavior. Work with cases was especially meaningful after completing a number of courses focusing on administrative theory.

As a result of working with case studies, I have changed my perspective of administrative behavior. Cases allowed me to apply knowledge and skills to specific problems. They prompted me to be more reflective about my decisions and more sensitive about judging the behavior of others. Cases provided an opportunity to critique my own approaches to making decisions. I really believe my problem-solving skills have improved. Finally, I have changed my perspective of how organizations operate. Educational administration seemed rather simple before—go in and provide management. Well, that perspective has certainly changed. No matter how many courses I could have taken, I don't think I would have changed my perspective about the application of knowledge without experiencing case studies.

First of all, working with cases has helped me understand that you must look beyond the facts which are obvious when you review a situation. In reading cases for class, I found myself searching for more information relative to the case, especially with regard to the culture in which the case is presented. I believe I have become more analytical of material as it is presented to me. I am more inclined to look for clues, to read between the lines. Lastly, I am better prepared to engage in reflection. This was a really fuzzy topic before working with case studies.

The case studies we worked with over the course of the year have not so much changed my perception of administrative behavior but have instead more clearly defined the need to view situations more globally.

The cases were helpful in the sense that they presented situations with multiple issues, all of which could affect your decision. The cases underscored the need for administrators to base their decisions on a thoughtful analysis of facts, both obvious and not, and to resist the temptation to act intuitively. I wish we could have spent more time with each case.

Working with case studies has changed my perspective of administration tremendously. Most importantly, the cases provided an opportunity to interface theory and practice. Prior to this course, I would rely heavily on the technical aspects of administration—you know, management ideas. I trusted my 'gut feelings' when faced with a problem. This is what I saw other administrators doing in schools. It amazes me that I spent so much time learning theories about administration but was never asked to make administrative decisions based on this knowledge. Now I think I am more inclined to weigh a number of factors before making a decision. I think about the consequences of my decisions a lot more before I make them.

The cases would be more meaningful if they were taken to their conclusion. It would have been helpful to know what each administrator decided and the consequences of their acts. Evaluating the decisions made by these administrators would have been very beneficial to our discussions. Often, I felt that the responses in class were based on political correctness and not personal convictions. Will these same solutions be used when all of us are sitting in the 'hot seats'? Overall, the experiences were informative and we had a chance to apply what we have learned over these many courses.

One experience that put things into perspective for me was the class discussion of a case involving what appeared to be an autocratic principal. When asked by you if we would like to work for this principal, most of us said no. We answered without much thought. Then you encouraged us to look at the principal's behavior from different perspectives. What are his legal responsibilities? What is his responsibility to students and the community? Everyone started to have second thoughts about the principal. The point is, the case made us look at this person's behavior in the context of his school's culture. I have learned to be more understanding and prudent.

Before this class, I had a tendency to view administrative behavior largely in a political domain. During my 15 years of experience as an educator, this view was reinforced by discussions with principals and superintendents. It seemed their views were always shaped by political problems and political solutions. Most of the administrators I know are oriented toward management. (And yes, they are all men who are pretty good managers.) Cases altered my perspective about the essence of administration. My perception of effective practice has changed. I have become more inclined to separate the personal from the professional. Our class discussions of cases always involved reflection, and this made the whole experience even more meaningful. I find myself with a different perspective of administration as a result of working with cases.

The case studies helped me realize that administrative behavior is more complex than I previously judged. My purpose in pursuing the Ed.D. is not to become a principal or superintendent, therefore I never thought a great deal about practitioner behavior. These cases have opened my eyes. The various dimensions of decision making discussed in class provided a framework for analyzing the cases. I had originally thought that answers to problems, such as the ones presented in the cases, were simple and straightforward. This proved not to be true. For example, when we were encouraged to consider the ethical and moral dimensions or the legal dimensions of a decision, I realized the danger of believing that there was always one right answer. I learned to place myself in another person's shoes as I read the case. How would I react if I was a school board member? A teacher? A parent or student? Currently, I am a college instructor, and exposure to cases has changed my thinking about my own teaching. I enjoyed being an active participant, and I am going to try to use some cases with my students.

My perspectives of administrative behavior have changed as a result of this seminar. This has occurred largely because of the discussion associated with the cases. The analytical activities forced me to look beyond my personal perspective. The dimensions of decision making provided by the professor were especially helpful. Prior to this class, I saw administrative behavior as being largely innate. We react and make decisions largely on the basis of personality, demeanor, biases, etc. While these factors remain in the mix, I have learned to pay far more attention to the professional knowledge base. We can't take for granted that our attitudes have been changed by what we learned in all these courses. My own thoughts were reinforced by my observations of other administrators whom I saw acting largely on the basis of emotion. The cases showed me the narrowness of my own experiences, because many of the schools in the cases are different from the ones I have known.

At first, I was frustrated because I wanted more information from the cases. I thought that the information provided was often insufficient to make decisions. I guess the real question is whether the cases are indicative of practice. How often are administrators required to make decisions with limited information? How often do they have to separate fact from fiction? I would have preferred more extensive cases that would have provided more facts.

I enjoyed the cases because the problems were so real. Many of them were similar to problems I have seen in schools. The greatest growth experience for me was developing my problem-solving skills. I liked being involved. Cases made me think about all the information I got from other classes.

I like using cases, but I am concerned that they might mislead students to believe that they can make important decisions without much practical experience. Some have never been administrators, and some have little teaching experience. Additionally, you don't have to face negative consequences when you make a decision in class. As a principal or superintendent, the political considerations are intense and the negative consequences are real. I just think some students see decision making as a purely intellectual task.

Most of all, I enjoy the opportunity to review 'real-life' situations rather than hypothetical examples. As an administrator, I know that you are better prepared for these problems when you have had the opportunity to discuss them in class. One concern focuses on students developing the tendency to second-guess. By that I mean that hindsight is always 20–20. We must remember that administrators have time constraints and information constraints. Even the best administrators get into trouble doing what they think is right. I'm not sure all students understand this when they work with cases.

CONCLUDING THOUGHTS

Possibly because of the past preoccupation with management in school administration, many students enter graduate study in this field with basic misconceptions. They frequently fail to challenge notions of rationality in organizations; they often believe that single best solutions can be applied across all schools and school districts with equally effective results; they believe that problem solving is largely a transactional process fashioned by self-interest (e.g., survival) or expectations to eradicate conflict. In truth, schools are not rational places, and the effectiveness of administrative de-cisions is influenced by a myriad of contextual variables. More specifically, there are no established structures of knowledge that suffice across all pos-sible applications. Accordingly, "it becomes imperative to focus on *how* knowledge is used in practice, rather than on *what* the knowledge struc-tures are" (Prestine, 1993, p. 193). For this reason, professors of school ad-ministration have a responsibility to increase emphasis on leadership and to associate this broadened professional knowledge base with critical processes such as problem solving, critical thinking, and decision making.

Almost uniformly, students react positively to working with cases. My observations lead me to believe that there are two reasons. First, grad-uate students in school administration are adults who prefer to be active learners; they respond more enthusiastically to problems cogent to their personal and professional lives. Second, they seek opportunities to use the vast amount of knowledge they have acquired. Many have never held an administrative position, and the vicarious experiences are espe-cially valuable for them.

Transitions occurring in public education require a rethinking of graduate education in school administration. In this vein, the case method can make valuable contributions in several critical areas. In ad-dition to addressing disjunctions between theory and practice, they help develop problem-solving skills, human relations skills, decision making, and reflection. Students who enter practice in the coming years must be better prepared for leadership roles. This requires a deeper understand-ing of the professional knowledge base and a deeper commitment to ac-cepting the responsibilities that accompany the public's trust.

REFERENCES

Ashbaugh, C. R., & Kasten, K. (1995). *Educational leadership: Case studies for re-flective practice* (2nd ed.). New York: Longman.

Burns, J. M. (1978). *Leadership.* New York: Harper and Row.

Capper, C. A. (1993). *Educational administration in a pluralistic society.* Albany, NY: SUNY Press.

Christensen, C. R. (1987). *Teaching and the case method.* Boston: Harvard Business School.

Culbertson, J., & Coffield, W. (Eds.). (1960). *Simulation in educational training.* Columbus, OH: University Council for Educational Administration.

Gorton, R. A., & Snowden, P. E. (1993). *School leadership and administration: Im-portant concepts, case studies and simulations* (4th ed.). Madison, WI: Brown & Benchmark.

Griffiths, D. (1963). The case method of teaching educational administration. *Journal of Educational Administration, 2,* 81–82.

Hamburg, M. (1955). *Case studies in elementary school administration.* New York: Bureau of Publications, Teachers College, Columbia University.

Hoy, W. K., & Tarter, C. J. (1995). *Administrators solving the problems of practice: Decision-making concepts, cases, and consequences.* Boston: Allyn & Bacon.

Kowalski, T. J. (1995a). *Case studies in educational administration* (2nd ed.). New York: Longman.

Kowalski, T. J. (1995b). *Keepers of the flame: Contemporary urban superintendents.* Thousand Oaks, CA: Corwin.

Power, F. C. (1993). Just schools and moral atmosphere. In K. Strike and P. Ternasky (Eds.), *Ethics for professionals in education* (pp. 148–161). New York: Teachers College Press.

Prestine, N. A. (1993). Apprenticeship in problem-solving: Extending the cognitive apprenticeship model. In P. Hallinger, K. Leithwood, and J. Murphy (Eds.), *Cognitive perspectives on educational leadership* (pp. 192–212). New York: Teachers College Press.

Sargent, C., & Belisle, E. (1955). *Educational administration: Cases and concepts.* Boston: Houghton Mifflin.

Sergiovanni, T. J. (1992). *Moral leadership: Getting to the heart of school improvement.* San Francisco: Jossey-Bass.

Waterman, R. H. (1987). *The renewal factor: How the best get and keep the competitive edge.* New York: Bantam.

Weaver, R. A., Kowalski, T. J., & Pfaller, J. E. (1995). Case-method teaching. In K. Pritchard & R. Sawyer (Eds.), *Handbook of college teaching: Theory and applications* (pp. 171–178). Westport, CT: Greenwood Press.

Yukl, G. A. (1989). *Leadership in organizations* (2nd ed.). Englewood Cliffs, NJ: Prentice-Hall.

14

TAKING PROFESSIONAL INSTRUCTION FOR TEACHING WITH CASES TO A HIGHER POWER: ISSUES TO EXPLORE

HENDRIK D. GIDEONSE
UNIVERSITY OF CINCINNATI

In the process of preparing this chapter I came to understand that I have been taught by case methodology since before college and graduate school. I have, on reflection, been engaged in the struggle to master its demands in my own teaching ever since. The preceding chapters cover familiar territory; they bring to mind the sometimes painful, often surprising, and ultimately deeply satisfying and still ongoing journey of discovery.

I have been a teacher educator for over 30 years. And yet, it would seem, I have never been very far removed from the formative experiences of the teaching to which I, as a student, was exposed during the 23 years of my formal schooling.

Very little of the instruction I received in elementary or high school could be classified as inspired. Nonetheless, it was among the best to be had in the early fifties. It was competent if pedestrian. That most of us learned so well from it was more a function of the kinds of people who taught us, and the unflinching support we were fortunate to have from our homes and families. Our teachers and our parents were instances of educated and caring adults. In our own learning and development, our achievements were in large measure a function of learning to emulate the "cases" of educated, caring, high-functioning adults we had before us day in and day out.

When I entered college in the fall of 1954, my exposure to learning via cases that were instances of adults as exemplars became augmented by case teaching; the model of learning shifted, if you will, to embrace more than apprenticeship. It now came to include the application of pedagogical imagination and application. Amherst College in the mid-fifties was, in retrospect, an astounding instance of a faculty-wide commitment to defining, and then implementing, a liberal arts curriculum of unremitting, (and, now, more than 40 years later) continuing instructional power. For example, the physics, math, and English courses we took in the first year were, in their deepest structures, and by careful design, intimately tied to one another. In particular, the physics course we took as freshmen required us to traverse the intellectual history of the field. We traced the steps of Kepler and Newton and engaged in exploration of the historically parallel domains of mechanics, electricity, magnetism, and optics. The course culminated in Niels Bohr's inspired conceptualization of atomic structure that, at one and the same time, explained phenomena that had heretofore been unconnected in the physical sciences. We took, in two semesters, a journey of 200 years, an extended case study, if you will, of the intellectual history of the development of physics to the first half of the 20th century.

Sophomore year exposed us all to two semesters of American Studies. The texts we used were the Amherst series of collected writings on several dozen topics of American history, economy, polity, and culture, all selected to reflect the damning diversity, to say nothing of out-and-out conflict, of understanding and interpretation of the great issues of America's development. Topics ranged from the role slavery played in the War Between the States, the frontier as a formative influence for America, industrialization and the accumulation of capital, the geographic, or economic, or philosophical grounds for rebellion from King George III, and so on. Each of those collections of readings was, in effect, a case, and we were obliged to choose a stance and defend it in biweekly papers that were subjected to withering analysis by the faculty, a withering that, in terms of our intellectual development, was more like weeding than anything else. ("I'm not throwing turnips away, son. I'm only trying to let a few grow well.")

When I was at Harvard's Graduate School of Education, Francis Keppel was our Dean. In 1959 he led a class of 80 or more under the title *The American School and its Social Foundations*. He convened it in the basement of old Lawrence Hall, a room distinguished by its windows on both sides, its long, narrow bolted-to-the-floor book-rest tables dividing the room into narrow rows, and rickety chairs being made progressively ever more rickety as generations of students tried unsuccessfully to seat themselves firmly on the uneven brick floor. Keppel would position himself some-what precariously on one of those narrow tables in the center of the room, his feet on the seat of a chair, and he would lead us in a spirited seminar whose principal vehicle was a case we had each analyzed, writ-ten up before class, discussed thoroughly, and then had critiqued by his section assistants. (Remember, those who think case study in teacher ed-ucation is a new phenomenon, we are not yet out of the 1950s here!)

A year or two later, at the start of an advanced graduate seminar on learning theory, George Goethals plunked down Ernest Hilgard's volume on learning theories and directed each member of the seminar to pick a chapter. Our assignment for the first six weeks of the semester was to go away and read everything we could get our hands on by and about the theorist we had chosen. At each of the remaining ten seminars of the se-mester Goethals would come to class with a scenario of learning. These seminars became vigorous exchanges as we role played our theorists at-tempting to explain what had been presented. Vygotsky was yet to be translated, but our competitive zeal as graduate students and the collab-orative endeavor in which the seminar engaged us were exercises in ex-panding our zones of proximal development, to say nothing of our social construction of knowledge. We debated one case after another, and by the end of the semester we knew our own and everyone else's theories with precision and balance.

Finally, my dissertation was a case study itself, historical, to be sure, the story of Henry Barnard's attempt to reform the common schools of Connecticut. It was a case study that turned out to be something of a century-plus-removed apprenticeship, for 12 months later Keppel per-suaded me to come to Washington to help with the preparation and im-plementation of the flood of federal reform legislation that began in 1965 following Lyndon Baines Johnson's overwhelming electoral victory the preceding fall.

Before Washington and after, too, I taught as I was taught, or at least I tried to. I used cases. For example, an advanced graduate seminar I taught for many years that focused on the theory, ethics, and application of educational research asked students to take particular published arti-cles as cases and subject them to analysis in terms of the extent to which the articles lived up to one or another ethical proposition. In courses in teacher education policy, curriculum, or management, I would routinely use cases as vehicles for learning. Students would conduct comparative analyses of the handful of curriculum documents or program descriptions in teacher education that could be found in print. They would compare and contrast policy statements governing faculty reappointment, promo-tion, and tenure in teacher education institutions of varying size, type, and mission. They would examine the unfolding developments in states like Texas, Virginia, or New Jersey (which, at various points in the recent past, summarily abbreviated the curricular space available for professional preparation for teaching), and consider implications for standards, accreditation, and the teaching profession in general.

In the late 1980s, a collaborative decision was taken within the Cincinnati Public Schools to revamp the teacher education programs completely at the University of Cincinnati (UC). The new program, stimulated by Cincinnati's membership in the Holmes Group, came to be called the Cincinnati Initiative in Teacher Education (CITE). At about the same time I was asked to assume responsibility for the old program's so-called *Student Teaching Seminar* required of all elementary and secondary candidates that nobody at UC wanted to teach (!). For seven years thereafter, through the phase-out of the old program and the inauguration and full implementation of the new, I undertook systematic experimentation with case instruction as we hoped to implement it in CITE. (I say "systematic" because I retained copies of everything students wrote, both individually and in groups, in response to seminar assignments and in summative assessment of the seminar, and used the data pool reflectively to make revisions in each upcoming quarter.) Students' summative reflections at quarter's end were an anonymous form of what the University of Pittsburgh's Learning Research and Development Center's Oakleaf School used to call "curriculum embedded tests," as well as an evaluation of their experience in the course. The student responses, plus my own independent assessment of their performance and progress during the quarter, became the basis for quarter by quarter revisions over six years, culminating in the first formal CITE case instruction offerings in the 1995–1996 academic year.

The point in sharing this personal history is two fold. First, one idea behind this volume of case teaching is to give voice to the personal in the experience. And, as all the previous chapter authors were invited to do so, it seemed fitting for this reflective chapter to share in that same character. Second, it also foreshadows my intent to use my own experiences to further illuminate observations arising from examination of the chapters. In other words, my responsibilities are not purely academic (examine the chapters and think about what they say), but arise equally from a longstanding interest and commitment to case instruction in my own learning and teaching life.

ISSUES TO EXPLORE

Five issues suggested themselves to me during the reading of the chapters. Some of them are things I have worried about before and were resurrected to my view; others are new matters to reflect on. A first one has to do with the conviction that cases constitute vehicles for systematically relating professional knowledge and values to the predicaments of practice. A second focuses on the extent to which case studies are, in fact, good representations of practice. A third issue focuses on assessment of the outcomes of case instruction. A fourth addresses the power of case instruction to serve as both candidate and program diagnostic. A last issue is the evidence of the apparent isolation of teacher educators from one another.

Cases as Ways of Relating Knowledge and Values to Practice

As part of the rationale for choosing to undertake case instruction, most of the chapters claim that it encourages and affords practice in applying theoretical principles and professional values to practical situations. In a sense that is unarguable. Where else but in practice would it be meaningful to think and talk about putting theory, epistemological or axiological, to use? Though it may seem unexceptionable, what exactly does it mean to talk that way?

We all assume we know what it means to apply knowledge or values to practice. In fact, I argue, virtually none of us were prepared to do it. Considering this assumption is, therefore, something that ought to be very high on our agenda. What we *were* trained to do is generate knowledge; in fact, major portions of our graduate preparation and our continuing professional development ever since have been in such domains as research design and analytic technique. True, we are taught to write sections in our research reports on implications, but as we all know (to make a small play on words), there's a big difference between the implicit and the explicit.

Knowledge

Let's take knowledge first. What makes for knowledge? What allows us to call something knowledge? Consider the following terms and concepts:

- Evidence
- Logic
- Validity
- Reliability
- Formal experiments
- "Wisdom of practice"
- Experience
- Observation
- Systematic review of the work of others

- Demonstration
- Evaluation
- Freedom from bias
- Theory/hypothesis
- Generalizations
- Site- or individual-specific

When a practitioner contemplates applying knowledge to practice, these terms and concepts like these suggest the kinds of epistemological criteria and concerns that should guide what is considered. For example, every time a student in case analysis would say something like, "Well, personally, I think . . . ," these are the kinds of concepts that I would seek to activate by jumping in with something like, "Well, that's fine, we're glad to know that, but what is it that you think *professionally?* What is the *warrant outside yourself* that legitimizes the judgment or the course of action you are contemplating?"

When talking about applying knowledge, it is also useful to consider professional taxonomies of knowledge, the topical domains and categories of knowledge for teaching. Of course, the taxonomy itself is a form of knowledge. It is useful as an heuristic for considering how many different potential issues and arenas for action there might be in a given predicament. In my case instruction with students, I refer to these domains as "frames of reference." By invoking these frames students may be led to useful lines of inquiry and analysis. For example, categorical frames I have urged on preservice teachers during case instruction include:

- Learning
- Individual differences
- Curriculum
- Content/subject matter
- Curriculum design
- Instruction
- Management of student behavior
- Evaluation/assessment
- Organization of schools
- Legal requirements
- Professional role relations
- Conditions of practice
- Family and sociocultural factors
- Professional development
- Professional ethics

So, finally, what does it mean to apply professional knowledge? At its most elemental, applying knowledge means at least:

1. Being clear about the epistemological warrant as rationale for what we do, and/or
2. Operating within a conceptual framework endorsed by the profession, and/or
3. Exercising constant judgment as to:
   a. what the task/circumstance confronting the teacher is;
   b. which domains of knowledge are implicated by the circumstances;
   c. what specific knowledge/theory/data are relevant.

This conception of what it means to apply knowledge to practice is demanding, to be sure. It is also quite compatible with the assumption underlying case instruction, namely, that professional practice is fundamentally problematic, that issues and circumstances are very often not necessarily as they first appear, and that, therefore, a skeptical and analytic stance about practice will always stand a teacher in good stead.

Values

Is the framework for thinking about values any different? In separating consideration of the two, I don't mean to endorse the notion that they can ever be considered wholly separate matters. Here we are all unwitting prisoners of the philosophical concept of the naturalistic fallacy that argues that one cannot derive a value from a fact, but acknowledging that this is so does not mean we can ever fully extricate knowledge and values from one another.

We can develop parallel analytic frames for values to those suggested above about knowledge. They can help us identify and think meaningfully about values, and help us recognize them when we see them. What terms and concepts come to bear that allow us to assert or recognize the presence of a value? Just as there is a variety of different concepts we bring to bear when we claim a knowledge warrant for an action, a parallel set exists in the value domain. By value we mean to enlist such ideas as

- Vector or direction
- Priority
- Great importance is attached (i.e., not merely preference or taste)
- Always incomplete, never finished, always subject to greater perfection
- A moral principle guiding thought and action
- A disposition or inclination
- Presumed to be shared across the profession (or ought to be)

Are there categories and domains, a taxonomy that might serve as an heuristic parallel to the topical domains of the teaching profession identified above in connection with knowledge? Consider for example: (a) relationships to one's students and their parents, (b) relationships to the society served, (c) relationships to one's professional peers, (d) stance toward one's own practice in terms of bases for action and effectiveness and impact.

A value formulation that I find persuasive touching on all these domains is that articulated by Kenneth Sirotnik (1990). Sirotnik identifies five fundamental values or moral ideals that ought to guide teaching:

Caring—deep empathic relationship between people based on mutuality, respect, relatedness, receptivity, and trust

Social Justice—commitment to individual freedom and to individual well-being

Competence—things worth doing are worth doing well, as professionals and as expectations for students

Knowledge—the commitment to practice based on information, theory, explanation, interpretation, and intellectual engagement

Inquiry—the commitment to the rational, to exploration, to validation, to deepening understanding, and to reflection

If these are the characteristics and the categories of values pertinent to teaching, then what may be said about how they are "applied" in teaching? Consider the following propositions:

- Values are a template that is always brought to bear in planning, in action, and in reflection on that action.
- All values must be continuously applied; a value sincerely held can never be ignored, one cannot choose not to attend to it.
- Struggle or conflict arises from the implications of possible contradictions or competitions among values in specific situations.

These propositions make the application of values different from the application of knowledge. One's professional moral principles are always applicable, in all situations and circumstances. While there is a value sense that one's overall professional knowledge must always be brought to bear, once the problem has been defined, the operational obligations respecting knowledge are delimited. For example, once a predicament is defined as instructional, curriculum knowledge can be temporarily shelved. Once we understand a problem to be essentially human relations, we need no longer look at knowledge of educational law or school structure.

But in the application of values, the "template" capturing the predominant set of values we would espouse is always relevant and must be honored. We cannot choose to ignore the obligation to care for clients or one's professional peers, or to skip being reflective, or to operate according to the state of the epistemological art.

Knowledge and value frameworks such as these are powerful guides to both reflection and action. I would not expect everyone who reads this to necessarily accept the particular formulations offered here. Their elements are open to honest debate and differences of judgment. But our obligation to give serious attention to what application of theory and values might mean and providing operative structures that will help teaching candidates and practitioners undertake their case analyses in these terms seems incontrovertible. Such structures have proven valuable to many students, particularly those who are determined to accept and address the professional obligation to think about their practice in terms of the extant knowledge bases and moral principles supporting and guiding teaching, and then to act accordingly.

How Close Is Case Analysis to Practice?

Among those engaged in case instruction for preservice teachers there seems to be fairly universal acceptance of the assumption that one of the reasons cases are so attractive is that they are closer to the realities of practice. The preceding chapters confirm that view, and, intuitively, the proposition seems unarguable. At the risk of appearing something of a contrarian, though, I propose to invest a few paragraphs in making some qualifications of the obvious.

I take my lead from three circumstances that have frequently arisen with my students. One of these is a negative reaction to cases that are anything more than a few pages in length. Some of that is related to the particular instructional context that I was operating in, the relatively small number of credit hours to be earned for the effort expended, as well as the other clinical activities ongoing for my student teachers when demands of case analysis were being made.

A second is the perception expressed by many students that teaching moves too quickly, on the one hand, and is too immediate and otherwise demanding, on the other, for teachers ever to be able to invest the kind of time and energy that systematic case analysis entails. Students will assert that case study as done in class is all well and good but, in the final analysis, it is just an "academic exercise" suited to preservice classes as part of their university experience but unrealistic in the swirling, pressured existence of classrooms and schools.

There is a third element, too. *Analyzing* a case prepared by someone else is one thing; *generating* the elements of a case in order to analyze and attempt resolution is quite another. They are two related, but quite different, skills. We have not done our job, it seems to me, if we expect to prepare teachers disposed to be complexly reflective of the problematics of teaching if we have only taught them to resolve predicaments, but not also taught them how to identify the intricate elements of new dilemmas as they arise.

In espousing case instruction and analysis, then, do we run the risk of academicizing practice when practice itself does not yet proceed very much in terms of the kind of thinking that case analysis entails? We are, it seems to me, only at the beginning of attempts to bring this kind of orientation to teaching. While Japanese teachers have been described as using portions of their planning and reflective time together to present cases for peer review and comment, this kind of professional collaboration and problem solving is not a common practice in this country by any means. And it should be.

But there are signs that are encouraging. The development of Individualized Educational Programs is a case review process involving teachers, parents, psychologists, and administrators focusing on one child's needs and aspirations. When schools are beginning to operate in local site decision making, when charter or thematic schools are being established, and when local site accountability and initiative is being undertaken, here are places where "case thinking" is beginning to take place.

My aim in raising these points is not to undermine the case for case instruction. It is, instead, to recognize that the development and review of cases is no less artificial, academic, if you will, in some of its elements than other forms of instruction we have used. Because case instruction has the focus on practice, the intrigue we find in complex predicaments and attempts to resolve them ought not to lead us to ignore the requirements of the kinds of thinking we are hoping to develop in our preservice and in-service teachers. We need to concern ourselves with looking for, and helping to expand, instances of this kind of thinking in the schools where our students will carry out their teaching careers. One might think of this as one more reason for the injunction of the proposition that the reform of schooling and the reform of teacher education ought to be thought of as intimately linked quests.

Assessing Student Outcomes of Case Analysis

There is some discussion of evaluation in these chapters and a few tantalizing hints of techniques that reflect the different demands and purposes of case instruction. There is more emphasis, though, on the resource demands of case instruction and less on the specifics of the assessment methods employed. The most recent review of the case instruction literature for teacher education (Merseth, 1996) also does not treat the matter directly.

It seems to me that the evaluation strategies applied to case instruction ought to be as "on top of the table" as the work we expect students to show. Awarding grades, for example, without keying those grades to explicit criteria linked to the purposes and aims of case instruction seems somehow inappropriate. Furthermore, given the constructivist thrust of case instruction, every effort should be made to render the assessment process constructivist as well. How can we help assure that the practices we employ in assessment contribute to further learning, that is, are pedagogical in their character, instead of merely signifying the terminal point of the most recently undertaken curricular experience? The challenge is to define and undertake assessment practices in case instruction that continue the process of learning rather than mark its conclusion.

The Koziol, Minnick, and Riddick paper talks of Likert-scaled rubrics. Kent's paper shows the ratings scales used in the Internet team competition. Herbert's paper references and gives one illustration of "explicit criteria by which I and others can assess students' abilities to engage in case analysis." Allen writes to the logistical and affective challenges of assessment, and offers his criteria and judgment processes. The difficulty in finding fair processes and criteria for assessment appears obvious and elusive. It seems likely that many of the chapter authors are still in the process of experimenting and struggling with their own assessment issues.

The paragraph just completed may sound critical, but my observations are deeply tinted by understanding. If case instruction is difficult, then assessment of case learning is doubly so. For one thing, wrenching students from their deeply ingrained mindsets about assessment, evaluation, and its unfortunate linkages to grades and grade point averages, to say nothing of the norms engendered by our teaching colleagues in and out of the teacher education program, can be excruciating. The 4.0 student whose case analysis performance in her last quarter of study, based on explicit criteria published in advance of student effort, doesn't rise above a C has no leg to stand on, on the one hand, and everything to be upset about in the larger scheme of things, on the other. But that's a familiar story to everyone. More salient here is the confirmation of my own experience as to how difficult it is to be explicit, to say nothing of both valid and reliable, in one's own assessments of intellectual activity as complex and all-encompassing as case analysis.

I started out my instruction by trying to remove the sting and the negative influences of grading by adopting a contract system that said, basically, do everything asked of you and you'll be assigned an A (e.g., prepare a fairly detailed analytic sheet on the case before class, attend all the classes, participate in the dialogue during small group, complete a decision agenda in class, prepare a case of your own, prepare and submit assessment forms on each of two cases prepared by your peers, complete a detailed evaluation response form at the end of the seminar, etc.). My rationale was that I wanted the display of energy rather than anxiety, as well as the generation of product on the basis of which substantive feedback could be given. The course accompanied student teaching, which was clearly students' preeminent worry, and this one-credit-hour course obligation was an apparent "addendum." Also, I quickly realized that by expecting students to do one hour's work a week in addition to the two hours of seminar each week, I was, in effect, expecting them to do *more*, challenging a norm about student time investment relative to credit hours that, after four years, was deeply ingrained.

The growing realization that many students were taking advantage of this contract (producing minimalist compliance with little thought or engagement) led me to reimpose assessment standards. That, in turn, obliged me to specify the levels of performance required to achieve specified grades. It was, therefore, necessary to devise both qualitative and quantitative measures of performance in case analysis and overall performance in the course.

Figure 14.1 displays the page in the syllabus that outlined for students how I assessed their case analyses each week. The prime vehicle for assessment of student work was the "decision agenda" each was asked to generate in response to a particular case stimulus. The concept of "decision agenda" arose from the realization that teaching predicaments were virtually never unitary in their resolution; almost always, the presence of multiple stakeholders, operating in different timeframes, in circumstances that engaged their elements interactively meant that resolution (and/or prevention of further recurrence) entailed several steps, not just one (hence agenda). An individual agenda item is an indicated action and the professional knowledge and/or values rationale for that action. Once again, the idea of asking preservice teachers to develop a "decision *agenda*" arose from the realization that complex cases have multiple causes, stakeholders, time frames, and modes of resolution, and that, therefore, predicaments almost always entail working on more than one thing in more than one time frame to resolve the current problem and prevent future occurrences.

As inspection will reveal, this rubric is not entirely successful in explicating or unpacking every domain of judgment. The four criteria (1, 2, 3, and 4), however, together represent a clear stance on the complexity of teaching predicaments: analytic frames are variable and multiple; time frames for onset and resolution of predicaments will vary; there will always be more than one stakeholder; and teachers have an obligation to identify a professional rationale for each course of action they propose

The decision agendas will be assessed using the following rubric:

1. Number of frames of reference addressed by decision agenda

a. One
b. A few (2–3)
c. Many (more than 3)

2. Linkage to professional knowledge and values (PK/V)

a. Not present
b. Categories of PK/V or frames of reference only
c. Limited knowledge principle(s) or value(s) identified (implied)
d. Substantial knowledge principle(s) or value(s) identified

3. Time frame/scope of indicated decisions

a. Immediate
b. Mid-range
c. Long-range
d. Combination of one or more

4. The decision agenda presented places the locus of responsibility for solutions to the problem on

a. The student or students
b. The beginning teacher (case protagonist)
c. Other professionals
d. Others
e. Some combination of a, b, c, and/or d

FIGURE 14.1   Case Analysis Assessment Rubric

5. Holistic judgment of the adequacy of the response overall

| a. Excellent: 9–10 points |
| b. Good: 7–8 points |
| c. Fair: 5–6 points |
| d. Marginal: 1–4 points |
| e. Unacceptable: 0 points |

NOTA BENE: Given the nature of teaching, the goals of the seminar, and extensive experience with case analysis during CITE planning, it is important for seminar members to know that, in undertaking assessment of decision agendas, several decision rules are followed:

For category 1, no "a" can result in a 5 "a" or "b" judgment;

For category 2, no "a," "b," or "c" can result in a 5 "a" or "b";

For category 3, no "a," "b," or "c" can result in a 5 "a" or "b";

For category 4, no "a," "b," "c," or "d" can result in a 5 "a" or "b"; and

For category 5, holistic judgment depends not only on the criteria being met as per the rules just explicated, but also on the adequacy of content and argument displayed.

EXAMPLE: A decision agenda assessed BBDBC 6 points means; only two or three frames of reference were identified; rather than specific principles or values being cited, categories only were identified; the case protagonist was the main decider or actor; actions embraced more than one time frame; and the agenda was judged, overall, fair. In virtually every case, the rubric assessment will be accompanied by analytic commentary.

FIGURE 14.1 *continued*

to take. In practice, the word *virtually* in the last line of the example was not needed; every student received analytic commentary on every agenda submitted explaining the basis for each component of the assessment received. Allen's description of the amount of time consumed by assessment for case instruction met, therefore, with instant recognition when I read it!

The last category, holistic judgment, is where shortcomings still exist. The value assigned depends not only on the degree to which the first four criteria are met, but also on the adequacy of the content and the judgment displayed, and it is here that, as an explicated criterion, considerable room remains for additional work.

Illuminating my criteria and the assessment process was important, though, not because it prevented students from making serious omissions early on (it didn't), but because it established an external frame against which they could address their own analytic performance and then struggle with developing the perceptions, or the energy, or the intellectual bases for proposing actions in their decision agendas.

Case Performance
as Candidate/Program Diagnostic

In the majority of the preceding chapters, instructors expressed surprise or chagrin over the students' hypercritical assessments of teacher protagonists in the cases, as well as the superficiality of their initial responses, or both. In most instances this was attributed to the naïveté of the students or their lack of familiarity with case analysis techniques and purposes. Additionally they may lack practice in applying problem solving, research, and writing skills. In some of the chapters the sequence or location of the class in the larger teacher preparation program is also clearly implicated; the course may be among the early ones students take and they may feel inadequate to tackle classroom dilemmas.

I want to raise the ante a bit on those observations. The responses of candidate teachers to cases should also be thought of as diagnostic about the suitability of candidates for their future roles. The earlier, the better! Equally importantly, however, preservice teacher performance on cases may also say a great deal about the design and adequacy of the program of which those students are a part. In this instance, the later, the more potentially damning!

First, student suitability. Case analysis and case resolution are deeply revealing of student dispositions, especially when what they are doing is not under the immediate eye of the instructor. Students who don't do their homework, for example, in a professional course sequence are not likely to prepare adequately or well for their own teaching work in schools. Students who are entirely comfortable with their own knee-jerk responses in the classes when they are *students* are very likely to commit them in the classes where they are *teachers*. Students whose performance illustrates they have not mastered metacognitive processes respecting their own perception, analytical efforts, and proposed actions and their likely consequences are not likely to generate them suddenly in the classrooms for which they are responsible as teachers. Students who cannot summon up curiosity about the problematics of a case presented to them, or the ins and outs of potential resolutions and the rationales for them, are unlikely to display such behavior when on their own. Students who are impatient or dismissive of the contributions of their peers in case discussion fail to display dispositions of great promise and sensitivity when dealing with future students that they will be responsible for and to, or to their teacher colleagues with whom they will be working.

Perhaps this is the subject of a paper in its own right, but cases reveal a great deal about students; the dismay more than a few of our authors express over the kinds of performances they have witnessed and worried over speaks volumes in this regard. In my own experience, the wisdom of what we did when we reformed our program at Cincinnati was confirmed when it became possible to contrast the dispositions of the CITE students to that too large a proportion of the students in the old program often displayed. There were only fleeting instances (usually associated with stress and fatigue) of the kinds of negative, bored, uninterested, obvious lack of commitment dispositions that would routinely drive me to distraction by these kinds of students (and, incidentally, equally worried their more engaged peers). Case instruction is holistic. It engages and displays the application of intellect, understanding, commitment, and the moral obligations of profession. Once we become aware of problems or shortcomings in any of these domains it is hard to justify not acting on them, first supportively, but ultimately judgmentally, if we must.

For much the same reasons—holism and close approximation to the complexities and realities of the craft—case instruction has powerful implications for quality control on the entry of candidates into the profession, especially relative to key dispositional characteristics, performance on case instruction has powerful implications for the assessment of program design, and its impact on teaching candidates as well. For example, if, at the conclusion of the preparation program, virtually no students are able to make sense out of the request that the rationale for action ought to be grounded in theoretical or moral propositions fundamental to the teaching profession, that would have to be a program shortcoming, not an individual failing. When the only arguments forthcoming respecting professional values are assertions that values are a personal matter or only pertain to ethical matters conceived to be generic to all human interactions, then program shortcomings loom large in the explanatory field.

When experience demonstrates to us the propensity of students to be sharply critical of the teachers they encounter in their cases, programmatically we have to ask what might be done earlier in the preservice teacher experience to expect this phenomenon and offer correctives, anticipatory explanations, and cautions against simplistic explanations of this kind. When students perform well in the course on managing students and instruction but then in their responses to cases reveal dispositions apparently untouched by their academic experience, larger pedagogical and program issues are implicated. As a final illustration, when students approach their terminal clinical experiences and reveal in their case analyses that they have not yet mastered the capacity to write clearly or analytically, the fact that they are where they are with such a shortcoming rests not so much with the students as it does with the faculty, writ large, and the program.

If, as this material is read, a modest sense of frustration is sensed, then I have achieved my writing aim. The point, in the final analysis, is that those faculty who facilitate case instruction may find themselves in a powerful, though perhaps unenviable, position to offer counsel to their colleagues if such be warranted. It is not always a pleasant role, but don't all teachers (which *includes* teacher educators!) have an obligation to their several clients to say "not yet" to their students when such a judgment is warranted by the data? And doesn't each of us as a faculty member in a program also have a stewardship obligation to both program and profession to note and then address any evidence suggestive of shortcomings in that program's design or effectiveness?

Evidence of the Isolation of Teacher Educators from One Another

It is hard for someone like me who has invested major blocks of time over the last dozen years in developing and implementing the concept of unit accreditation for the National Council for Accreditation of Teacher Education to read these chapters and not see evidence of the distance yet to be traveled before fragmentation of effort in teacher education is finally overcome, and genuinely integrated and articulated preparation programs become the standard. One can do nothing but applaud the individual initiative revealed in these chapters, but they communicate, still, a sense of isolation and disconnectedness.

For example, Herbert talks about the infrequence of conversation about pedagogical matters as compared to administrative and logistical. Allen pleads for collaboration between educational psychology and teacher education faculty to achieve a more developmental and systematic use of cases in the program. Kowalski gives no indication that his characterization of teaching as isolated does not apply to teacher education, too. The pride with which Hunter notes the redesign of teacher education at the University of Calgary underscores the (dare I say it?) "go it alone" flavor of the chapters as a whole.

There are, without a doubt, major issues to confront for any faculty seeking to develop integrated and articulated programs of teacher education. The links requiring formulation are numerous. They lie within the teacher education faculty *per se*. They must be found between teacher education and support faculty in the school or college of education, between the teacher education faculty writ large and the arts and sciences (especially as we get more and more serious about pedagogical content knowledge as well as modeling good teaching), and, finally, between college and university teacher educators and our practitioner teacher educator peers in schools.

The number and types of collaborative relationships only begin to define the additional demands of collaborative practice in teacher preparation. Collaboration takes time and lots of it. Participants need to inform one another, come to understand, and begin to get comfortable with the real "cultural" differences that exist between the component communities in the teacher education enterprise. Collaboration also entails conflict, a phenomenon that many teachers and academics find aversive to the point of avoidance. Finally, collaboration without mutual accommodation and adjustment, resulting in changes in behavior and understanding, would be empty and meaningless. Collaboration is not just a process; it has products, too, and among the most demanding and difficult are the alterations we must all make in what and how things are done. This is a far cry from "business as usual" or "the way things have always been done."

Because of its holistic and summative character, student performance in case instruction provides a point of focus for the attention of all teacher education's protagonists. It could become a powerful catalyst for the processes of program design, interlinkage, delivery, and assessment.

FINAL REFLECTIONS

The issues addressed above suggest the wisdom of thinking of the import of case instruction in more than just pedagogical terms. Its reemergence in teacher education comes at a time when other reform developments are under way that parallel it and/or that can receive additional impetus from it.

The holistic character of case instruction and case learning is a cohering force for a program and its participants. The performance of preservice teachers in case learning provides a focal point for the several protagonists in the teacher preparation enterprise to examine how their work contributes to the desired end result, and the ensuing work stimulates the kind of (self-)consciousness that supports the development of carefully integrated and articulated programs.

Maybe the holistic and summative character of case instruction and case learning will have an unanticipated reform influence all by itself. The quintessentially constructivist character of case learning has the felicitous consequence of virtually requiring instruction to match. Case instruction proceeds by processes on inquiry and dialogue. The learning that takes place focuses on the problematics of teaching, learning, and schooling.

The highly visible nature of student responses to cases insures availability to instructors of the perceptions and constructs of the preservice teachers as they go about their learning, thereby enabling instructors to make the kinds of adjustments, both immediate and long-term, necessary to achieve ever closer approximations to the desired ends.

The tendency of case instruction to problematize the practice of teaching is also healthy. There are two senses of this. The first is the encouragement it gives to apply intellect to the art and craft of teaching, to think deeply about its elements, requirements, and outcomes, and to be prepared to apply the products of one's own thought, and the thoughts of others who have gone before, to the day-to-day obligations. The second is to encourage examination of the extent to which case learning for teaching does, in fact, approximate the practice of teaching, and what needs to be undertaken, in both practice and preparation for it, in order to reap the greatest benefits. At least one implication is that, if beginning teachers are to be able to reap the benefits of case analysis in their own teaching, they are going to have to know something about case development or recognition. Addressing a case and building one are different; they are as different as the ability to live well in a building as compared to actually designing and constructing it. While the latter entails prior attention to the former, the converse does not hold. Developing the ability to problematize teaching will tend to assure that skills of analysis built through case learning can come to be applied fully in practice.

In sum, the promise of case learning and instruction is not just a matter of pedagogy. It entails thorough attention to the very conceptualization of the many functions and obligations of teaching for effective learning, the recurring patterns and puzzles implicit in those tasks, and how best to assure the effective collaboration of the protagonists for preservice teacher education. Finally, teaching with cases provides teacher educators with ongoing feedback to take professional instruction to a higher power: that of building carefully integrated and articulated teacher preparation programs that turn out professionals capable of educating all America's children even as they pursue their own continuing growth and development as teachers.

REFERENCES

Merseth, K. K. (1996). Cases and case methods in teacher education. In J. Sikula, T. J. Buttery, & E. Guyton (Eds.), *Handbook of research on teacher education* (2nd ed.) (pp. 722–744). New York: Macmillan.

Sirotnik, K. (1990). School, schooling, teaching, and preparing to teach. In J. Goodlad, R. Soder, & K. Sirotnik (Eds.), *The moral dimensions of teaching* (pp. 296–327). San Francisco: Jossey-Bass.

INDEX